ALL KINDS O

Mollie Harris still lives in Oxfordshire. She has written articles for local newspapers and has made many radio broadcasts on country topics. She is perhaps best known for her performances as Martha Woodford in 'The Archers'.

All Kinds of Magic

Mollie Harris

Oxford   New York

OXFORD UNIVERSITY PRESS

1995

Oxford University Press, Walton Street, Oxford OX2 6DP

Oxford New York
Athens Auckland Bangkok Bombay
Calcutta Cape Town Dar es Salaam Delhi
Florence Hong Kong Istanbul Karachi
Kuala Lumpur Madras Madrid Melbourne
Mexico City Nairobi Paris Singapore
Taipei Tokyo Toronto

and associated companies in
Berlin Ibadan

Oxford is a trade mark of Oxford University Press

A Kind of Magic first published 1969
Another Kind of Magic first published 1971
The Green Years first published 1976
First published as an Oxford University Press paperback
in a single volume 1995

British Library Cataloguing in Publication Data

Data available

Library of Congress Cataloging in Publication Data
Harris, Mollie.
All kinds of magic / Mollie Harris.
p. cm.
Contents: A kind of magic—The green years—Another kind of
magic.
1. Oxfordshire (England)—Social life and customs. 2. Cotswold
Hills (England)—Description and travel. 3. Working class families—
England—Oxfordshire. 4. Country life—England—Oxfordshire.
5. Harris, Mollie—Childhood and youth. I. Title.
DA670.09H29 1995 942.5'7—dc20 94-31327

ISBN 0-19-282413-9

1 3 5 7 9 10 8 6 4 2

Typeset by Best-set Typesetter Ltd., Hong Kong
Printed in Great Britain
by
Biddles Ltd
Guildford and King's Lynn

Acknowledgements

Parts of *A Kind of Magic* have already appeared in different form, in broadcasts by the BBC, and as articles in the *Witney Gazette*, the *Oxfordshire Roundabout*, and the *Oxford Times*.

In writing *The Green Years* I would like to thank my late brothers and sisters, cousin Harry, Mr R. Beckinsale and Mr H. Wheeler, and many others, who, from conversations, have helped to make the book a colourful portrayal of village life in the 1920s and 1930s. My thanks also to Mary Hathaway, my Mother's friend, for kindly sending the poem *Ducklington* to me. Some of the characters' anecdotes have been broadcast on the BBC *Countryside* programmes.

Some parts of *Another Kind of Magic* were originally published in the *Witney Gazette*, 'Ship Dags' appeared in *The Countryman*, and many of the characters' anecdotes have been broadcast on the BBC in country magazine programmes.

Contents

Introduction   ix

A KIND OF MAGIC
1 The Village   3
2 The Family   9
3 There was a Time   22
4 A Cotswold Christmas   27
5 The Little Farm   35
6 School Days   39
7 Hop, Skip, and Jump   51
8 Lotions and Potions   59
9 Village Life   62
10 Magic Moments   72
11 Village Activities   82
12 Characters and Neighbours   92
13 Growing Pains   99
14 Pig Killing   103
15 Good Times and Bad   108
16 A Time to Remember   113

THE GREEN YEARS
Ducklington
1 Come Summer   125
2 Cotswold Days   132
3 Wireless Sets and Home-Made Wine   138
4 Hatching and Dispatching   146
5 China Dogs and China Cups   157
6 Where the Windrush Flows   166

Contents

7 Caravans and Kings   173

8 Poaching Tales and Tall Stories   180

9 Come Day, Go Day, God Send Sunday   189

10 Uncle Jesse and Pigsty Passion   197

11 Dumble Dads and Foster Mums   211

12 Rhymes and Relations   224

13 Summer Days, Summer Ways   235

14 Winter   245

15 The Green Years   254

ANOTHER KIND OF MAGIC

1 A Cotswold Shepherd   273

2 'Me Operation'   281

3 Amos and Rosie   288

4 Sorting Spuds   296

5 Hoppy the Roadman   304

6 Missus-Next-Door   314

7 Cotswold Friends   320

8 'Tempory Move'   329

9 'Tatering Tales'   333

10 Ship Dags   343

11 Bill Brown and his Missus   349

12 Cotswold Spring   356

13 All on a Summer Day   365

14 World Without End   372

15 Whitey Smith   377

Conclusion   386

Glossary   388

Introduction

ALL KINDS OF MAGIC is a collection of my very early writings, and of course of my very early memories, mostly of when we were a large poor family living in the village of Ducklington.

But hard up as we were, for me it was a magical time. As you get older you are inclined to remember all the happy times; the unhappy events are but a blur. There was a wonderment about our everyday lives—sliding on a frozen pond in those bitterly cold winters, seeking the first wild flowers in spring, wooding, mushrooming, blackberrying—all gifts from heaven, along with the joy of living and growing up in the wonderful Oxfordshire countryside. The kindness of friends and neighbours in those hard-up carefree times; the closeness of a big family in an overcrowded but happy home; our Mother's indestructible gaiety and sense of amazement—some of which thankfully rubbed off on to her children. All this is covered in *A Kind of Magic* and is continued in the second part of this trilogy, *The Green Years*. This contains episodes which I didn't have the space to write about in the first book, with me being young and green, and still wet behind the ears!

But in *Another Kind of Magic*, we move on apace. It is not so much about me, but about the Cotswold friends that I had the privilege to meet and who lived in those 'wide high hills'. (Surely it is some of the loveliest countryside in England, whether shrouded in snow, mist, or rain, in the cold green of early summer or the brilliant patchwork of autumn.) In *Another Kind of Magic* you can read about some of the delightful characters I have met, and share with me their simple happy way of life.

A Kind of Magic

To my grandsons

PETER LEIGH & JONATHAN

with love

I

The Village

WHEN I look back, the days of my childhood seem to have had a kind of magic about them. They were colourful, exciting, demanding days, full of wonder and discovery, joy and adventure.

The village where we lived was set in the low-lying valley of the Windrush—it was long and straggly, stretching a mile and a half from the milkman's in Little Ducklington to the flour mill cottages in Ducklington proper. It seemed always to smell of cows—a sweet, grassy, pungent smell, a mixture of milk, warm animals, and manure.

Apart from the ordinary cottages there were several farms dotted about—Pudney Wilsdon's, Hoppy Druce's (Hoppy because of his bad foot), Holtoms' and Stranges'. Good-living and hardworking, they employed a number of local men, mostly who lived with their families in tied cottages near the farms. Men who were known by their calling—Carter Temple, Shepherd Spindlow, Carter Porter, Cowman Godfrey—names they were known by all their lives, and nobody thought of addressing them any differently.

Men who didn't work on the farms in Ducklington puffed up to Witney on their bicycles to the blanket mills. Most of the ordinary girls worked on the looms at one or other of the blanket factories, too, often walking over 'The Moors', a short cut to the town; few could afford a push-bike. The more genteel girls served in the shops and in-betweens worked in the big steam laundry. But a few still went away to domestic service.

Most of the cottages in the village were built of Cotswold stone, roofed with grey stone slates quarried at Stonesfield near by.

3

Others were thatched in deep thick yellow thatch that seemed almost to touch the ground. And the long gardens at the backs were filled with cabbages, potatoes, rabbit hutches, pigsties, and earth closets.

A few houses of red brick were dotted about. The flour mill, too, was red-bricked, and its continuously throbbing engine, chunk, chunk, chunk, could be heard all over the other end of the village.

The heart of our small community was the wide square, dotted with cottages, near the church, close-knit and protecting. Over the road was the school and pond.

There was a chapel up the other end, as well as two pubs and two small shops—these were in the front rooms of cottages, their tiny windows bursting with glass jars of brightly coloured sweets, sherbet dabs, liquorice pipes, and aniseed balls—a haven for a child with a penny to spend. There was Baker Collis to bake our bread, and the milkman who came clanking up the path in his hobnailed boots to dole out milk from a shiny can.

We had travelling men who came puffing down the dusty road. One weekly visitor was Hog Puddin' Walker, a giant of a man who pedalled his hog puddings—black and white puddings—and beautifully plaited chitterlings, in a yellow wicker basket fixed on the front of his huge black bicycle. His wares were kept covered with a whiter-than-white cloth, and there was always fresh green parsley dotted about among the puddings.

Saturday was something of a field day for us—that was when Benny Clements, the oil and rag and bone man, paid us a visit. He was small and ragged and wore a long overcoat winter and summer; it reached nearly down to the ground, almost covering his boots. He brought paraffin oil right up to the doors of the cottages. Amongst his rags and rabbit skins were tall shiny tins of sweets. 'Benny's Blackuns' we called them, and for a handful of rags the old man would dole out a few of these black peppermint sweets, although the flavour was often lost because Benny handled them with black-grimed, paraffin-soaked hands.

Many a duster or house flannel found its way to Benny's cart. 'Yes, you little hounds,' Mother would shout, 'no wonder I can't find a duster anywhere—halfway to Witney on Benny's cart, I'll be bound!'

We called another tradesman 'Spetter' King, because he spat on his hands a lot, although some people said he was called this because he stuttered. Whatever the reason was it didn't matter. All we were interested in were his sweets. In his shop in the town nearby he made a wonderful assortment of boiled sweets, clove, lemon, aniseed and cinnamon, acid drops, and peppermints. And once a week he would cycle out to the village to try and sell some. We would hang round him, a dozen or more of us.

'Giss one, giss one,' a big boy would say.

'Du—du you want to to buy any?' Spetter would splutter.

'How du we know if we shall like 'um? We ain't tried 'um yet,' another would say.

And we would nudge each other, pressing forward till we nearly knocked Spetter over, and his bike and his wares as well. Then he would give us each a sweet to taste, popping them into our open pink mouths like a parent bird feeding a brood of young fledglings. Perhaps one of the boys would buy a ha'p'th; then he would slink off with half a dozen more kids following him saying, 'giss a lick, giss a lick', knowing darn well they would never be given a whole sweet.

Packmen called too; sometimes our mother bought thick, warm, twill sheets and boots for us all, paying perhaps a shilling a week onto the dog-eared card until the debt was cleared. By then the boots were worn out, so more were ordered. With seven growing children skipping and scauting about it must have been boots, boots, nothing but boots to pay for on that dog-eared card.

Tramps and gypsies were other visitors; tramps always called on us, the middle cottage in a row of three. It was funny they never called at the others that stood either side of us. Our mother said that the tramps left signs for their fellow travellers by scratching marks on the wall with bits of stone. We would search the walls for signs but never found any. But whatever time of day it was our mother never turned a tramp away with an empty billycan. Gypsies she wasn't too fond of—they used to cadge water from our well, dipping their dirty buckets down into the depths of the cool spring water, sometimes breaking the well hook into the bargain.

When it was the annual feast several families of show people ('Gypoes' we called them), would arrive on 'Chalky', the village green, and because the row where we lived was the nearest to the green, we had to put up with them. They were in and out of the yard all day, bringing hordes of children and dogs with them.

The children would snatch gooseberries from Mrs-next-door's bushes and the dogs would chase cats all over the neatly dug gardens. If you refused them water or grumbled about the kids and dogs they would fling out a string of abuse and curses. The best thing to do was to let them get on with it for a couple of days while the feast lasted. Then they would pack up their stalls and kids into the brightly coloured caravans, harness their ponies, and were away to the next village fair.

The nearness of the close-knit village enveloped us every day. We youngsters and our mothers were a little community on our own; only the men and girls who worked in the town knew a different sort of life. We knew everything that was going on—birth, illness, death were everyday topics—we children knew little of their proper meaning, but talked about them as our elders did.

Always somebody's mother was having a baby—we saw birth and death in the farmyards and fields—but we didn't probe or bother to find out why or where—many of us were thirteen and fourteen before we started to pick up the facts of life, and then these were whispered and giggled to us by other girls a little older who had already started work and had picked up snatches of conversations from people they worked with.

I must have been nearly fourteen when a gang of us stumbled across a village girl and boy lying close in the thick standing grass. 'I'll bet he is giving her a french letter,' a fifteen-year-old girl whispered. But I wondered what this youth could be doing with a french letter—he had only attended the village school. It was as much as any of us could do to master English, let alone read a french letter lying down in a grass field.

Then two of the older girls that I was with started singing and cat-calling to the courting couple:

> Down in the meadow
> Where the nuts are brown
> Petticoats up and trousers down. . . .

they sang. The young man in the grass half-rose and shouted to them, 'Shut up that singing or I'll clout your ears.' 'If the cap fits, wear it,' answered the cheekiest of the girls, and we all ran off squealing and laughing.

At Michaelmas other families moved into the tied cottages, bringing new children to the school, often very shy; probably they had lived miles from anyone, up in the fields somewhere before coming to Ducklington.

One family, the Goodsons, were like this—the Mother was a timid, white-faced person. She made the most lovely chocolate cake—at least I thought it was marvellous. She told me years afterwards that it was only flavoured with cocoa—she did not have the money to buy currants and things.

The pond was just opposite the church and in winter became a meeting place for every able-bodied person. The hard cold frosts of January froze the surface solid. We would spend most of our time sliding there. In the evenings men, women, boys and girls would congregate down there—someone might bring a lantern if there was no moon, and we would cut great long slides from one side of the pond to the other. Dozens of us, tearing along through the frosty night on those glassy slides.

When the thaw set in we were lost for a while—then it was back to the fireside and our stepfather trying hard to get 2LO* on

---

* The name of the first wireless station.

our crystal set. 'Be quiet or you'll all go to bed,' he would shout, 'and take that dratted kettle off the fire, I don't know whether it's that or London I can hear.'

On Saturday nights poor people walked up to Witney. After eight o'clock you could buy 'bits': oddments of meat and bones. A shilling's-worth would make a lovely meat pudding or pie, enough for the biggest family. Many of the villagers kept a couple of pigs. One would be killed and salted for the family's use, the other would be sold to pay for the toppings (pig food).

Everybody had big allotments as well as their gardens. Both men and women toiled on these; into the late evenings they would work, growing enough potatoes and other vegetables to last all the year round. Children, too, helped their parents with picking up potatoes, hoeing, and weeding. Nobody could afford 'boughten' vegetables or fruit.

This then was how most of the folk managed. 'Rough and enough' the women called the heavy meals they dished up for their families. Some did not have enough to eat, and pale, skinny children either grew up as weaklings or died. But for most of us, we thrived on stews and suet puddings, bread and dripping, home-made jam, and fat bacon.

2

The Family

$\mathcal{M}$Y first and most lasting memory of my mother is that of a tall, majestic person. She was five-feet ten, well-built, and with fine features. She had a mop of thick black wavy hair coiled on top of her head and laughing, sparkling eyes, and she was as strong as an ox. Of course, over the years she became grey and bent but the sparkle in her eyes was always there.

She had started her working life at thirteen when she was packed off to service, never earning any more than £8 a year. Of course she had good food in the gentry's houses and uniforms were found.

Then she met and married my father, a mail-van driver. When they set up house their furniture was not the ordinary cottage type, but upholstered chairs and a good sideboard and a really nice bedroom suite. For he was a hardworking, steady fellow and had not squandered his money.

Then just two months before I was born my father died. Our mother already had three children, my two elder brothers, Bern and Bunt, and my sister Betty, and they were all under five years old. Apparently our father, normally a very fit man, had been taken to Oxford Infirmary with acute appendicitis. Within a week it had turned to peritonitis and he died.

Then for our mother the long struggle began. Her parents begged her to go back to their quiet village in the Cotswolds, but she refused, thinking that we would stand a much better chance to get on in life if we stayed where we were. 'A little bit nearer civilization,' as she put it. So with the help of neighbours and friends lending a hand or keeping an eye on us she took a job in the town at the local cinema, 'The People's Palace'.

Her job was to take the money and show customers to their seats, but her generosity was her undoing. She would let old Susie go in free. Susie was a dirty woman who picked up dog-ends and sorted over people's dustbins. She did not want to look at the pictures but just to sleep in the warm cinema. Our mother used to say: 'You go down and sit in the front row Susie, you'll be all right.' The front seats were the very cheap, hard ones. But Susie, looking for comfort, used to sneak up to the more expensive red-plush seats at the back. One night the house lights went up and there, between a Colonel and a Major, sat Susie, snoozing. Susie was banned from The People's Palace and our mother got the sack.

She did other jobs—one was gloving at home. Quite a number of the village women did this hand-stitching of gloves, brought out to them from a local factory. The work was tedious and very poorly paid and our mother, who always hated sewing, did not do this for any longer than she could help.

At this time we were living in a tiny low-windowed cottage down Hell Corner near the church. One day we children were all crammed by the bedroom window while our mother mopped and dusted and changed the bed. Suddenly there was a knock on the door and four small faces surged forward to see who the caller was. I was first to meet him, straight through the glass panes onto the dirt path below, suffering no more than a badly cut leg. The caller was our future stepfather and he was tall and good-looking, with a mop of curls and bright blue eyes. He was dressed in his army clothes and I could feel the prickly material stinging my legs as I sat on his lap to be comforted. He became a regular visitor, and looked at our mother as I had never seen anyone look at her before.

He was a dispatch rider and told us tales about the countries he had been to and brought us presents—serviette rings (which we never used), carved in wood from the Mount of Olives, and a

Bible too, with the same fine wood for its covers; a red fez with a black tassel for each of us; and a photo of him taken on a camel and one of him standing with a guide half-way up a Pyramid. From him we heard about places with strange names—Mesopotamia, Dardanelles, and he sang cheeky army songs to us—and we loved him.

After he married our mother we all moved from Hell Corner to a bigger cottage in Little Ducklington, a small community of thirteen houses separated from Ducklington by the village green. Here, three more children were born, my stepsister Mick, and brothers, Ben and Denis. Our cottage called 'Wayside' was a two-up and two-down affair with a large landing that served as a third bedroom, and it was to be our home until the older ones began to leave and marry—with our parents and seven growing children it must have been crammed, to say the least, but we didn't notice it.

The meals were all cooked and eaten in the living-room, but the washing-up was done in the back kitchen where there was a small larder and a place we called the dungeon. It was really a cupboard under the stairs, where we kept sacks of potatoes in winter time, and the brooms and brushes and things.

Somehow on a great black grate our mother concocted wonderful meals—tasty and filling. In a great oval pot that was suspended over a good fire she cooked hunks of fat bacon along with potatoes and cabbage. The vegetables were put into string nets to keep them separate. When they were cooked she would fish them out of the steaming saucepans with the aid of a fork. Then into the same water and along with the bacon she would drop a suet pudding, perhaps a roly-poly or a currant 'spotted dick', and sometimes just plain suet to be eaten with golden syrup on it as a special treat.

Occasionally an uncle and aunt who lived in the Cotswolds would send us a couple of rabbits by post. They usually came at a particularly hard-up period. 'If the Lord don't come, he sends,' our mother would shout gleefully, holding up the furry objects. In no time at all the skins were pulled off. Sometimes we would get sixpence for these from Benny, the old oil man. Then she would make up a good fire, poking the red coals underneath to heat the oven which was at the side of the fireplace. Into the oven went the jointed rabbit covered with thickly sliced onions and halved potatoes covered in dripping. And later we would all sit down and have a meal fit for a king.

In our house jam was made from anything that was going, and during one bad period for about three years we almost lived on blackberry and apple jam. It came out of the jars in great solid lumps—we had it on porridge, boiled rice, suet puddings, toast— three times a day sometimes, till we were all sick of the sight of it. But at least it was wholesome and nourishing. Blackberries were ours for the picking, everybody had an apple tree in the garden, and sugar was no more than 2*d.* a pound.

Once when dried apricots were cheap our mother bought some—soaked them in water till they 'plimmed up'* and then set about making jam. It only cost about 3*d.* a pound to make, but she made one mistake—she cooked it in an iron saucepan. By doing this she killed all the apricot flavour, but we had to eat it. It was much too precious to give to the pigs. We waded through about fourteen pounds of the stuff, and after all these years I still expect apricot jam to taste of iron.

But except for an occasional slip-up like the iron saucepan, most of our mother's cooking, although prepared in a slapdash fashion, was the best I've ever tasted. She never weighed or measured anything.

Sometimes she would buy three penn'orth of bones, set them in water in the oval pot, throw in every sort of vegetable and herb that was available, and top it all up with suet dumplings as big as tennis balls. 'That'll put a good lining in your insides,' she'd say to us as she ladled out the thick, warming stew.

When it began to get dimpsy† in the evenings the paraffin lamp was lit and carefully stood in the centre of the table where it cast

* Made soft.
† A lovely country expression for when it is just starting to get dark.

a soft, gentle light over the room. Through the years, in spite of crowded families in the village, I never did hear of anyone's lamp being knocked over. Candles were used to light the rest of the house.

The only fire scares we ever had was when our mother, perhaps late back from shopping in the town, or just wandering over the fields, would fling paraffin on to the fire to 'jostle it up' ready for cooking. Then there would be a minor explosion and flames and wood ash would shoot out into the living room covering everything, and sometimes setting the chimney on fire as well. 'Quick!' she would shout to one of us, 'fetch me a sack'. She would plunge the sack into a bucket of water and stuff it up the chimney with the end of the broom handle, and quell the fire. When the danger had passed she would fetch the sack down, bringing with it great lumps of black smelly soot. 'Never mind,' she'd cry, 'that'll save me having it swept.'

Washing day, always on a Monday, began before we left for school. First, every drop of water had to be drawn from the well out in the yard. Our mother hooked the bucket onto the long-handled well hook, plunging it down into the cool depths, bending and pulling up the dripping bucket time after time, until she had filled the old washing copper which was built into the corner of the wash-house. It stood away from the cottage and in it we kept our stock of coal, wood, old bikes and tools. When the copper was full she would light a fire underneath to get the water good and hot. All day long she would be washing, blueing, and drawing more water. The only aids she used to get the clothes clean was a big bar of yellow washing soap, and soda. A few years later, when Hudson's Washing Powder was put on the market, housewives thought they were really in clover.

In summer our mother would drag a heavy table out from the wash-house and do her work in the sun. Some women in the village had huge wooden roller mangles—not us though—and our mother, the world's worst wringer, often slapped her washing over the line dripping wet. The copper was still hot at the end of

13

the day so she would fill it up again and the next morning the water was quite warm, for Tuesday was the day when the bedroom floors were scrubbed in a mixture of soda water and paraffin. This was done to make sure that there were no fleas hiding in the floorboards, for fleas, like head-lice, were easily picked up.

There were no mats or lino in the bedrooms—such luxury was kept for the living-room only. This was warm and cosy; the stone floor was covered in fawn coconut matting, but by the fire stretched a lovely rag rug, one our parents had made and the sort of thing to be found in most of the cottages. They were made from old coats and dresses. We children used to help cut up the strips of cloth into pieces about six inches long and an inch wide. From somewhere our stepfather would get a good big strong hessian sack which was washed and opened out flat to form the base of the rug.

It was quite simple to do: you just made two small holes in the hessian with a wooden meat skewer and poked a strip of material through, and each time you did this it made a double tuft. You just kept doing row after row until the hessian was covered. The colours used would be mostly browns and black but people usually managed to find a bit of bright material, blue, green or red, to make a little pattern in the centre and the corners.

In the summertime the living-room got very hot, because the fire had to be lit in the afternoons for cooking. But later on, when things were a bit easier, our stepfather brought a paraffin stove and the vegetables were cooked on this.

Then, if on a Sunday we had a joint or a tin of potatoes or a rabbit to be baked, we would take them down to Baker Collis's. In his bread oven he would cook any of the villagers' dinners for a penny. We had to walk to and from the bakehouse with the baking tin, and the lovely smell that rose from it on the return journey was almost unbearable.

But on one day each week in the summer the fire had to be lit specially, so that our mother could do the weekly ironing. As soon as the fire was nice and red she would hang a metal stand onto the fire bars, and the irons were stood on it—the fronts against the fire.

Two irons were necessary, one heating while the other was being used. She used to test the hot irons either by holding them up near her face or by spitting on them—then the little balls of bubbling spit galloped down the iron onto the hearth mat.

Such a lot of ironing there was too: knickers and nightgowns, pinnies and petticoats, working shirts and overalls, as well as bed linen. Then the freshly ironed clothes were hung on the fire-guard to air. Ours was a big oblong one, made of wire mesh with brass round the top. The guard was always kept round the fire when it was alight, so that the little 'uns were safe from it. But when we children had gone to bed our mother used to take it away so that they might get more comfort from the fire.

When we had weeks and weeks of rain the washing had to be dried indoors, either draped round the guard or slung up on lines in the back kitchen where it dripped damp and dismal, fogging up the windows, giving us colds and coughs.

Further down the garden, and quite a walk from the house, were ours and Missus-next-door's lavatories, side by side. These, when we first lived there, were 'privies' or vault type, a huge deep hole in the ground that was emptied about twice a year. Over the top of this hole was built a box-like contraption with two holes or places to sit. This was a 'two holer' and what most villagers had, although some had three and four holers. In ours there was one large hole for grown-ups and a smaller one for children. These really should have had wooden lids on when not in use, but not ours; they had most likely gone up the fire copper hole years ago.

After we had been living at 'Wayside' for about seven years these awful vaults were replaced by bucket lavatories, but not before an incident happened that could have easily been a tragedy in our family. I must have been about nine at the time and young Ben, one of my stepbrothers, about four. He had got into the habit of wanting to answer nature's call in the evening just as he and Denis were undressed ready for bed. He would say 'Mum, I want to go to the lavatory,' and our mother would say 'Mollie, take him down,' and I, no bigger than two penn'orth of 'apence, would stagger down the dirt path with Ben on my back, our light a candle that often blew out on the way down.

Ben was a cheeky, spoilt show-off, and each night as I carried him down he would jog about on my back and whine, 'I wants tu go on the big seat, I wants tu go on the big seat.' I suppose he thought he was old enough, but of course he was much too small.

As the weeks went by I got fed up with this nightly ritual, and suddenly, one night, I didn't bother to sit him carefully over the small hole but backed straight on to the big one and let him go. He folded up just like a shut-knife* and went down the hole backside first, leaving only his head, hands and feet showing. He let out a blood-curdling scream and I yelled at the top of my voice—the noise brought the whole family running pell-mell down the garden path. They hauled Ben out, smelly and frightened. I got a darned good hiding and Ben a good hot bath. But that 'larned' him. He answered nature's call earlier in the day after that.

Our stepfather, after working for a couple of years on a farm, got a job as a lorry driver for the 'Bewry', the local name for the Brewery in the town. He liked this varied job; it took him to many of the towns and villages within a radius of fifty miles where he delivered great barrels of beer and bottled stout to the firm's pubs and sampled the beer at each one.

At weekends he was glad to do a bit of seasonal work for the farmer who had previously employed him. I've known him take on the job of cutting and laying a hedge just for the privilege of taking the wood home, which was mostly blackthorn that burnt like coal. We kids would help by dragging the piled-up truck

* A pocket knife.

home time after time, with the smaller children carrying the wood chips.

He kept many of the habits he had acquired in the army and he was very strict with us. No going out in the morning without a clean pair of boots and no talking at meal times. If we were disobedient it was 'quick march' up to bed whatever the time of the day. He kept himself as smart as it was possible to do with such a big family, and his military moustache was kept clipped and twirled. He sang a lot too, mostly army songs, sometimes sentimental ones, sometimes cheeky—

> Put me on a hiland where the girls are few
> Put me in a cage with the lions at the zoo.

This he would sing to the tune of Mendelssohn's 'Spring Song'. My favourite was—

> Round the corner behind the tree
> Sergeant Major made love to me.
> Oh when are you going to marry me?
> For I should like to know
> 'Cos every time I look in your eyes
> I feel I want to go
> Round the corner behind the tree.

In his younger days he had emigrated to Canada and would tell us hair-raising stories of that great continent, but he got fed up with the life there and saved to pay his passage home—soon to settle in our quiet village with a ready-made family.

Often on a winter's night we would sit at home in the dimpsy light, gazing into the glowing embers and playing a game called 'Pictures in the fire'. Usually it was just the four of us younger ones, Mick, Ben, Denis, and myself, curled up on the warm hearthrug. The game was nearly all imagination but such fun to play.

'Look,' Mick would shout. 'Look, there's a fairy castle like the one in my Christmas picture book.'

'No it isn't,' Ben would butt in. 'It's an army fort with turrets and guns coming out of it.'

'It's not either, it's just like Windsor Castle where our King and Queen live,' I told them seriously.

While we were arguing, the picture would change as the coal and wood burnt away in the shiny black grate. Now the castle became a man's bearded face—a bit like Brummy Edwards. Now it was a dog. 'Our dog,' Denis the youngest would cry. And for a moment a dog's head, his mouth open as if barking, would glow clearly in the fire. Now it became a bird—its fine etched wings outstretched—and then, as if by magic, it changed to a lovely lady, her hair piled high, her dress full and flounced.

Suddenly the door was flung open and a wave of cold air would sweep round the room as Bern, Bunt and our stepfather came in from work, cold and hungry. Our mother would jump up, 'Time I lit the lamp,' she'd say. 'Didn't realize the time had got on so, listening to you kids.' And in a moment the warm glow of the oil lamp filled the room. You could still see pictures in the fire, but they never seemed quite so vivid and real as they had seemed in the almost darkened room.

'Come on,' my brothers would say, 'move back a bit you kids, we bin out at work all day.' Stiff, hard boots would be taken off and stood in the fender so that they might be warm and dry to put on in the morning.

Our mother would dish up the cooked meal, serving the men-folk first; then we children had ours, dipping chunks of bread into the gravy or thick stew.

'Jam roly-poly for pudding,' our mother would cry, brandishing a great knife, 'whose turn is it for the end bit?'

'Our Mollie's,' came a chorus. 'No it isn't, it's our Bern's,' I would protest. Arguments followed and excuses were made; nobody wanted the end bit, there was never any jam in that piece anyhow.

'You can wash up in here tonight, you girls,' our mother would say if the weather was cold. I would fetch the enamelled bowl from the freezing back kitchen and an old tin tray to turn the crocks on to drain. Mick was supposed to dry up. But she often invented a surprise trip to the lavatory or a bad hand or headache, cunningly getting out of her stint.

I would try to slip the kettle back empty on the hob. Someone would notice. 'Come off it Mollie, go and fill it up.' Nine times out of ten I'll bet the bucket was empty, so it was out into the ice-covered yard to the well, thrusting the well hook, simply freezing, and slippery with ice, down into the depths. The stars in the clear sky were sparkling and crackling in the frosty air as I drew up the heavy, full bucket.

Then it was off to bed for all of us children, so that the grown-ups might have a little warmth and comfort. Sometimes we might be allowed to stay up a bit late if one of the neighbours brought in their gramophone, and we would sing to the accompaniment of the singer on the scratchy records. But mostly we went to bed much earlier than lots of the village children. Our mother said it was good for us and that we grew while we were sleeping anyhow.

But sometimes when she was feeling tender and sentimental she would tell us stories of the past. Of how, when she was a schoolgirl, she used to have to go up to the big house every night during the winter-time to get jugs of rabbit soup. This was during the late 1800s, when times were very hard and in some places people were starving. Not in their village though. Thousands of rabbits were shot on the estate and made into stew in the great kitchens of the big house, and anyone from the village could go and get some daily.

'That stew,' our mother would say, with a far-away look in her eyes, 'was the best I've ever tasted. It was supposed to be for my Dad's tea, but walking back across the park with that lovely smell wafting round my nostrils was too much. I kept having a swig, it was nearly always half gone by the time I got home.'

And another tale she never tired of telling was the romantic one of our great-grandfather, and we children never got tired of hearing it. A dreamy look would steal over her face when she told us:

'Years and years ago your forbears lived in a little village called Preston in Gloucestershire. They were well-off farming people, and lords of the manor at one time. They had three sons, bold, black-haired and good-looking they were too. All over six-feet tall and as strong as the oxen that pulled the ploughs at a nearby farm.

'Job, the eldest of the three, was wild and wilful and a charmer—charm the hindleg off a donkey if he wanted to. When he was about twenty he fell head-over-heels in love with Emily, the pretty daughter of the shepherd who worked on his father's farm.

'What a good-looking pair they made too, he tall and dark and she a fair, shy little thing. At first they met quite openly, then Job's father got to hear about it. 'Course the fat was in the fire then. There was a most awful row and he dared his son never to speak to poor Emily again. "No son of mine is going to marry a shepherd's daughter," he said.

'Then the couple began to meet on the sly. Job would make any excuse to go out in the evenings, down to see if the cattle were all right or over to the blacksmith's to get the plough mended, just so that he could see Emily for a few moments.

'And do you know what happened then?' Mother would ask us as we sat spellbound listening to her—'they ran away and got married. After a little while the money ran out and they returned to the farmhouse at Preston to find the door closed against them for ever. My Grandfather never had a penny of the family fortune.

'And that,' Mother would add a bit sadly, 'is why we are so darned hard up. But at least you are all big and strong and healthy, and that's something you inherited from him.

'Then there's your own Gramp,' she went on, 'he'll never have a penny to bless himself with—give his head away if he could get it off. Now your Granny, she's different, good job she is else we should never have had a stick of furniture in the house, he'd give it away to anybody. And although we never had any of the family money officially, your Great-Grandfather's younger brother, Sam Broad, saw to it that your Gran wasn't entirely penniless and he

20

helped her no end secretly. He had a business in London besides the farm at Preston.

'Then suddenly it all ended. One day when Sam had been up to London on business, and most likely had a lot of money on him, he boarded the train to come home but he never reached there. All sorts of enquiries were made and at last the police came to the conclusion that he had been set upon and robbed, then murdered, and his body thrown out at some lonely spot. Anyhow nothing was ever heard of Sam Broad again, and the link with us and the rest of the family was broken.'

Some years ago I took my mother back to the little village of Preston and we searched the overgrown churchyard and found tombstones erected to our farming forbears.

One old fellow there told us that when he was a boy the names of some of the Broads were clearly marked on stone slabs in the aisle, but he added 'They be either all worn away or bin took up when they done some building alterations yer a few years back.'

3

There was a Time

MY idea of heaven was to go and stay at the home of my
grandparents who lived in one of those lodge houses on the
outskirts of a lord's country estate in a little village in Gloucestershire. My Grandfather was shepherd for this lord and my Grandmother was gate opener, for the lodge where they lived was
situated at the main gate that led to the great house that had as
many windows as days in the year.

That was how my grandparents met—in the big house. My
Gran was head cook there and one of my Grandfather's weekly
jobs was to kill a sheep and take it to the great kitchen where it
was basted and baked, steamed and boiled for both the gentry and
the dozens of servants that were employed there. By the time I
came along my grandparents must have been in their late sixties
but were still both at work.

The lodge was a sort of bungalow with one large living-room,
kitchen, back scullery, and two bedrooms. The one that I slept in
was filled with the smell of ripe apples and lavender. Under the
bed were boxes and boxes of apples carefully packed away for
winter use, and the cool clean sheets that I slept in seemed filled
with the scent of a summer garden.

They were great gardeners, both of them; more than half their
living came from the well-kept plot. All summer long we picked
and potted, pickled and chutneyed anything that was possible to
preserve for the coming winter. Such crops they grew! Giant
cabbages and potatoes, row upon row of broad beans and peas,
such as I have never seen since. My Grandfather liked to eat his
broad beans old: 'pitch-eyed' he called them. 'As big as a baby's

ear—six on a fork, that's how I like 'um,' he would say, 'an' boiled in a drop of bacon water too.'

Still, they had most everything at their advantage to grow good stuff: a couple of pigs in the sty, and the midden—the useful countryman's compost heap where both kitchen and garden waste was thrown—gave them a good supply of manure.

As well as this there were the yearly 'sheep dags'* that formed part of my Grandfather's perks. About a month before the sheep shearing, the flock had to be tidied up a bit, because mucky fleeces were not accepted at the wool staplers. So on a mild spring day my Gramp would round up the sheep, driving a few at a time into a smaller pen, where he would proceed to cut off wool that had become messy at the animal's rear end. For this work he used a pair of hand shears.

Sheep's wool is impregnated with lanolin and this, along with the clinging manure, makes a wonderful base in which to plant kidney beans, and the wool holds the moisture in the roots. It was a job to keep insects off the growing kidney beans and Gramp believed that soot was the best deterrent. But soot is harmful unless it is at least a year old, so it was carefully kept dry and left to mature before they sprinkled it liberally over the young plants.

My Gran and I would sit for hours, stringing and salting the beans for winter use, packing them tightly into fat yellow stone jars.

Another thing my Grandfather believed in was ' "Tater 'Awks' as he called them. Living on the edge of a great park, their garden was at the mercy of hordes of woodland birds, and the only thing that scared them away was ' "Tater 'Awks'. Each spring he would say, 'I shall have to get old Nathan (the head keeper on the estate) to shoot I a sparrow-'awk or two.'

Then he would get several nobbly potatoes—they had to be nobbly so that he could tie a piece of string round them. The largest feathers from the sparrow-hawks were stuck into the

---

* The country name for the mucky wool on a sheep's backside.

potatoes. Then these feathered contraptions were hung on a piece of string about a yard long and tied on to a stick which was pushed into the soil at a slight angle, leaving the ''Tater 'Awk' swinging and twirling at the slightest breeze. The finest bird scarer I've ever seen.

Any vegetables and fruit that were not wanted for immediate use, or for pickling and jam, were used to make home-made wine. Both my Gran and Gramp made all sorts which they imagined cured any complaint.

The gallons of agrimony that my Grandfather consumed! He really believed that this wine kept him free from rheumatism— most likely it did for he was out on the Cotswold hills for the best part of sixty years in all winds and weathers, with never a day off for illness. Each wine, they believed, had its own medicinal properties; clover for bronchitis, parsley for clearing the blood, beetroot for anaemia, mulled elderberry to sweat out a cold, dandelion for a sluggish liver, and metheglin, made from honey and sweet herbs, for a real good pick-me-up.

In the back scullery there was always wine of some sort or another fermenting. Gleanings from the garden and the hedge-rows and fields filled the floor of the stone-flagged scullery. Sometimes my Gran and I would go off on a drowsy summer afternoon to gather dandelions and agrimony, burnet and clover.

She never hurried her wines; after boiling they were allowed to settle in a big red earthenware pan. Then she would place a slice of barm-covered toast on top, leaving the concoction to ferment and bubble before straining it off into bottles and casks.

Several journeys I made during the summer to Northleach— three miles there and three back—to get a penn'orth of barm from the local brewery. I was given a two-pound stone jam jar to collect it in and on the way back I often poked my fingers into the barm, sniffing and savouring the sharp beery taste.

We drank wine after the midday meal and again before going to bed and if anyone called they were always asked, 'Will you have a glass of wine?' At seven years old I was quite a confirmed wine drinker!

I like to think that some of the wine-making, pickling, and chutneying that was so very much part of my youth has rubbed off from my Grandmother onto me, and the urge to rush out and pick dandelions and cowslips, elderberries and sloes and transform them into sparkling, brain-tickling wine is most compelling.

My grandparents' flower garden was a riot of colour whenever I saw it, full up with pansies and pinks, stocks and hollyhocks. Old-fashioned sweet briar roses and phlox tumbled and bloomed everywhere. Seeds were carefully gathered and saved each year and cuttings and slips swapped with other villagers.

Visitors never went away unless they were armed with some of my Gran's best blooms. She would scratch and bob about amongst the greenery like an old hen selecting the choicest flowers for them. 'Never give a bunch of flowers away unless you slips a sprig of rosemary in, my dear,' she once told me. 'It'll bring the receiver good luck, and bad to you if you forgets.'

I must have been a favourite grandchild because I was the only one of our family that was allowed to stay with her for any length of time. Although once, I remember, someone drove my mother, Bern, Bunt, Betty, and myself all the way to Sherborne to visit our grandparents. We went in a pony and trap and all I remember of the journey is that it was perishing cold and that the driver had piled hay on the floor of the trap—up to our knees it came. This was to help keep us warm during the long ride.

We must have stayed at the lodge overnight because I vividly remember we kids slept four in a bed, a single one at that—my sister and I at the top and our brothers at the bottom, with our feet meeting in the middle.

And the next day we had a scrumptious lamb-tail pie for dinner, something we had never even heard of before. My sister got quite distressed because our Gramp kept telling us that he 'bit 'um off' the young lambs, but it made no difference to either my brothers' or to my ever-eager appetite.

For our return journey our Gran packed us up one of her special apple cakes. It had brown sugar and cinnamon sprinkled on the top which gave it a sort of sweet crackly crust. We stopped to eat some and to give the pony a rest at a place called Worsham Bottom where a ghost named Black Stockings is still supposed to run across the road.

It was beginning to get dimpsy and we were scared stiff; owls were hooting and great black bats skimmed over our heads. A stoat ran out of the grass as the pony cropped it for a moment and my sister let out a blood-curdling scream and clung to our mother. Bern and Bunt would have liked to have stayed there longer but we others were eager to get moving again.

I loved visiting my grandparents. I used to travel by the carrier's cart part of the way and then get a lift from the baker or butcher to get to the lodge. There was no other way, no railway for miles and miles, and it was 1928 before the motor coaches started to operate between Oxford and Cheltenham. (The lodge is on the now very busy A40.)

4

A Cotswold Christmas

Such excitement there was in our house one Christmas—well, at least for me—for I was getting ready to go and stay with my beloved Gran and Gramp, just for the festive season. At six o'clock in the morning I'd got my flannel nightgown and my pinny packed, and all the little presents we had been busy making for me to take to the grandparents.

Our mother bundled the two youngest, Ben and Denis, into the pram and we set off for Witney where I was to be put in the capable hands of Mr Groves, the carrier. I was wearing one of my sister's coats that was miles too long and it flapped round my legs as I skipped alongside my mother. She had knitted me an emerald green tammy with a fluffy bobble on, and my stepfather had made me a muff from a rabbit's skin that he had cured. It was cold and frosty and I snuggled my hands deep inside the warm muff, my new shiny boots squeaking in rhythm as we hurried along.

I'd been to Sherborne by carrier cart several times before, but never had it been so crowded as it was on this day. The inside was stacked high with boxes and bundles and sacks of apples, and there were hares and rabbits hung on the sides, and some chickens in a crate at the back.

It took the carrier ages to get to Burford because he had to call at several of the cottages in the villages that lay along the valley of the Windrush, delivering boxes of groceries and things.

There were two women travelling in the cart and we chattered and laughed and stamped our feet in the hay that had been put on the floor to help keep our feet warm. I told them where I was going and all about my grandparents. Round, red-faced country women they were and they sat opposite, listening to me. 'You be a mighty fine story-teller,' one of them said. 'Never met a child with such an imagination before. 'Ow old did you say you was— seven? My Nellie's going on fer nine an' 'er can't chatter like you can.'

When they got down from the cart at Asthall one called back to Mr Groves, 'You 'ang on and I'll bring 'e out a hot drink, you'll both be froze to the marrow betime you gets to Burford.' She brought out hot cocoa and great hunks of bread and fat bacon, and it was lovely.

When Mr Groves went into the cottages to deliver things I could hear squealing and laughing and he would come out red-faced and beaming. Then I noticed that he'd got a piece of mistletoe tucked into the peak of his cap. 'What have you got that in there for?' I asked him, and he threw back his head and laughed a big, throaty, hearty laugh. 'Comes in very 'andy, do that bit of mistletoe,' he replied. But it was years before I realized how handy it must have been.

When we got nearer to Burford Mr Groves said that I could come out front with him. It was freezing cold and getting dimpsy. He flung a smelly horse rug over my legs. Then, hearing some children carol singing, he started, booming out in his rich voice 'Good King Wenceslas', and I joined in. Even his pony seemed to trot along better for our carolling.

The lamps and candles had been lit in the cottages and Mr Groves kept banging his hands across his chest to warm them. Then he lit the lamps on the cart and they glowed warm and bright, and as the pony's feet hit the stony road they sent out a shower of sparks like the sparklers did on bonfire night.

We dropped down the last hill into Burford—the lights of the town winking and blinking in the gathering gloom. Mr Groves pulled up outside a house and lifted me from the cart—I could hardly walk, my feet and legs were so cold. This was where he lived and we went into the hot, welcoming kitchen. His wife sat by the roaring fire making toast for our tea. They had four or five children, merry curly-headed kids they were too. After tea we sat up at the table and made paper-chains to decorate the room with. We cut strips of paper from brightly coloured tea packets, sticking the ends together with home-made flour paste.

About six o'clock Mr Greig, the baker, called for me. He was to take me on the last few miles to Sherborne. He lifted me up the front of his high cart and wrapped me in a couple of thick coarse flour sacks. He had to deliver bread at three more villages before we got to my Gran's. I was so tired, I'd been travelling since twelve o'clock, and I kept dropping off to sleep, but woke with a start every time the baker shouted, 'Whoa there, Jinny!' to his pony.

Then he brought me out a cup of hot, home-made wine from one of the cottages; it smelt sweet and strong. I took a sip. 'Go on,' he said, 'open your shoulders and let it down, it'll do you good. It just bin hotted with a hot poker.' I could feel the red liquid dropping into my stomach and soon a muzzy feeling crept over me; it was much stronger wine than my Gran's.

Next thing I knew, my Gramp was carrying me into the warm kitchen. My Gran took off my shiny new boots, and my long black stockings, and I cried as the life gradually came back into my frozen limbs. 'Yer Harry,' my Gramp said to the baker, ''ave a jackety 'tater, warms yer 'ands an' fills yer belly, that's what 'ot 'taters does.' My Gran cut open a steaming potato for me and spread it with home-cured lard. After a bit the baker got up to leave and my Gran handed him a bottle of 'me matheglum wine'* as she called it, and my Gramp gave him a hen pheasant, one of a pair that his employer had given him for Christmas.

Presently my Gran said 'Come on my little maid, you must be tired out—time you went to bed.'

My Gramp swung me up in his great arms—'Have you put that hot brick in the bed, Mother?' he called. And I was slipped into the lavender-smelling sheets. The heat from the brick that had been in the fire oven all day warmed me through and I was soon asleep.

---

* A drink made from honey, herbs, and water (metheglin or mead).

Next morning when I woke, the pale sun was shining on the window. There had been a sharp frost overnight and the panes were covered with frosty forests of Christmas trees, that seemed to glisten with a million fairy lights. I sat up in bed and scratched the frost with my finger-nail, then huffed on the pane, making a small clearing.

This was the day before Christmas and my Gran had lots to do. I knelt up in a chair by the big white scrubbed table and helped her to prepare the herbs for the stuffing—parsley and thyme, sage and onion. Gleanings from a summer garden they were. After picking and carefully drying the sage, parsley, and thyme, she had rubbed the fine leaves from the stalks, afterwards storing the leaves in jam jars tied down with brown paper. The onions came from a big thick rope that hung out in the back kitchen. Roping them had been Gramp's job after he had harvested them the previous autumn, and as we chopped and mixed the herbs together the kitchen was filled with lovely, country, stuffingy smells.

We were going to have such a dinner on Christmas day—that's all we talked about as we plucked the feathers from the bright cock pheasant. I'd never tasted pheasant before—not that my Gran and Gramp had it often, only when his employer, the old squire, presented each of his workmen with a brace at Christmas-time.

My Gran showed me what she had had from her ladyship. 'Look, my dear,' she said, holding up yards of red flannel. 'Make me some good warm petticoats—needs a bit of wool round yer bones in this climate.' There was a pound of tea too, in grey-coloured packets with pictures on them, showing black men and women working in the fields. 'That's where the tea comes from,' my Gran told me. 'Hundreds and hundreds of miles away where it's ever so hot. So hot that the sun turns everybody black.'

Every housewife whose husband worked on the estate had had a present of some red flannel and tea, as well as boots for the children who were still at home.

Every now and then, my Gran had to leave what she was doing and go and open the park gate to let people through to the big house. 'Drat the visitors,' she'd say after several interruptions. 'Don't give a body time to settle at nothing.'

My Gramp came home from work about five o'clock. He was a giant of a man and he wore trousers that squeaked as he walked. He had leather straps round his legs, just below the knees. They were used to hitch the trousers up so that the bottoms would not get wet and muddy. All farm workers seemed to wear them. His face was the colour of a russet apple and he had a mop of black curly hair which he washed every day, and screwed-up, bright blue eyes. I asked why he screwed his eyes up and he said, 'Ah! against that pesky old wind out there,' nodding in the direction of the hills.

There was no trouble to get me off to bed that night. My Gramp said that he would be sure to see that the fire was out before he came to bed so that Father Christmas wouldn't burn himself when he came down the chimney. Hopefully I hung one of Gran's black stockings on the brass bed knob. Yet I wondered how Father Christmas would know that I was not still at Ducklington.

Next morning, almost before it was light, I crawled to the bottom of the bed. He had been. I could feel the nobbly, filled stocking. It was packed with things—sugar-mice, a liquorice pipe, nuts, an orange and a rosy apple, a painting book, a chocolate watch, like my Gramp wore in his wesket pocket, and best of all, a beautiful little doll dressed in pink.

I squealed with delight—I had never had a real doll before, only black ones our Mother used to make from old stockings. My Gran found one of her crocheted shawls and I sat by the roaring fire nursing my lovely doll while she got on with the cooking.

Into the oven went the pheasant and potatoes for baking while on the hob a monstrous Christmas pudding bubbled and boiled in the great saucepan. Up to her elbows in flour, my Gran made pastry for mince pies. Her face was red and shiny where she kept bending and peering into the oven as each batch was drawn out.

For the hundredth time I peeped at my doll, then I let out a loud scream. 'What ever is the matter my little maid?' my Gran said, rushing over to my side.

'Look Granny, look,' I cried, my cheeks streaming with tears, 'my doll's face, it's gone.'

The heat from the fire had melted the pretty wax face; now all that was left was a shapeless lump. I cried for the rest of the day. I couldn't even eat. I never did taste the pheasant we had prepared so excitedly the day before. As my Gramp ate his Christmas pudding he kept finding shiny threepenny bits. 'Come on my little maid,' he said, 'you might find a florin in your piece.' But it was no use—nothing comforted me.

We went to church the next evening, walking down the beech-lined drive to the village. As we went up the church path a horrid boy snatched my green tammy off by the bobble and I punched him so hard he soon dropped it. 'Proper little spitfire en't you?' he said, but he didn't try it again. My grandparents were slightly ahead of me, chattering, otherwise they would have chastised me for such unseemly behaviour so near to the church.

As the lord and lady of the Manor took their seats in the cold, grey, candle-lit church, the women all curtsied. Her ladyship was dressed in deep purple and sat stiff-backed and regal. Like a proud foreign bird she looked. The brilliant feathers round her turban-shaped hat wriggled and fluttered at the slightest movement. She showed up like a jewel against a sea of the Sunday-best black of the village folk.

Out in the cold moonlight night once more; goodnights and ''appy New Year if I dun't see 'e agen' echoed again and again. Then back through the park, quiet now, save for the hooting owls and scurryings across the leaf-strewn path of things I couldn't see; and I held my Gramp's hand tight for fear of being whisked away by witches and hobbly-goblins into the trees.

The next day one of the footmen from the big house knocked at the door of the lodge. He handed a big brown paper parcel to my Gran. 'It's for the little girl,' he said. We stood there for a moment, speechless. 'What ever is it Mr Carter?' my Gran asked.

'Well Mrs Broad, her ladyship heard that your little grandchild had had a most unfortunate accident with her doll. There's a note inside,' he said, and was gone.

Still bewildered we went back into the house and I snatched at the wrappings, tearing the paper with excited fingers. 'Careful, child,' my Gran warned, 'it might be something breakable.' She read the note pinned on the top of the box, 'For the pretty little girl in the gay green tammy'. Inside was the biggest, most beautiful doll I had ever seen. My Gran said that it must have belonged to one of her ladyship's children when they were small. It was dressed in fur-trimmed satin and all the clothes took off and I undressed that doll a hundred times or more that day I'm sure. Excitedly I told my Gramp about the doll when he came home from work. He lifted me on his lap and said, 'It's worth all the tea in China to see you laughing again.'

A few days later the baker picked me up. I was to travel back home as I had come, and although I'd got my lovely doll and a parcel of things for the rest of the family I cried when I left my grandparents. 'Come again soon little maid,' they said, but I never did.

During the next year my Gran died and my Gramp went to live with my uncle and aunt at a nearby farm. But I spent some very happy holidays with him there.

We used to sit on the wall near the road and he'd sing to me. His favourite was 'Pretty Polly Perkins from Paddington Green'. I've only to hear the tune now and I'm back in that quiet Cotswold village sitting on a wall with my Gramp.

His hair that was once so very black had now turned to what he called 'pepper and salt'—really sprinkled with grey—his eyes brightest blue, crinkled and laughing. And that's how I last saw him, waving goodbye to me as I rode away in the baker's cart that was to take me to Burford. He had given me two super ripe pears to take home but I remember eating them before we got out of the village.

Sometimes I pass the lodge where my grandparents lived for so long and where I spent such happy times. The last occasion was on a cold November day. The place was empty and deserted, the curtainless windows had a ghostly air about them, the Cotswold mist hanging thick in the beech-lined drive, and the last remaining leaves fluttering quietly to the ground. I had a great urge to stop and peer in at the windows. Never go back they say, so I turned away, leaving undisturbed all the lovely memories of the past.

5

The Little Farm

THE farm where my uncle and aunt lived was set right down in the village of Sherborne, about a mile and a half from the lodge where my Gran and Gramp had lived. And during the school holidays I always went to stay with them for a few weeks.

It was a little farm—I say a 'little' farm because at that time they had only six or eight cows and delivered milk round the village. They had a hand cart they used to push around with a big milk churn in it, and my uncle and cousin would call at the cottages with the milk in steel cans that held about two gallons. Hanging inside the cans were pint and half-pint measures, and at intervals they would refill the cans from the big churn on the hand cart.

The other side-line to this little business of theirs was the lovely buttercup-yellow butter my auntie used to make. First of all she poured the milk from the wide steel pans into a separator, a large mincer-like contraption, hand-turned, and this separated the cream from the milk by some ingenious device so that the cream poured into one pan and the skim milk into another. This skim milk was often fed to the young calves, but poor people with large families would sometimes buy it for about a penny a quart to make milk puddings and other things.

I still seem to hear the monotonous drone that separator made as my auntie tirelessly turned the handle until all the milk that had been set aside had gone through. Then she would pour the thick cream into a wooden butter churn and stand it on the table on its side. Hers had two little wooden legs. Then she would turn the handle which operated the small wooden paddles inside, and before she'd been at it long the wet, sloppy, slap-slap of the paddles changed into a firm and solid sound which meant that the cream had slowly turned into butter.

She'd tip the rough, solid lump of yellow fat out of the churn, then reach for her butter pats. These were flat and made of wood, scrubbed white, and finely ridged, about five inches long and three inches wide, and they had handles. Grasping one in each hand she would pick up one of the yellow lumps, deftly turning it and patting it again and again till it resembled a half-pound slab of butter.

If the weather was very hot my aunt would stack the neat half-pound packs into a large steel bucket, tie a rope to the handle and gradually let the bucket down in the cool well. When the water was about three parts of the way up the outside of the bucket, she'd secure the other end of the rope to a heavy iron bar in the yard—it was always known as the butter bar and I never remember it being used for anything else.

In those days a good deep well was the housewife's only form of keeping food cool, and often meat and milk would be put into buckets and slung down the well until they were needed.

Sometimes if I paid a surprise visit to my aunt's, she would make enough butter specially for my tea. She'd scoop a little thick cream into a jam jar, then, keeping her hand tight over the neck of the jar, she would sit in a chair, shake the jar for about five minutes while we were chatting—then suddenly a lump of yellow would emerge from the cream and she would plop it out on a plate, sprinkle it with a little salt, and cut wafer-thin bread— leaving *me* to spread that wonderfully flavoured rich butter on, topped with home-made strawberry jam. I don't care what anybody says, and this is not just a fancy of my youth—like perpetual sunshine and things—but that butter my auntie made did taste very different from anything you can buy today.

My Auntie Sarah, like my Gran, was a great wine maker. She was also a good chapel-going body and had a number of friends who were of the same religion. One hot summer I remember she had a couple of lay preachers staying with her for a few days. They were going round to some of the remote villages to preach the gospel and made my auntie's home their temporary headquarters. Both were very much the 'holier than thou' type and firmly believed that any form of 'drink' was a sure passport to hell.

Before they arrived at the farm we carefully moved all the bottles and casks of wine up into a loft over the kitchen. The farm had once been a mill and this loft was where they stored the flour. We had to handle it very gently because some of the wine was still at the fermenting stage, but at least it was out of sight.

As soon as they arrived they started ranting and raging about a young couple who were camping out in a tent near the farm. They had met them as they came down the dusty road—the couple had just come away from the off-licence with bottles of beer under their arms. They did this most days, laying them in the shallow water at the edge of the River Windrush to keep the beer cool and drinkable.

All we heard from the lay preachers was the hell fire and damnation that would surely be the fate of the camping couple and anyone else who took any sort of intoxicating drink. They never stopped. My uncle would catch my eye and look heavenwards as if to say, how much longer have we got to put up with this?

But suddenly their visit was cut short. The afternoon was very hot, threatening thunder, not a breath of air anywhere, and the worthy gentlemen were leading off for the umpteenth time about the sins of the world, and how they were going to convert everybody, when the air was shattered with a loud report, then another and another. Up jumped the black-coated lay preachers, eyes blazing, arms flung heavenwards—'There are the warning notes,' called one in a ranting voice. 'Yes, hell fire and damnation!' shouted the other. 'Judgement on all sinners!'

Just at that moment a red, gory substance started pouring down the walls and onto the white, scrubbed stone floor and settled in a puddle at one of the visitor's feet, and a strong fruity, winey smell filled the room. I took one look at my red-faced aunt and we both went off to get buckets and house flannels to sop up the mess. The visitors stamped out of the house and up the road toward the next village and we never saw them again.

And the only damnation came from my uncle because his favourite wine (raspberry, red- and black-currant) had ended up all over the kitchen floor.

6

School Days

THE village school, like others of that time, was small and overcrowded. How teachers managed to cram anything into the heads of a bunch of rough country children was a miracle. But with the exception of a few that even a genius could not have taught, we did not turn out too badly—or else where would we be today? Like most of the children, I started school at the tender age of three—five was the proper age, but my mother, like others with large families, was only too glad to get another child off her hands for a few hours.

But those first early days proved to be quite disastrous. It happened that Bern and Bunt, my elder brothers, had taught me a jingle. They seemed to find it very funny and on our way to school kept saying it to me: 'You wants to ask if you can say it to Sir,' Sir being our one-eyed school master, quite kind and very clever.

All that first week we infants played with sand and beads and listened to the frizzy-haired girl who was in charge of us telling stories and nursery rhymes. But I liked the one my brothers had taught me better. And I kept asking 'Miss' if I could tell it to the Headmaster.

The first morning of the second week I was called out front. 'We are all going up to the top class, Mollie. Mr Westwell wants to hear your poem,' Miss said. We traipsed up; I walked boldly, swaggeringly, showing off. I was to say my piece in front of the whole school! The Headmaster lifted me up and stood me on his desk. 'Silence!' he said. 'Let the youngest pupil in the school recite.'

Beaming boldly I began,

> Nipple, Nipple with one eye—

From the back of the room I could see my brothers, taller than the rest of the kids. Bunt had gone very red and Bern was waving to me. I waved back and went on,

> Went to Church on Sundays,
> Prayed to God to give him strength
> To whack the kids on Mondays.

There was a deadly hush and then suddenly the air was rent with the loud whacking of Mr Westwell's cane as it came down on the desk, and I nearly fell off with fright. I noticed he had turned the colour of my mother's geraniums. Something was wrong—no clapping from the class, just silence. Suddenly I was seized, turned over and tanned on the backside several times. Bawling and screaming I ran out of the room, round by the pond and the church and home. And my first public appearance was ended.

Because of this incident our mother took us away from the village school and we all trailed up to Witney for a little while, but I remember nothing of this short period. Then the old school master at Ducklington retired and we returned to the village school.

By then, fortunately for us, a Mr and Mrs Preston had been appointed. He was Headmaster, teaching standards 4, 5, 6, and 7, and his wife taught the lower classes. They were a marvellous pair, kind and understanding and just what we needed in the village. They were fresh and young and loved by all.

After school some of us would stay behind and practice for the concerts that they tirelessly arranged. Dressed in clothes that Mrs Preston contrived, we became Kings and Queens, Princes and Pages. To a bunch of uncouth village children this was wonderful. Our stage in the parish room where the concerts were performed consisted of a number of trestle tables, erected carefully to make them safe to walk on. Everybody turned out to these events to see 'ower little 'uns' perform. We did not realize that these brief concerts were helping us to grow up—to talk properly and make it possible to converse with people.

To our school came children from outlying villages and hamlets. They often had to cross a couple of muddy fields before walking the two or three miles to Ducklington. One of these small places was called Yelford, just a manor house, a farm, four cottages, and a church in a field. One very big family who lived at Yelford used to pick up eight or ten loaves of bread after school, carrying it home in hessian sacks slung across their backs. To keep the bread moist their mother used to stack it in the church font. Their cottage was very near to the little church and it was easy to slip out and get a loaf. The big family left little storage room in the cottage for such a lot of bread.

Another family who lived in one of the hamlets took on the delivery of the newspapers, both in our village and where they lived. They walked from their home for three miles to collect the daily papers and delivered to most of the cottages in our village before school. Then during the dinner-time they delivered the rest. But the people who lived in their own hamlet had to wait until after school for theirs.

At school, boys and girls played together in a small playground where there were four bucket lavatories for the girls and four for the boys, separated by sheets of corrugated iron. The boys used to try and frighten the girls in all sorts of ways, and once one of them put a great hedgehog in a newly emptied bucket. Then they waited for the first girl to go in.

It happened to be a timid, rather shy girl and fairly new to the school. She saw the animal just as she was about to sit down and, letting out a loud scream, came rushing out with her long, white, lace-edged drawers hanging round her knees. Then they fell to her ankles and she went headlong, full length onto the hard playground. The screaming and shouting brought out Mr Preston and all the boys got six of the best.

In the playground kids fought and played and called each other names—

> 'Oodley, 'oodley,
> Stick stack stoodley,
> Eyeball, beball,
> Long-legged 'oodley.

someone would chant to us Woodleys, although the same rhyme could be used for other names. For the short-legged Fishers, for instance:

> Fisher, Fisher,
> Stick stack stisher,
> Eyeball, beball,
> Short-legged Fisher.

A favourite way of answering back was:

> Sticks and stones
> May break my bones
> But names will never hurt me.

Children who told tales had this bawled to them in the street:

> Tell-tale tit,
> Cut your throat a slit,
> All the sense that you've got
> Is in your mother's teapot.

When there was a General Election children proudly wore a coloured ribbon according to their parents' politics—although grown-ups would never admit which party they fancied. We Conservatives would link arms and chant:

> Vote, vote, vote for Major Edmondson.
> Who's that knocking at the door?
> If it's Bennett or it's Fry [Liberal and Labour candidates]
> We'll sock 'um in the eye
> And never see their faces any more.

And we'd snatch ribbons off other children if they happened to be wearing anything other than blue.

At school you could catch head-lice quicker than measles and our mother dreaded the time when we might be sent home by 'The Bug Nurse' or 'Nitty Norah', as some of us called the health nurse who came to our school about once a month to examine everybody's head. As soon as she walked in our teacher would say 'Heads down, children,' and we all folded our arms across the desks and rested our heads on them. Before this public examination the teacher would have a whispered conversation with the nurse, probably about those children who were known always to be cooty.* These were sent out to wait in the porch, where we hung our coats, then they were sent home and told not to come back until their mothers had got their heads clean.

During the very cold weather we used to take our dinner to school. Our mother would pack up great hunks of bread and dripping or lumps of cold bread pudding and give us each a screw of paper that contained a spoonful of sugar and cocoa. Our teacher would put a kettle of water on the tortoise stove† so that we might make a hot drink—that is, if we hadn't eaten the dry mixture beforehand.

After a couple of years Mr Preston fell ill and they left, and a Miss Spencer became Headmistress. The lower classes were taught by shy, kindly, plump Miss Evans. She was young and pretty and I worshipped her. She did her hair up in a knot at the back and wore crocheted jumpers that I could see through and she had dimples in her arms just above the elbows. Her voice was quiet but firm and when she read poetry to us it used to make me cry.

One Christmas she gave me a present of a lovely handkerchief. Stamped on it was a figure of a Spanish lady, dressed in red. It was the first handkerchief I had ever possessed—bits of old sheeting

---

* Children, dogs, or cats that had fleas or nits in their hair.

† A single coke-burning stove (with a tortoise stamped on the lid) that was supposed to heat the schoolroom.

were doled out to our family for nose-blowing, and always pinned on the jersey or frock of the younger members so as not to lose them. I could do nothing wrong while I was in Miss Evans's class. 'Teacher's pet' they called me while I was there for I was always top, except for sums.

Too soon it was time to move up to Miss Spencer's. She came from somewhere in Lincolnshire and pronounced her words in a different way from us in our small Oxfordshire village. We would be in the middle of a singing lesson—suddenly she would stop playing the piano, jump up, stamp her foot and say—'It's moon, moon, moon, not moo-oon as you say it.' Words like 'round' and 'bound' and lots of others she tried to make us say differently. But it was useless for her to try to alter a dialect that our mothers and fathers and the whole family spoke. One prim little miss couldn't alter centuries of speech. Whereas Miss Evans brought out the best in us, Miss Spencer seemed to do just the opposite—at least for me.

I don't think she was used to country children anyhow. She was small and pinched-looking and had soft white hands, and catching hold of them in country dancing was like holding a sponge. She wasn't used to our rough ways and would squirm when kids brought in frogs and frog spawn, and fat-backed toads. One boy, Doungey Clarke, brought a couple of harmless grass snakes into school, hidden in his cap, and she squealed the place down. We had no respect for her at all.

Older boys of thirteen and fourteen were sometimes head and shoulders taller than Miss Spencer. When she called them out to cane them for some trifling offence they just snatched the cane from her. And once Chris Goodwin, a great lump of a lad, picked her up and dumped her down on the tortoise stove—thankfully it was summertime. How we giggled and sniggered to see her skinny legs dangling in space!

Then suddenly one Monday morning she was not there. She had gone back to Lincolnshire in a hurry. Stories flashed round the village like wildfire—she was supposed to have been secretly in love with a confirmed bachelor. The poor fellow would have nothing to do with her and, filled with frustration, she packed her bags and left.

That summer our school lessons were continued by a Miss Seed who came pedalling over the Aston Hills to fill in for our departed Miss Spencer. She arrived on an old upright bicycle—'Seedie's bedstead' we called it. But she was jolly and understanding, and above all fair. In the past there had been too much discrimination between the very poor kids and the better-off ones.

It was while she was in charge of us that I won 'The Bishop's prize' for scripture. As my hand shot up to answer the examiner's questions I could see her encouraging smile time and time again almost saying, that's it, my girl, you can do it. I still have the prize, the only thing I have ever won. Inside the worn, red-covered Prayer Book is written: 'Presented to Mollie Woodley, Ducklington School, after an examination held on the 17th of June 1927. Signed: William Preedy, Assistant Diocesan Inspector.

As it was a church school we often attended services during weekdays—Ascension Day, Saints' days, and Empire Day, and once a year we all solemnly took an egg to a church service, carefully laying our small offering in a yellow wicker washing basket that was placed near the altar. The eggs were afterwards packed up and taken to Oxford on the train, and then on to the Radcliffe Infirmary.

On Empire day we all got up early to go into the meadows to pick daisies, which we made into daisy chains to drape on our dresses and garlands for our heads and waists, wrists and ankles. Then after a short church service we would all troop out to the small green by the school and march round saluting the Union Jack.

On the 29th May, bedecked with sprigs of oak apple, we linked arms on our way to school and chanted—

> Shick Shack day,
> Twenty-ninth of May,

If we don't have a holiday
We'll all run away.

And woe betide any kid not wearing a sprig of oak. Gangs of us set on such offenders, stinging them all over with nettles.

There were no facilities for anything other than just ordinary lessons at our small school. It was a three-roomed building with part of one room screened off for the infants. When we reached the age of thirteen we girls walked up to Witney once a week to attend cookery and housewifery lessons and the boys went on a different day to learn woodwork. We girls were taught how to make cornflour moulds and rice puddings, and how to turn out rooms and do laundering, while the boys made stools and tea trays, and we all learned a new way of life in town.

Some of the town kids looked upon us as a bunch of hobbledehoys; they called us names and teased us about our rough clothes. 'You be one a they dungle-bred* 'Oodleys from Duckleton' a pale-faced, runny-nosed girl said to me one day, and I set about her and we fought like a couple of cats—nobody called me 'dungle-bred' after that.

Sitting in school on hot summer days we could hear the cows going by, to and from milking, with Mr Druce calling them, 'cup, cup, cup', and occasionally shouting to Blossom or Jenny for stopping to pull grass from the churchyard. The village pond was just outside the classroom and we could hear the cows splash into the green slimy water where they would stand like statues, cooling their great hot bodies; then we would hear the slosh-slosh as their long pink tongues picked up the water.

There were always ducks on the pond, just a few. They belonged to Mrs Lija Collis who lived near by. Any time of the day her precious birds could be seen waddling across the green that separated her cottage from the pond, or swimming or standing on their heads searching for food on the slimy bottom. A reward if we

* Someone born in a remote part of the village where there was likely to be many dung-heaps.

46

ever found a duck's egg was a super piece of home-made cake—how we searched and prayed to find an egg in the rushes or in the rough grass near the water!

Recently I came across these few lines in a book—

> Four ducks on a pond,
> A grass-bank beyond,
> A blue sky of spring,
> White clouds on the wing:
> What a little thing
> To remember for years—
> To remember with tears!

They were written by William Allingham and someone had scribbled on the top in pencil, 'Ducklington Pond'.

Not that there was always a blue sky of spring; in winter the pond was often frozen solid for weeks on end and we would spend many happy hours sliding there. In summer we made mud pies on its fly-filled sides and most all of us at some time fell in, but our parents were probably none the wiser because, as we played all through the long hot summer days, our clothes just dried on us.

Some of the carters were very kind and would give us a ride up the village or from Witney if we had been on an errand. I loved to ride on Holtoms' flour carts. Carter Porter used to sit up front, covered in a fine white dust of flour; even his eyelashes were powdered with the stuff. Sometimes he would have three, other times four, great cart horses in the shafts depending on the weight of the load. The great sacks of flour were stacked in the long Oxfordshire wagon and in the summertime the horses wore little white caps with blue and red bobbles on over their ears to keep the flies from worrying them, and their tails would be tied up with red and blue too. And always the horses wore harness brasses that winked and shone in the sunshine.

When Carter Porter drove the team to Witney he would start tapping the horses just before he got to the station hill so that they could pull the great load up better. When we got to the top he would stop and jump down and slip under one of the back wheels a thing he called a shoe brake. It was flat and about a foot long and it stopped the wheel from turning, and this helped to steady the loaded wagon downhill.

At the goods station he would skilfully back the horses and cart right up the track where he and the railway workers unloaded the flour into a railway wagon. But not before he had hung great brown nosebags filled with chaff round the horses' necks, and they would stand and munch contentedly, occasionally blowing into their food. When the bag was nearly empty they would toss it up, flinging their heads high, to enable them to get all the bits at the bottom of the nosebag.

When it was raining, carters and farm workers used to sit hunched up on their carts with sacks tied over their heads and shoulders. Some of them disliked us kids hanging on the backs of the carts and they would give a backward flick with their whips, narrowly missing, just to let us know that we were not to hang on, let alone ride. But when you had walked backwards and forwards to school twice and then had to run an errand up to the town, a little help, even from a muck cart, was welcome.

At harvest time we used to go out into the fields where the men were busy loading the sheaves and cadge a ride on the leading horse. Up and down all day from the farm to the fields I've ridden on the fat brown rump of old Turpin; so big he was he filled the shafts of the yellow farm wagon.

Then one day on our way home from school we came across a little knot of people, so we joined them, pushing forward to see what had happened. Turpin lay helpless in the roadway, his huge brown eyes rolling, his once active body now still and useless. 'Dun 'is bit, no good to nobody now,' one of the old men said. Someone sent for the knacker man, and crying bitterly we watched them drag the heavy animal, now dead, onto the floor of the cart. Then, roped and chained, he was taken away.

The incident worried me for days, until our mother took me quietly on her lap and explained that Turpin's soul had gone where the fields were always filled with sweet grass and scented clover. There would be no more hard work—no more clouts on his brown rump for not going fast enough—nothing to do all day but roam about in those evergreen glades with other animals. And the picture of a heaven filled with cropping horses put my mind at rest.

A little while afterwards Clarke's horse fell down and died, and I didn't feel too bad at all.

One day I was sent up to Witney to get two twopenny oranges for Bunt who was in bed with tonsillitis.

When it was fine we never went the road way to the town but took a short cut through 'The Moors', across a footpath that lay over three or four fields with tiny wooden bridges spanning the green-slimed ditches.

I was dawdling back home, lazily dangling a plimsolled foot into the almost stagnant water. It was scorching hot. Fat cows grazed in the fields, tails swinging like pendulums. Clouds of flies hung over the manure-covered paths. I grabbed a handful of azzies (the local name for haws) and chewed away as contentedly as the cows.

Suddenly from behind the hedge came one of the village lads—he was a great gangling boy of about fourteen and a bit on the simple side.

'Hello,' he said. 'I got summut fer you,' and he came towards me, cap in hand. In the cap were about a dozen bright-red crab-apples.

He handed them to me with one hand and grabbed hold of me with the other. 'I got summut else fer you too,' he whispered hoarsely, with a wild animal look on his face. 'You come down yer with I,' and he half-dragged me towards the hedge.

I struggled, wrenching myself free, tossing the cap full of crab-apples in his red sweaty face and rushed stumbling over the grass. I lost my oranges as I ran over the fields, blindingly crying, breathless and terror-stricken. I reached the stile and roadway before I dare look round to see if he was following.

Just then one of the carters from the flour mill came riding by on his wagon. He pulled up the horses to a stop.

'Come on young Mollie, what's up wi' you? En't never sin you cryin' affor'.'

He sat me up beside him. I tried to answer him but no sound came out. 'I've lost me oranges,' I blurted out at last. 'They're for our Bunt. 'E en't very well.'

'Never mind, one of the others 'ull go an' find 'um,' he said, as he set me down outside our gate.

Our mother was in the garden. 'She's lost her oranges, poor little mite. Proper upset 'er is too,' he called out.

'I'll give her "lost her oranges",' she cried. 'That was my last few coppers till Saturday,' and she boxed my ears as I ran indoors. 'Go on off to bed with you. That'll teach you not to waste good money,' she called after me as I crept upstairs.

Betty was sent back over 'The Moors'. She found the oranges all right. 'There was crab-apples scattered all over the place,' she told our Mother. 'Bin wastin' 'er time picking them sour things I reckon.'

7

Hop, Skip and Jump

THERE was no special time to start certain games. For weeks we all might be skipping madly, then one day someone would come to school with a bag of marbles or a whip and top, and suddenly all the other children did the same. For when errands had been run or our small daily tasks had been completed we would spend the long summer evenings playing contentedly, all the while trying to play our chosen game as well as or better than our brothers and sisters, or the kids next door.

Probably many of the games had been handed down from earlier generations—ring games and ball games with singing and rhymes to accompany them, although some of the words most likely had lost their original meaning.

Some of the games needed more than one child to play them, but it was nothing to see a small solitary figure, pig-tailed and pinafored, bouncing a ball against a wall while counting, reciting, chanting, or singing. The idea was to keep the ball in play through an ever-changing, intricate sequence of movements. The first dozen times it was simply thrown against the wall and caught, then bounced under the right leg, then under the left leg and finally bounced onto the wall again while the player spun round and caught it in mid-air.

Another ball game was Alary:

> One, two, three, alary
> My ball went down the cary
> Serves you right for playing alary
> On a Sunday morning.

All Kinds of Magic

The first time each word of the rhyme was spoken the ball was bounced, but on repeating it the pattern was changed. We would bounce the ball, throw the right leg over, and when we could bounce it with the left hand and throw the left leg over, then our cup was full. To perfect these games was our aim and it did not matter how long it took.

Skipping was often done by solitary children. Our mother disliked the skipping craze because we wore out so much boot leather, but skip we would. Some of the children possessed proper ropes with nicely shaped wooden handles all painted red and blue. Poorer children had to be contented with any old bit of thick string they could get hold of. Skipping games usually started with a slowly spoken jingle. 'Salt, mustard, vinegar, pepper', we would chant, then speed up the rope to finish with an exultant 'one hundred'.

Other Oxfordshire rhymes were—

> Black-currant, red-currant,
> Raspberry jam,
> Tell me the name
> Of your young man

or

> Cups and saucers,
> Plates and dishes,
> Here comes a man
> In calico breeches.

As we progressed we could skip backwards—at least the rope was twirled backwards, or with the arms across the chest. And if you could jump in the air while the rope was twirled twice under your feet then you were really happy.

Whips and tops were most popular in the spring when the roads began to dry and clean from mud and muck. You could buy a top for a ha'penny. There were different sorts, and we had a special name for each: Carrot, Granny, Window Breaker, or Spinny Jinny. They were usually made of plain white wood but we would crayon the tops so that when they spun round they looked quite pretty.

The shortage of string for the whips presented problems, and who could afford to buy string? If we could get one of the older boys or girls who worked in the blanket mills at Witney to bring us a bit of 'mill bonding', a thickish, strong white string—only used in the mills—then we were well away.

There was an art in keeping a top going by just thrashing it with a whip. The trouble with the 'window breakers'—sleek, slim tops they were—was the fact that they flew in the air as you whacked them, and if your aim was bad they often smashed straight through somebody's front window. Then there was hell to pay—at least the offender's parents were expected to buy new window glass. In the meanwhile the precious top and whip were flung on the back of the fire.

Hoops was another game that was hard on boot leather. Some of the boys had large iron hoops which they steered skilfully with an iron hook; for miles and miles they bowled them. Girls, if they were lucky, had smaller wooden ones which they tapped gently with a stick—mostly we used old bicycle wheels or tyres and got just as much fun out of them.

Of course, marbles was a summer craze, a slower, quieter game, and if you had a penny you could buy twenty chalk marbles. A Tally, which was the one you scattered the smaller ones with, usually cost a farthing and was often made of clear glass with bright, multi-coloured wavy threads in. If you were lucky enough to find an empty lemonade bottle that had been thrown away, a sharp crack on a stone broke the bottle and released a super glass Tally for nothing. Boys *and* girls played the game, but it was really considered more of a boy's game. The marbles were carried around in flannel bags secured tightly at the top with a thread of tape.

Once, from somewhere, I'd got four marbles and a glass tally and one night after school I plagued the champion of the village to play. He was a big bully of a lad and sniggered as I challenged him. 'I shall take your few fust game, you see if I dun't! Hark at 'er challenging I, thur yent nobody in the school as can beat I.'

It was true too, and he and his followers used to walk to the other villages and challenge the kids there. 'Set 'um up then Mollie, we en't got long to 'ang about yer, we be awf up to Witney tu beat some a they tonight.' We placed our marbles on the dusty road against the school wall. 'You go fust,' Bert said, 'cost if you dun't you wun't 'ave no chance at all tu play.'

I took careful aim and scattered the row of chalk marbles. 'Coo!' one of the other boys said, 'that was a lucky aim.' I quickly picked up my winnings.

'Beginner's luck—thas what that was,' Bert sniggered. He stood well back, took aim at the fresh row we had set up—and missed!

'Crikey! Wass up wi you?' Percy Russell said. 'Strikes I you be nervous Bert.'

For the next half hour we played and Bert the Bully never won a game. The other boys were shouting and cheering me on and Bert was swearing and getting redder and redder. Then it came to the pitch when he set his last few marbles in a row. Spitting on his hands he swore he'd beat me yet. But he didn't, and mad with temper he flung his super lucky tally at me, hitting me sharply in the face.

'There, take that!' he said. 'I'll win 'um all back tomorrow, you see if I dun't.' Then he and his gang moved off, shouting and swearing. I stuffed my winnings into Bert's flannel marble bag that he'd left lying on the ground and ran off home.

When I got to school next morning Bert and his gang were bowling their iron hoops in the playground. 'En't you going tu try and win 'um back?' I asked, clutching my bag of marbles.

'No I blumen well en't,' he said. 'Shove off. Marbles is a girl's game,' and they tore away and charged round the playground like a herd of young bullocks. In fact nobody wanted to play. They were all too busy bowling their hoops.

During the dry weather we girls played hopscotch—we would mark out the 'beds' with a bit of rough stone, which acted as chalk if you found a good white piece. Sometimes the 'bed' would be six large squares joined together and in each square a number was written. The art of the game was to slide a small, flattish stone from one square to the next. This was done by hopping on one foot and gently kicking the stone along with the other so that it landed right on the number. If the stone slid too far or landed on a line then the player had to start again. The winner was the one who could complete the game without any faults.

Another hopscotch 'bed' was marked out like a giant snailshell. This was a much more complicated way of playing, and all sorts of instructions were written in the different squares. You had to concentrate like mad to be able to master this game—still on one leg. You could play this on your own, but it was much more exciting if two or more took part.

There was little or no traffic on the roads and so, as we walked to school, many of us played games on the way. Six or seven of us would link arms—right across the narrow road we would stretch, singing:

> Queen, Queen Caroline,
> Dipped her hair in the turpentine.
> The turpentine made it shine,
> Queen, Queen Caroline.

(I planned to try this when I grew up.)
Or

> Here we go gathering nuts and may
> on a cold and frosty morning,

fitting other words to this tune as we rushed along:

> This is the way we run to school

or

> Jump in the air and clap our hands,

and before we know where we were we'd walked the mile and a half, and were boiling into the bargain.

The most popular game for boys was 'Fox and Hounds'. On clear frosty winter nights they would run for miles and miles. The lad chosen for the fox had to be a pretty good runner. He would dash off into the night and a little later the hounds would follow, shouting as they ran, 'Come out wherever you are, the dogs are on your tracks.'

Sometimes the fox would 'holler' and give his pursuers an idea as to where he was. Then the hounds would be off in full cry, but the 'fox' often doubled back and they would be lucky to find him. Often, after hours of chasing and running, the 'dogs' failed to catch their man and the game would be continued the next night until the fox was caught; then another was chosen to take his place.

Then a change came over our lives. About the middle of the 'twenties a travelling concert party settled on the outskirts of the town near by.

They had a huge tent with wooden forms stacked in tiers. There were thre'penny and sixpenny seats down front. The ha'penny seats, very high, were just rows of boards set almost underneath the tent top. 'Going to the ha'penny leg dangle?' we'd say. And halfway through the 'Death of Little Willy' like as not you were all suffering from acute pins and needles. But they were exciting nights.

We saw 'Maria Martin in the Red Barn' or the 'Death of Little Eva', 'Uncle Tom's Cabin', and many others.

It was a family affair, this concert party. Mother, father and sons and daughters-in-law. I had a silent crush on one of the lads performing. He looked so handsome as I worshipped him from the ha'pennies. Then I saw him close-up one day with all his make-up on. He looked like a Red Indian and was ever so old— quite thirty! That cured me.

Of course there was a picture house in the town but the cheapest seats were three-ha'pence for Saturday afternoon matinée. Most of the children went then.

When I got a bit older (I think I was about thirteen at the time), I was asked to deliver to every house in the village a pamphlet on which was printed a month's programme of what was on at 'The People's Palace'. For doing this I was given a free pass once a week.

They were all silent films, of course, with Mr Lewis playing the piano down front. Many of the children could not read and bigger brothers or sisters read the captions out loud—when half the audience was reading out loud there was a tidy din going on all the time.

But it wasn't all games—there were errands to be run, often up to the town after school, or kindling wood to be gathered from the nearest hedge. And younger brothers and sisters always needed to be taken for walks while our mother was cooking the evening meal. 'Take them down the Curbridge Road,' Mother would call as we started off. The Curbridge road was very quiet, just a country lane really.

As we walked between the thick, berried hedgerows we gorged ourselves with wild berries, fruits and leaves, suffering no more than severe stomach-ache. 'Bread and cheese,' the new leaves of the May bush, were eaten as fast as they grew. Even to this day, when the warm spring sun opens those tender green leaves, I still greedily gather some, savouring those halcyon days.

Somehow we all knew what not to eat when it came to poisonous berries and things. I suppose it was something that was automatically handed down from one generation to another for I never ever remembered anyone being poisoned. But we did have a pet jackdaw who, attracted by some poisonous berries that we had picked to decorate the home with, decided to sample them. We found him dead on the sideboard. Everybody cried and we buried him in the garden, and for a few days placed flowers on the tiny mound.

We knew where the first dewy mushrooms grew, and the fattest blackberries, and called every field around by its special name—not the official one, but by association with something or other:

'The Devil's nutting ground', 'Stranges' lucerne', the 'flower field', 'Parker's forty acres', 'Clark's moon daisy ground'.

There were green lanes between some of the fields and these provided short cuts to the next hamlet or village. And double hedges where we would find our 'first of the year' primroses and violets or where we'd play for hours in bramble caves.

We would climb trees and make swings by half-bending, half-breaking willow branches. Then catching firmly hold of the branch and with our feet pressed against the trunk of the tree, we would push off, letting the branch swing us high into the air before dropping down again. It was a tremendous thrill—but we had to be quick on the down-drop for if our feet missed the trunk we were bashed against it. Up and down, up and down we would swing, for hours on end.

There was great competition in our house as to who found the first flowers as they started to bloom. We had no other reward than a good warm hug from our mother and a little praise because we had been more observant than the others. But this made us sharp-sighted and keen, always on the look out, a gentle way of instilling in our minds knowledge that we were to find useful for the rest of our lives.

8

Lotions and Potions

OUR childhood illnesses were either cured or treated by our mothers; having a Doctor was almost unheard of unless someone elderly was dying of a painful and incurable disease, for it cost money. So home cures were widely used, some of them quite primitive too. Our mother had some magical cures handed down to her from her mother—hot, spicy, and almost medieval they were; a pinch of this and a sprinkling of that, and taken so hot they nearly seared your throat.

I can see her now, bending over us, in one hand a tablespoonful of one of her special concoctions, and in the other a spoonful of jam—the offending medicine was pushed into our unwilling mouths, our eyes shut tight so as not to see. Then immediately afterwards, the jam was thrust down our throats in an effort to camouflage the horrible taste. Mind you, if you could keep the concoction down, the cure for whatever you had was certain.

Our winter salvation, apart from the great suet puddings we ate, was surely our 'possibles', a name we christened the flannel weskit we younger ones were annually sewn up in. At the beginning of the cold weather our Mother slapped goose-grease thickly on our backs and chests, then sewed us up in a piece of real flannel—next to the skin. This was kept on till spring! No proper baths were taken during the winter; we were merely topped and tailed—washed up as far as possible and down as far as possible, 'possible' being that smelly greasy flannel weskit that was in such a state at the end of the winter that it was simply cut off our bodies and flung in the fire.

When we were small the only thing we were ever given to cure a bad head cold was a steaming hot basin of bread and milk. But when we got older home-made wine was the answer, heated with a red-hot poker and drunk at once. We would stagger upstairs after a hot toddy of elderberry wine and fling ourselves sweating into bed—and get up the next morning as fit as a fiddle. Other people swore by blackcurrant tea for colds and coughs. This was just a good spoonful of home-made blackcurrant jam in a cup of boiling water.

Some of the villagers had originated from different parts of the country, bringing with them their own special potions and lotions and beliefs. Our next-door neighbour's daughter was supposed to be 'weak in the chest' and she was never seen without her 'velvety band' as her mother called it. It was a narrow, black velvet band fastened tightly round her neck, and this was only taken off when she washed. She wore this well into her teens and for all I know she may be still wearing one.

Some of the older men and women carried either a potato or a nutmeg about with them believing that this warded off 'The Rheumatics', the symptoms being any ache or pain they had anywhere in their body.

Others walked around with a number of little leather bags hung round their waists next to the skin; this was really a secret way of believing, and what was in the bags was anybody's guess. Once our mother, very unwillingly, was forced to help lay an old man out ('get him ready to meet his Maker' was the expression often used). And he had a number of these little leather bags tied round his waist; how long they had been there remained a mystery. They opened some of the bags and whatever had been in them had completely disappeared.

There was never any need to put up with warts for long. One old lady could charm them away simply by rubbing them either with the inside of a broad-bean pod or with one of those huge black slugs, the latter being used when broad beans were not in season. Always in the winter we would rub our chilblained feet with raw onions to try and ease the itching, and a small piece of real silk was carefully hoarded away by most families to be used if anyone had a stye on the eye: first the silk had to be drawn through a gold wedding ring and then the stye was stroked with the silk twelve times night and morning. A general relief for earache and toothache was a small flannel bag filled with common salt. The salt-filled bag would be put in the oven to get it well and truly hot and this would be held against the pain.

My elder sister used to get up very early on summer mornings and go out to Pudney's field and bathe her face in the morning dew in an effort to get rid of her crop of freckles. Some cottagers swore by nettle beer for clearing the blood, others made a concoction with pearl barley, liquorice, figs, and raisins. And one old lady used to make buttercup ointment by boiling flowers and vaseline together, and her almost wrinkle-free face was a proof of its worth.

One of my Gran's special herb salves was made simply with home-cured lard and freshly gathered groundsel, elderflower, and wormwood all boiled up together. This was kept and used for any sores or to bring a bruise out, and if my Gramp had a lame sheep he would rub the animal's foot or leg with the same stuff.

Our mother was a great believer in bread poultices to bring a boil to a head or to slap red-hot on to any gathering or festered place, but a farm labourer who lived near by swore by hot cow dung.

Friday night was 'jollop night' in our house whether you needed it or not: either the juice from soaked senna pods or brimstone and treacle was the order of the day. Later on we had Beecham's Pills and I remember reading on the wooden lid the words 'worth a guinea a box', and wondered how on earth our mother could afford these.

9

Village Life

*I*N spring, when it was warm enough, we all took a weekly bath in the old wash-house where coal and wood was kept and the washing done. The copper would be well stoked up with hedge wood and filled up with water from the well. Then we would take it in turns to sit in our mother's zinc washing bath, just adding a drop more hot water as each of us stepped in.

In summer there was no need for baths; dozens of us would go down to the River Windrush, bathing and teaching ourselves to swim. Every now and then we would take a bit of soap and have a good wash in the river and this saved our mother the job of filling up the old copper.

Older men who didn't go swimming had what was called 'a swabble down' during hot weather. I've seen my stepfather stripped to the waist, sloshing water over his arms and shoulders. This was always done outside in the garden and the soapy water left in the bowl was usually tipped over plants—nothing was wasted, not even soapy water.

One of the villagers, Mrs Pye, used to make a song and dance about their washing habits. She'd say to our mother on a warm day: 'Ah, Missus, I be goin' tu light a fire in the hovel [wash-house] an' when that water's good an' hot I be goin' tu wash my fit an' legs an' ower gel, 'er's a goin' tu wash 'er fit an' legs, and then George [her husband] he's goin' tu rurely wash 'is fit an' legs'—so we always thought of George as a person with much dirtier feet and legs than his wife or daughter.

They came from a remote village north of the county and pronounced their words differently from most of us, and had the most peculiar expressions too. Mrs Pye was as thin as a whip stick. She would pull her skirt out at the waist and say 'Lar' Missus, I be slipping 'ud'—like a woodnut slips its hud she meant, and when she was hungry she'd say, 'My back varnear touches my belly I be that lear, proper famaled I be.' When she did her housework she always wore a coarse 'epern'—an apron made from a clean washed sack—and a man's cap perched on top of her bun of hair. A great long hatpin kept the cap firmly in place, and her skirts were long and black.

When her daughter was engaged Mrs Pye came along to our house and asked our mother to come and have a look at the present that the young man had given her daughter. ''Tis lovely Missus, a sort of pos-set thing, creamy white with roses on.' At that time young girls were using a thing called a 'poshet'. This was a small flat handbag, often made of raffia, and this was what our mother thought she was going to see. Imagine her surprise when she walked into Mrs Pye's cottage to see, set out on the white scrubbed kitchen table, a full set of bedroom ware, jug, basin, chamber pots and all, creamy white with roses on.

A year or so after this Mrs Pye's daughter and the young man decided that they would be married. So about three weeks before the great day Mrs Pye, eager to show the fellow what a good steady thrifty girl he'd got, suggested that he should be invited to see what the girl had saved up in her bottom drawer. It was rather cold weather just then, so she said to our mother, 'Ah, I be going tu light a fire in the bedroom and ower gel's going tu show 'er young man all 'er got.'

There was a woman who always seemed to be having babies and she had a rather nice way of telling folks that she was pregnant. She would hug her stomach and say, 'Well bein' as I be as I be'. And sometimes the menfolk could be heard to say, without any hint of vulgarity, when their wives were having another child, 'Damn me if 'er en't bin an' joined the puddin' club agen'. And illegitimate children were referred to as 'Sun-hatched' or 'Love children'.

Since a visit from the Doctor was so rare, if anyone had to call him in they would remember for years what he had said. This would be repeated and savoured to relatives and friends, although the teller sometimes got the words a bit mixed—'The Doctor says thur's nothin' 'e can do for I, its summat *eternal*, but 'e wouldn't say no more'—a story one woman was very fond of telling.

And a new young Doctor at his first practice called on one old lady and enquired how she was: 'Middlin',' the woman replied, and the Doctor used to tell the tale against himself of how he went straight back and searched the medical journal to try and find out what 'middlin'' meant.

Villagers just didn't greet each other with a simple 'Good morning' but would probably follow it up with 'how bistthis morning then, George?' 'Ah,' the other would reply, 'I be rough an' ready like a rat catcher's dog'; or seeing his pal looking a bit glum, he might say, 'I be in the pink, but you looks as if you worked hard for a bob an' found 'twas a bad un'. Or, 'you looks as crusty as a barrow-load of muck on a frosty morning'.

When people spoke of walking anywhere they often used to say that they were going by 'Walker's bus'. Ask how they were and the answer would most likely be, 'Ah! Bad abed an' wus up' or 'None the better for your askin''.

Typical Oxfordshire expressions were heard every day: 'bissent' was used instead of 'you are not', and 'cyassent' instead of 'cannot'.

They called left-handed folk 'keky-handed', thin folk 'herrin'-gutted', and loud-mouthed men and women 'chopsey'. A person who talked a lot was called a 'chattermag' and an awkward one was 'tiziky' or 'cussed'. Anyone slow-witted or stupid was 'dummul-headed'.

If Mr Pye, who lived near us, was talking about going to the parish tea and our mother might ask politely, 'Well, who else is going?', instead of saying everybody in the village he'd say 'Well, thee and I and all of us'.

Young men spoke of 'wenchin'' when they went out after the girls, and when people roamed about the fields it was called 'pelvering' or 'traipsin' '—never walking. 'Ketch holt', they'd say, if they wanted anybody to catch hold of anything, and if you sat thinking you'd be 'mumchancing'. 'What's 'e gawpin' at?', villagers would remark if a stranger was staring at them.

The times, when I was small, I've asked grown-ups where they were going, only to be put off by them answering 'Round the park to see the shops' or 'Thur and back to see how far 'tis'!

The sky over to the west was always known as 'Round Will's Mother's way'. The expression came from a girl who had married a fellow called Will from Brize Norton, a village that lay west of Ducklington. And if the clouds were black and lowery in that direction she'd say, 'That looks black round Will's Mother's way', and to this day all our family, wherever they are, still use the expression.

The word 'unkid' was used instead of horrible or nasty, and 'flummoxed' instead of worried or bothered. 'He do ugger mugger I so', the old lady next to us used to say of her husband who was one of the world's worst worriers.

Men who came home from the fields with muddy boots came home 'all clapered up'.

If a child came home with his clothes ragged they would be 'torn to lickutts' instead of to pieces.

Children were called 'childern' and stones 'Stwons', and the word 'dillin' was the name for the smallest pig in a litter, but was also used to describe a child who was small and undernourished.

Grown-ups referred to a tall thin child as gawky, but we kids would sing out after one as he went by, 'You be long and lanky, thin and cranky'.

Superstitions, bad and good luck omens, ran riot in the village, especially with the older folk, although we children believed in them too. There were, and still are, women who never dreamt of washing blankets during the month of May.

> Wash blankets in May,
> You'll soon be under clay.

There were old ladies who always curtsied to the new moon or turned their money at the first sight of a new one, and thought that bad luck would surely befall the person who saw a new moon through a window—unless the viewer went straight out and flung salt over the left shoulder. This should always be done if you spill salt and the old saying,

> Spill salt for sorrow,
> Spill sugar for joy.

is still believed by some country folk.

Very good luck would come to the person who saw a dapple-grey horse. Catch sight of his tail and your good luck became bad—unless you wetted your finger with your tongue immediately and made a cross on the toecap of your boot.

Speaking and bowing to magpies was quite a common thing and to this day I still nod my head and politely say 'Good morning, Sir', when I catch sight of one.

May blossom was never taken indoors and holly never before Christmas Eve. And some people still think that having lilac indoors or white flowers of any sort will bring bad luck. Once I took a little posy of spring flowers to a woman who was ill in bed and her husband refused to take the flowers indoors until I had removed the snowdrops.

Village funerals were very simple affairs. The undertaker most likely had a motor hearse that conveyed the coffin to Church but the few mourners would walk, all wearing deep black. When our Gran died our mother had to borrow a bicycle to get to the funeral. It was sixteen miles each way up and down hill through Cotswold country. I remember her sending my elder sister down to the village to Mrs Fisher to ask if she could borrow her best black coat and hat to go in.

Villagers were like that. If they had anything to lend anybody worse off than themselves they would do so without any second bidding. When my young stepbrothers had to go to the Radcliffe to have their tonsils out, Mrs Frank Townsend lent them a nice white shirt each to go in. She had a biggish family and was always sending for our mother if the children had anything wrong with them. She was a good mother but not one for home doctoring. 'What do you think's wrong with our Bern?' she's say, eyeing one of her sons thoughtfully.

'Nothing 'as a good dose of physic won't put right,' our mother would reply. And one of us would be sent home to bring back 'Some of me special' as she called it.

Some of the older people had what they referred to as 'Me best black'. The men's were often their wedding suits, green with age, and smelling strongly of moth-balls. These would be kept for what were called 'High days and holidays and bonfire nights', but were really for weddings and funerals, christenings, and church on a Sunday.

Some of the women, like Mrs Fisher, had their best black; not our mother though. She borrowed again when our Gramp died a few years later. The first brand-new coat that she had during her married life was one I bought her during the last war. But not having new clothes never bothered her; hers, like most of ours, came from jumble sales—'better quality than I could afford to buy new', she'd say, after picking up a worn Harris Tweed coat for 2s. 6d.

Living down the bottom end of the village was a deaf and dumb woman called Sally Castle, and for a few shillings Sally would unpick a faded second-hand coat, and then make it up again on the wrong side to fit one of us. Our mother could manage to make all sorts of things on her hand-turned sewing machine, but coats were a little beyond her. Our stepfather used to make us things on the machine too, and once, as a special treat, he bought some cheap red velveteen and made us three girls a dress each for Christmas.

Not every family in the village could afford a clock, but then it didn't matter really, for there were several ways by which the time of the day could be reckoned. For one thing, old Mark used to drive through the village at the same time every day, winter and summer; folks reckoned he was never a minute out. He drove a float, a sort of open-backed cart, with a good trotting pony in the shafts, and took the milk in huge churns from the farm where he worked at Yelford to Witney station to catch the 'Lunon' train. Mark always stood while he was driving, near the back, the float slightly tilted with his weight and that of the churn, the reins held high in his strong hands. He looked for all the world like a proud Roman in a chariot, with his weather-beaten face and fierce eyes. The daily journey to the station must have been a real treat, for at least he had a glimpse of the outside world—and that was something the other farm workers at Yelford rarely had.

Although a clock could be set on the outgoing journey, sometimes Mark would be late coming back—he often had to run errands in the town for his employers or sell rabbits to the housewives in Ducklington. In his strange sing-song voice he would say to us, 'If yer Mother waants a rabbit I'll skin 'er one fer ninepence.' And we used to shout this to him and tease him as he tore by in his float.

Thursday was market-day in Witney, though the locals called it 'Hurdle Thursday' because of the hurdles that were set up in the market-place. And the sheep and things that the farmers brought in to sell would be put into the hurdled pens. It was a meeting place where whiskered, gaitered farmers prodded the animals for sale and chattered over prices with friends or joined them in the local for a hard-earned pint. On these days Mark's employers, two lady farmers, would drive their smart pony and trap from Yelford to Witney, bringing with them lovely half-pound pats of yellow dairy butter to sell to people in Ducklington and Witney.

Another way we knew the time, at least if the wind was in the right direction, was when the whistles blew in the blanket mills at Witney. First at eight o'clock, when the workers started; at 12.30 p.m. when it was dinner-time; at 1.30 p.m., calling the weavers back, and then at six o'clock when it was time to go home. And on a Sunday we always knew when it was getting on for dinnertime for Mr Amos who lived near us, whether he had anything to carve or not, always walked over to the wash-house where he proceeded to sharpen their carving knife with a great, long, blue sharpening stone. We could hear the noise as he swiftly drew the blade over the stone. 'Ah,' our mother would say, 'must be one o'clock, old Bert's tiggling his knife up.'

And then again, if the wind was in the west, we could hear the whistle of the Bampton Flyer, a local name for the train that puffed to and fro on a single track between Witney and Fairford, calling at some of the small villages in between, including Bampton. In those days they pretty well ran on time. 'Best get back to work,' our stepfather would say. 'Just heard the flyer's whistle, must be two o'clock.'

Some of the old men had big weskit-pocket watches hung on chains that stretched across their chests. One even had sovereigns dangling on his. Ask them the time, and with one movement the fat watch was pulled out and the thumb automatically moved over the face, cleaning imaginary dust off. 'Ten o'clock by God's time,' they would say. The older people would have no truck with Will Willett and his daylight-saving bill. Not wishing to offend, one had to do a quick bit of arithmetic according to whether it was summertime or wintertime.

I suppose, on the whole, we at Ducklington were pretty well catered for one way and another. There were two tiny village shops and the milkman's, the church and the school, Baker Collis's and the travelling men. We also had Snobby Castle to mend the boots of those who were not clever enough to mend their own, and Brummy Edwards to cut our hair. Once, and once only, Mother sent Bern and Bunt down to him to have a penny haircut.

Brummy sat them on an old box out in the garden and went over their heads with a pair of mule shears, the same pair that he clipped his old mule and donkey with. I think Brummy must have been the originator of the crew cut. When the boys got back home our mother burst out crying. Their hair was cut so short they looked almost bald. She gathered them into her arms saying, 'If I have to gnaw it off myself you'll never go down there again. Look at them,' she said to one of the neighbours, 'they look like a couple of old men, all their lovely curls blowing about on Brummy's garden.'

'Missus,' Brummy said when she went at him about it, 'thas what folks comes to I for, to have thur hair cut, and I likes to give full value. Any-how,' he added, 'it'll grow thick and strong now— a head of hair's like a grass field: cut it off short an' it'll grow all the better.' Brummy went on bragging a little, 'I got what the papers calls "the monopoly", thur yent nobody else in the village what can manage the job besides I.'

But when our stepfather came on the scene he cut all our hair. We had to kneel up in a chair while he snipped away at our locks—'keep your blessed head still, young Mollie,' he'd say to me, 'or we shall be having pickled ear for tea tonight.'

A very handy man our stepfather was; night after night he used to sit up mending our boots, tacking leather onto the soles to keep our feet warm and dry. He used to say that his iron foot, that was the thing he slipped the boot or shoe onto so that he could mend it easily, was worth a pot of gold to him. It really must have saved us pounds and pounds during the years when we were all at home; always it seemed one or other of us needed our boots mended.

He was something of an inventor too. He could make a mincing machine out of a worn-out grandfather clock's inside, or a lathe from an old treadle sewing-machine.

His one luxury when we were all small was a melodion which he could play beautifully. Sometimes on summer nights he would sit outside the house and go through all the tunes that he knew— the wartime songs, the up-to-date ones, and the dirge-like ones: 'Don't Go Down the Mine, Daddy' or 'Break the News to Mother'. Then he'd have a go at hymn tunes, sometimes singing as well, with young Ben, only about three at the time, joining in, knowing all the words too.

But from this happy-go-lucky singing man he changed over the years, becoming moody, staying out late and drinking. His pals thought he was a marvellous fellow, yet he had rows with us all and kept our mother short of money. For years I wondered why the rot had set in, but not until after he died did I know. Apparently our mother found out that he was more than friendly with a young widow at one of the pubs he called at. And that was that; she just never forgave him. Slowly, through the years, she grew further and further away from him and so did we children, not really knowing why.

IO

Magic Moments

THE fields around the village were our playground, almost our whole environment.

In spring, the flat green meadows that lay either side of the banks of the Windrush were filled with fat yellow kingcups; water bubbles or water buttercups were local names for them. And in two or three special places we searched for the rare fritillary, darting backwards and forwards to pick the lovely snake-like flower heads. Sometimes we would find a few white ones, but mostly they were speckled, pinky purple, and for a few weeks our schoolroom window-sills, set high in the building, were lined with tightly packed jars of them.

In fact most of the year the jam jars were filled with our gleanings. From early spring when we gathered our first yellow catkins, that spilled their pollen on our desks, until winter, when we dragged the lovely fluffy trailing plant called Old Man's Beard (Traveller's Joy), from the hedges on our way to school.

And it was in these same fields that we found watercress in abundance, that is if Watercress Charlie hadn't got there first. This wasn't his proper name—just one we had given him. And gathering these dark green leaves was the only job he seemed to do. What he did in the months when it was not considered fit to eat the stuff we never knew, for to country people watercress is only eatable when there is an 'r' in the month.

We would sneak down to the 'Meds', our name for these special fields, and start to pick the cress, and I'll bet we hadn't gathered much before Charlie would come skulking up the hedge and run us off, although he had no more right down there than we had.

But while ours was for our own eating, Charlie's was for selling. He would bunch his up and stack it in his little home-made rush basket and take it up to Witney to one of the shops.

Another place down the 'Meds' we used to go to was Buffy's Raddum. This was a specially planted willow copse that belonged to Mr Tremblin, the local basket maker. And the Raddum was where he got his willow for making shopping baskets, clothes baskets which women used to collect their washing in, cradles and other things. The slim willow sticks, which were stacked upright in bundles to dry, had to be cut just at a certain time so that they did not become brittle but remained supple and easy to handle. We really should not have got into the Raddum at all, but in that damp, low-lying ground the kingcups were always bigger and better than those in the sur-rounding fields.

When spring had really come and the warm sun had brought out more meadow flowers, we would pick baskets of cowslips so that our mother might brew some home-made wine. We used to keep some of the best blooms ourselves to make what we called a 'tisty tosty ball'. Taking off the main stalk we would bunch up the thick flower-heads together, tying them in the middle with wool, and this made a lovely soft sweet-smelling ball. Then for hours we would play a game called 'Tell me true', each girl tossing a ball in the air, keeping in time with this jingle—

> Tisty tosty, tell me true,
> Who shall I be married to?
> Tisty tosty, cowslip ball,
> At my sweetheart's name you'll fall.

Each of us had our own favourites where the boys were concerned and we'd chant them—Percy, Charlie, Jimmy, Tom, Billy, Frankie, Bob, and Bert, and, strange as it seemed, the ball always managed to fall at the name we wanted it to.

A little later on in the year we gathered armfuls of moon daisy, ragged robin, bloody butchers (purple orchid), meadow-sweet, and bright yellow flags—always there were plenty of wild flowers for the picking.

Each summer when Pudney Wilsdon cut the grass in the field just over the road from where we lived, we knew it was time to take our tea outdoors. We would arrive home from school to find a mountain of bread and jam cut and stacked on a plate, and a great big white jug filled with hot, strong tea. 'Go on, off you go, the lot of you,' Mother would say, 'and stay out and play in Pudney's field till I call you.'

Carefully carrying the precious food, we would file over to the hay field and make ourselves a house by scooping up armfuls of sweet-smelling hay, piling it up to make it look like a room.

Then we would pick thickish grasses from the sides of the field where the mower had failed to reach and make ourselves drinking straws. When all the food and drink had gone we would dismantle the house and throw the hay over each other, filling our hair with millions of hay seeds which also stuck to our sweating bodies. Whatever the farmer thought when he saw what we had done to his neat rows of hay I don't know, but it was such fun.

'Let's make pea shooters,' someone would say, and we'd all make a dive for 'The Mound', a thick double hedge where the biggest, strongest pigweed grew. These hollow stalks made super pea shooters, but we didn't use peas—no—'azzies' were our gun fodder. We'd grab handfuls of the berries, not yet ripe, from the may bushes, and fill our mouths with them, and holding the pea shooter to our lips we'd blow the berries through, hitting anything and everything. I know I got a clip round the ear for taking a pot-shot at old Mr Judd, stinging him in the face with a volley of azzies. 'You be too cheeky by half,' Mr Judd said. 'All you Woodleys be the same.'

Tree-climbing was another pastime that we all enjoyed, and most of the girls could shin up a tree as quickly as any boy.

The hedgerows in summer were festooned with dog roses, honeysuckle and waywind (bindweed). From most of the summer flowers we would suck honey, holding tiny flowerets of clover, waywind and honeysuckle up to our lips, savouring the sweet, fragile taste.

Long days were spent just sitting and playing in the fields making buttercup and daisy chains, holding bright buttercups under each other's chins to test if we liked butter, or chewing the sharp tangy leaves of the sorrel plant. We made hideous noises by holding a blade of strong grass between the thumbs, pressing it to the mouth, and blowing hard; the result was earsplitting, and heard a mile away.

We would pluck scarlet poppies from the growing corn and make poppy dolls by turning back the petals, tying them down with a piece of grass, making a red-skirted dolly with one green leg.

And there was one certain grass that we picked and curled each other's hair with, resulting in a tight frizzy tangle. I know once my hair was in such a state after Alice Spindlow had curled it for hours that our mother in desperation cut it off as short as a boy's. There was another sort of grass with little seeds growing alternately up the stalk. With this we tried to find out what sort of man we were going to marry. As our fingers moved up the stalk touching each seed we would chant—

> Tinker, Tailor, Soldier, Sailor,
> Rich man, poor man, beggar man, thief

—hoping that the last seed on the stalk was 'rich man'.

The boys often made whistles from thin sticks cut from the elder trees. First they would scoop out the white pith, then cut holes along the wood, and this gave them a few notes. Ben, one of my stepbrothers, could play anything you would like to name on one, for they were as good as any tin whistle.

And where birds had at one time dropped the seed into the forks of the gnarled old willow trees that stood drunkenly along the banks of the river, blackcurrants and gooseberries would grow. Perching precariously on a branch, we would gorge the fruit, often before it was properly ripe, while below in the rushes we would find wild duck and moorhens' eggs that we took home by the dozen. Our mother always cracked these into a basin first in case they were addled. They were strong and rich, with bright orange yolks. Nine or ten of these completely filled the frying pan and made us a nice nourishing tea.

Other days we pinched swedes and turnips from Parker's fields, first gnawing the skin off with our teeth. Then we sat down in the middle of the field and had a good feed, eating the small circle of swedes that surrounded us. Once Mr Parker caught me turnip-pinching. Our mother had always drummed into us that if we were caught doing anything we shouldn't, we were not to run away, but stand our ground. So I stood there, watching Mr Parker's long thin legs getting nearer and nearer, his face purple with rage.

'What du think you're doing then?' he bellowed.

'Just eating a turnip,' I answered timidly.

'Well,' he said, 'you tell your stepfather I want to see him. (This was the farmer that he did weekend work for.) 'And if you don't tell him I want to see him I shall let him know that I caught you pinching me turnips.'

But I never did tell him—I knew that I would have got a hiding for pinching and I don't think Mr Parker, for all his faults, ever split on me either. Mind you, if he caught us mushrooming or blackberrying or gathering crab-apples for jelly in his fields he would simply tip them out on the grass and send us home with empty baskets.

A short cut across his forty-acre field led to Gorsehill woods where we gathered primroses in spring and wild strawberries in summer, and filled our pockets with woodnuts* in autumn; and where sometimes in later years Denis, the youngest, went poaching and brought back plump cock pheasants.

We lived in a limestone district so our river was well-stocked with crayfish. And in the late summer or early autumn the lads of

---

* Wild hazel nuts.

the village would go off on dark nights with a lantern and lie on the bank by a deepish pool. Here they would set their buckets and bait, often a bit of smelly meat, and wait. You had to be very quiet and still; a slight shadow cast on the water, and the little beggars would scuttle off.

Our brothers used to go, bringing back dozens of the crab-like creatures. They would put them live into the big black saucepan to cook over the fire, a pot full of wriggling red things. Then we would all sit down and have a nice feed of these delicacies.

So many things that were part of our quiet life still remain in the mind. Once, always during the summertime, we paid an annual visit to Yelford. Our mother usually took Kitty Moore with us. Kitty was a cripple girl who lived up the back, and the only way she could get about was if someone took her out in her bath-chair.

It was one of those two-wheeled wicker chairs with a small extra wheel in front, attached to a long handle which was held by the rider who guided the chair—it just needed someone to push. Kitty would have young Denis on her lap, with Ben riding at the bottom by her poor mis-shapen feet. We others trotted alongside, holding on to the bath-chair when we got a bit tired.

The object of going to Yelford each summer was because, in a disused garden, there were several gooseberry bushes. The trip took nearly all day—it was over four miles each way. Several times on the journey we sat by the side of the road to rest on the cool grass. One trip I remember vividly.

We passed a few cottages on the way—two after we left Ducklington, and we called at both of them for a drink, greedily gulping the ice-cold well water. We knew the women at the cottages and our mother stopped to chatter for a while before we pushed on. 'We might drop in on our way back,' Mother called to Mrs Shepherd as we set off down the dusty road.

When we reached the garden at Yelford we fell on to the gooseberry bushes like a swarm of locusts, stripping off all the fruit, filling our baskets, bags and stomachs, prickling ourselves to death with the sharp thorns.

That morning on our way through the village we had called at Baker Collis's and bought a crisp new cottage loaf. 'Come on, grub up,' Mother cried, pulling the bread apart with her fingers. Then she spread dripping on it, giving us each a chunk. Like manna from heaven it tasted as we lay sweating in the overgrown garden, gnawing at our food.

I never taste dripping without remembering that day. There were clumps of columbines and rambler roses, and a rosemary bush and lots of weeds and birds everywhere, and the hot sun bore down from a cloudless blue sky.

We played for a while in the ruins of the burnt-out cottage, pulling a few remaining stones from the walls, dropping them into the garden. Then it was time to start for home and the long walk back.

When we reached 'The Plantations' Mother cried, 'Look at all this rotten wood lying about!' So we rushed around picking up the chunky bits, piling them on to Kitty's lap, squeezing lumps between her and Ben. Suddenly we were all tired. 'Let's have a bit of a sing-song,' Kitty said. 'We'll sing everybody's favourite in turn,' and for a while our steps were light as we strode along, piping out 'It's a Long Way to Tipperary' and our mother's special, 'Keep Right On to the End of the Road'.

We reached the village. In the twilight the gardens looked luminous and beautiful. We trailed along the last half mile, quietly tired. Denis was fast asleep.

The night smells rose up from the cottage gardens as we passed—damp grass and middens, stocks and roses. The evening star winked from a westerly sky; it was the end of a lovely day.

The great event of making the Christmas puddings each year is another that is particularly vivid. Try as she would, our mother never managed to get all the ingredients together by the allotted time—Stir-up Sunday—the first Sunday in Advent, usually in late November. No, ours more often than not were cooked about two weeks before Christmas and were the loveliest I've ever tasted. The preparation often took days. Suddenly the great red earthenware pan was set on the table and little by little the ingredients were thrown in. There was no weighing or measuring, all just guess-work. One messy job we children had to do was to stone the raisins. We would sit up at the table with a basin of water near at hand so that our sticky fingers could be dipped in now and then. Otherwise, after the stones were taken from the fruit, they simply remained stuck on the fingers.

Our stepfather always bought a quart of old beer with which to mix the puddings. The mixture was never put into the basins until we had all had a stir and a wish, the younger children standing on a chair so that they might take part. We all had to have a taste of the uncooked mixture just to see if anything had been left out. 'Something's missing,' our mother would say, and we'd poke our fingers into the raw pudding and taste, gazing heavenwards, trying to decide what it was. One year it was nutmeg, another spice, and another time it was sugar. Then one of us would be sent rushing up to town to get whatever was missing.

The next day the copper in the old wash-house was filled up and the fire lit, and there the puddings would bubble and boil all day long, our mother continuously having to make up the fire and add more water as it boiled away.

One year a Mrs Hathaway who lived in the Square cooked her puddings nice and early. Afterwards she tied clean, dry cloths over them and set them up on a high shelf in the kitchen. She had made eight, the first to be eaten on Christmas Day. Early on Christmas morning she climbed up to get one. The first basin was empty, although the cloth was still tied on neatly. She reached for the next—that was empty too. And so were all the rest. The culprits were two of her sons. They used to come in at nights after the others had gone to bed and over the weeks had completely eaten the half-cooked puddings.

The excitement of pancake day in our house had to be seen to be believed, for no other day in the year could we afford such luxuries. The fun began as soon as our mother brought her big wash-stand jug from the bedroom and set it on the kitchen table. Into it went a quart of skimmed milk that one of us had fetched from Sarah Clarke's, and several eggs from our own hens, all whipped up together with plenty of plain flour into a creamy frothy mixture.

A new frying pan—another annual event for the great day— and a pound of best lard to cook the pancakes in, and we were all set to begin. Our mother's face was flushed and happy, her hair untidily wispy as she bent over her task. The fire burnt fiercely, so that she had to hold the pan above the flames. As each pancake was cooked it was doled out to the members of the family in turn, according to one's age, the eldest first.

The room was filled with squealing and laughing as our mother skilfully tossed each pancake high in the air. Blue smoke rose from the boiling fat and there was a strong smell of lemon as she slipped the long-awaited treat on to each plate. At last it was Ben's turn, he was last-but-one on the list. He had waited patiently for almost an hour, and as she tossed the pancake mother cried, 'Whose turn is it this time?'

'Mine, mine,' Ben shouted excitedly, and he rushed forward, plate in hand, and tried to catch it as it came down—our mother tried to do the same thing. She gave him a quick shove and he went backside first into a bucket of water and she herself, slightly off balance, stumbled a couple of steps sideways on to the sleeping cat. The hot pancake landed right on top of the squealing animal who made a bee-line for the door. Someone rushed to open it and the cat streaked out, completely enveloped in the cooked batter.

'That's yours boy, go and get it,' Mother yelled to him above the din as Ben heaved himself up from the bucket; with water dripping from his trousers he rushed out into the garden. Minutes later he came back, stuffing lumps of fluff-covered pancake into his mouth, having cornered his quarry in the wash-house.

The incident only lasted a few moments but the memory of that particular night will never be forgotten by the family.

II

Village Activities

FILLED with untold energy we threw ourselves into the few village activities. We romped along from the fair to Harvest Festival, from Christmas to the parish tea, and so on through the year. Our eyes were filled with stars and our hearts light, for everything we did was an adventure. There was little or no money to spend, yet the joy of those simple, unforgettable affairs remains always.

The village green where the two-day fair was held was just near our house. On the Sunday before the fair we were up long before it was light, to watch the caravans 'draw on'. There were never more than eight or nine, but to us it seemed like a colourful, magical parade. The vans, all horse-drawn, were painted in exotic colours, with shiny brass water buckets and jugs hanging and clanging outside. Dozens of children were packed into the quite small caravans.

Sometimes one giant steam engine would come to the fair. We could hear the chugging and the rattling of the wheels roaring over the flint roads miles away, and a gang of us would rush up a couple of miles or more to meet it. Then we'd run behind until it reached the green; like the children of Hamelin we followed the mechanical pied piper.

The coming of a steam engine to the fair meant there would be more than just stalls—perhaps roundabouts, and once a set of chair-a-planes came. We had never seen these flying chairs before and were scared stiff of them; we younger ones couldn't be persuaded to go on them at any cost. Grown-ups offered to pay for the ride but we hung back, saying we should get chucked out. 'I should be frit tu death,' said Willy Weaver, and we nudged one another in our shyness and fear. When evening came some of the older lads took their girls on this tearing, swirling monster and we stood dumbfounded at their flying legs, and were greatly surprised to find that after a short ride they returned to earth none the worse.

If any of us could cadge or earn a penny it would most likely be spent on a breath-taking ride on the 'Gallopers'—those beautiful, galloping horses with gaping mouths and flaming nostrils. We would mount these gaily painted animals, hanging onto their necks as if they were fiery steeds. They were fixed to the round-about with brass rods that looked like giant barley sugar sticks. And the organ with its colourful, stiff-jointed figures of men and women who played cymbals, drums and bells, blared loud, lovely tunes:

> I'm one of the nuts from Barcelona,
> I clinkety clonk,
> I cassidy blonk.

or

> I'm for ever blowing bubbles. . . .

—tunes that we hollered and bellowed for months after the fair had gone.

We would stand, mouths watering, watching the gypsy women make the 'Claggum'. This was the name we called the cream and brown 'fair rock' that they sold for 1*d.* a lump. The women would sit crouched round an open fire, their faces grimed with smoke, stirring treacle and brown sugar in a big black saucepan. For ages they seemed to sit there stirring and talking and smoking clay pipes. When the Claggum, or 'teasing candy' as it was sometimes called, had reached the right consistency, it was tipped out onto a wooden board.

When it was cool enough to handle the gypsies would spit on their hands and start to 'tease' the Claggum, first by flinging it over an old hook that was fixed to the side of the caravan, then they would pull it out from the hook—like a huge hank of cream wool it looked—flinging it back over the hook time and time again. Somehow they managed to get a thick brown stripe all through the rock. As soon as the Claggum had been teased to the right length it was whipped off and slapped back onto the board. Then, wielding a huge knife, the women cut the rock up into lumps.

In the evening the naphtha lights round the stalls hissed and flared, lighting up coconut shies and hoop-la, casting weird shadows over the fairground. A gypsy who always came to Duck Feast was Mrs Topper, a black-eyed, fierce-looking woman with two wild-looking sons. She had no coconut shies or hoop-la, but made her money by selling water squibs. She would set up a small table—on it was a bucket of water (drawn from our well), and a pile of small shiny tubes, not unlike toothpaste tubes.

She would fill these with water from the bottom end and skilfully twist the open end up tightly with a pair of pliers. These she would sell for a penny. Many a love affair was started or strengthened at Duck Feast—this was how the fellows showed their affection, by chasing the girl of their choice and generously squirting her down the neck with one of Mrs T.'s squibs.

'Tigglers' were sold at the fair too; they were just a bunch of soft strings of coloured papers fixed to a cardboard handle. These were a more gentle way of 'getting to know you', but served much the same purpose as the water squib, and the girls raced round and round the vans squealing in protest, but longing to be caught.

One year Bern, the eldest of our family, and about thirteen at the time, had earned and saved about 1s. 4d. to spend at the fair. He told us he had hid it away where none of us would ever find it. On the feast Sunday when the caravans had drawn on and settled down to their short stay in the village, Bern suddenly burst out crying. 'What's up with him?' Mother said. He had hidden his money away in an Oxo tin under a clod of earth on Chalky (the village green), but a caravan, with two lurcher dogs safely tied to the axle, had parked on the spot.

Bern mooned about the fair with nothing to spend. Early on the Wednesday he was up before anyone else—the caravans had moved out, and so had his treasure. The dogs had evidently smelled something and had scratched the tin out. He found it empty in some rushes near by.

Bonfire night was the next event, not that we had any fireworks, but we did go round the village and peer over the gardens of those who were well-off enough to have a few sparklers. And although many of the cottages were thatched I can never remember any of them catching fire. A precaution against this was a bucketful of water and a bit of cloth fixed to the end of a long pole kept outside at the ready.

Before we knew where we were it was time to go carol singing. Our mother wouldn't let us 'go plaguin'' people until three or four nights before Christmas—not that there were many places to sing at. It was no good going to ordinary cottagers like ourselves.

Real carol singing was confined to 'The Big House' and a few large houses where the people lived who were much better off than most of us. With candles set in jam jars we would set off. At some of the places we just received 'kind'—mince pies or lovely sweet-smelling apples, hot soup, sometimes a little money. At one or two places our carol singing was a sort of ritual.

One house we loved to sing at was the elderly Miss Holtoms', two spinster ladies whose lives were devoted to the church. Dressed in long full skirts they would swish along the cold stone passages of the house where they lived and invite us to step inside out of the biting wind. Our first carol always, for them, was 'While Shepherds "Washed"' and then 'See Amid The Winter's Snow'. The Miss Holtoms' mince pies were the best we ever tasted—all fatty and crumbly. 'We will tell the Rector how beautifully you sang,' they would call as we hurried down the dark drive. But our mouths were too full to answer.

Every year we had a wondrous Christmas party at school. It was given by Major Feilden and his wife. Trestle tables were brought from the parish room and were absolutely bowed down with food: thin bread and butter—you could put a slice straight into your mouth it was cut so fine—and lovely square chunks of dough and seedy cake made by Baker Collis.

We would fill ourselves to bursting point, then slyly sneak a piece of cake and slip it into our pockets so that our mother might share the treat with us, but like as not it would be a crumbly mess by going home time.

As well as the lovely feed, we had another treat. In the 'big room' was a most wonderful Christmas tree. It touched the ceiling it was so tall, and it dripped with toys, dolls and drums, books, and games. It was lit with real candles and dressed with shiny baubles such as we had never seen before. Everyone in the school received a present off the tree.

Then some time in January another special event was held. This was more a grown-ups treat. I think you had to be at least fourteen before you could go. It was the Parish Tea, which cost a shilling. Men and boys all scrubbed clean, red-faced and shiny, their hair plastered down with tappaleen (water) and dressed in navy-blue best suits smelling strongly of moth-balls or lavender, would stand in shy groups at the back of the hall. Women and girls also in their best, hair crimped with curling tongs, stood about in gossiping groups. First of all there was dancing—this was where we learned the Lancers, the Veleta, the Boston Two Step and the ordinary dances. We would plague the older women to take us round—clumsy, gawky, great country girls we were too.

All the music both for the dancing and the 'turns' that came later was played by a Mrs Fowler who would tirelessly thump away on the old upright piano. The thing was, there probably wasn't anyone else in the village able to play.

We certainly had our shilling's worth on those wonderful nights—for the ladies of the village had prepared sandwiches and cakes and urns of thick brown tea. But those turns that each year were performed by the same stalwarts are what I remember best—

Shade Franklin—Charley Edwards—Albert Hickman—Claude Collis—these were the men who sang and joked and made us very happy—year after year after year.

Before the end of the evening we were all red-faced and sweating, though the only heat came from a tortoise stove. But it was the excitement and the dancing and the fun, and the fact that all through those cold winters we were stuffed with great suet puddings and potatoes and mountains of bread and dripping that must really have been our very salvation. And it was these annual events that bound us, as a village, tighter together—making our own fun, sharing and giving.

Sometimes there would be a school concert—weeks and weeks of practice were needed to get some of the children to walk on the makeshift stage, but on the final night, when the parish room was again packed to bursting point, we all excelled ourselves. Except once, when Mavis Killmaster forgot her words as she was rendering 'Some people love to fun and frolic'. She had a good voice and we were all rather envious of her.

Once, I remember, Percy Bayliss brought the house down in a Nativity Play by saying to Mary, 'Blessed art thou, for thou art highly flavoured,' although he didn't realize what he had said.

On these concert nights the Rector would sit in the front row, his plump body perched uncomfortably on the bench-like seats. He would clap eagerly at all our efforts and dab his eyes with joy at the end.

Sometimes in the summer Bible meetings would be held on Chalky, and although we as a family were 'church', we used to love to go to these open-air meetings that were organized by the chapel; camp meetings they were. Most of the crowd was made up of children—although one old chap used to say of these meetings, 'all the 'nominations will be there'. We would gather round, staring wide-eyed as the lay preacher ranted and raged about the sins of the world. These men would fling their arms about and gaze heavenwards, as if the vision was written up there in that summer sky.

Brother Irvings used to play a little squeeze box thing, a melodion some folks called it, and this provided the music for the hymn singing. We loved the hymns. It didn't matter how loud you sang—in fact everybody seemed to try and outdo one another in efforts to be heard. Not like church, where we sang in quite subdued voices and the Rector preached his sermon in a more dignified manner. Not that the feeling of the Lord was any less out on Chalky—it was just that we put more into it, and bellowed 'Jesus wants me for a Sunbeam' or 'At the Cross, at the Cross', loud into the summer evening.

The bigger boys, those who had started work, used to stand at the back of the meeting and would sing, quite loudly, parodies to the hymns—and when we got home we would sing them—only to get our ears boxed for taking the Lord's name in vain. The one that was sung to the tune of 'At the Cross' ended like this:

> They were eating currant buns,
> When they heard the German Guns,
> And the bottom of the bucket rolled away.

But the really rude part came before that.

In the summer we had another school treat. This one was always held on the rectory lawn—the same trestle tables would be carried from the parish room—the same lovely wafer-thin bread and butter and Doughy Collis's cakes. After tea some of the children from the top class would give a display of country dances. I wasn't often chosen to dance because I was big and clumsy and probably Miss Spencer, our teacher, thought that I would not be able to produce the white dress and plimsolls that were required for those taking part in the dances.

But one year I assured her that I had a white frock to wear— really, it was the one my sister had worn when she was confirmed. My mother declined to have me confirmed because of my tomboyish and unruly behaviour—but I could wear the dress. White lawn it was, with white embroidery on, and the edge of the skirt was scalloped, but as it was several sizes too big for me this lovely scalloped piece didn't show because of the huge hem my mother had put on it. Never mind, I was going to be able to do 'Rufty Tufty' and 'Gathering Peasecods'* with the rest.

But first we all sat down to eat. Mrs Edwards came round with a big white enamelled jug full of hot strong tea. She was just pouring some out for me when Chris Goodwin shoved his great arm across to grab the last bit of cake on the plate, and sent the jug flying out of poor Mrs Edwards's hand. The tea went all over me and the white lawn frock. When it came to dancing time Miss Spencer eyed the big brown stain on my frock and 'tut-tutted' and said, 'You can't possibly dance in front of the Rector looking like that—Nellie Clark can take your place.' How I hated Nellie Clark as she simpered through those dances while I sat and sulked.

Never mind, I had my own back later when we ran races, three-legged, sack, and just ordinary fast running. I beat her every time and went proudly home with eightpence winning money—but had a darned good hiding for spoiling the frock.

The only other big events were the Harvest Festivals held at the church and chapel, both lovingly decorated year after year.

The church were first to hold theirs—the almost bare sanctuary suddenly sprang into life, stooks† of wheat greeted us as we entered, outsized marrows filled the windows, onions, leeks, and apples were heaped on every ledge, great bunches of Michaelmas daisies and giant dahlias nodded from earthenware jugs, and an unusual crowd filled the pews. The Rector preached of 'my faithful few', those stalwarts who attended always. 'I thought he was quite rude,' Mother said, but turned up just the same next Harvest Festival.

We looked forward to the chapel one, at least to the sale of produce held on the Monday. We would get there early, completely filling the front seats. Of course we had no money and

* Authentic names of old country dances.
† Bundles of wheat.

gazed open-mouthed as people passed over a few pence for cabbages and apples, carrots and pears.

Always in pride of place was a beautiful loaf of bread, much larger than the ones we had at home, and all down the middle, and running along the top, it had a pattern of wheat ears, shiny, golden and brown. Placed on either side of the big loaf were several minute cottage loaves—this was our interest because dear, hunchbacked Mr Irvings always bought these little loaves and distributed them amongst us. We never waited until we got home to eat them, but stuffed them into our ever-hungry mouths as soon as he gave them to us.

Just before Easter we children made a pilgrimage to Gorsehill Woods to gather primroses to help decorate the church, bunching them up with the pale green leaves, tying them carefully with wool. Then the Miss Holtoms would place them lovingly round the font and surround them with tangy moss.

This was our small contribution. There was never any money to chink into the plate that Mr Spindlow brought round as the last hymn was being sung, although when we got a bit older we used to pretend to put something on there, but he knew we didn't—there was the absence of that chink as the pretended money failed to land. But I don't suppose that the dear Lord thought any the worse of us for that.

Our beloved Rector at Ducklington was the Reverend Tristram. He was an ideal village parson and was kindness itself to the villagers. There was a little charity money that he gave out to the poor but our mother often told us that he gave much of his own money away too. 'There's some people for ever in and out of that rectory just for what they can get from him. Not good Christian folk neither. Still,' she'd go on in her independent voice, 'nobody can ever say as I've had a penny charity money. My father used to say to me "Ah my girl, an independent woman an' a beggar's purse en't worth a curse"; perhaps it isen't but it's a nice feeling inside.'

Most mornings the Rector came into the school, sometimes taking us for scripture lesson. He had been educated at Magdalen

College, Oxford, and taught us the correct way to pronounce it (Maudlen). It was his idea to have an ancient barn converted into the parish room, and this is still the only meeting place in the village. He started a reading room there too, and got Miss Polly Holtom to run the lending library.

Old Mr Hill who lived up the other end of the village, near the milkman's, used to toddle right down to get a book for himself and his ailing wife. One day Miss Polly was trying to help him choose a book and said to him in her high-pitched, educated voice, 'Oh Mr Hill—have you ever had *A Night Out?*' 'Yes Miss,' Mr Hill replied cheekily, 'I've had several,' and everybody burst out laughing; Miss Polly moved quickly from the fiction to the history shelf.

At the Rector's suggestion a girls' club was formed. You had to be between ten and fourteen to be able to join. It was held in the parish room every Thursday and the fee was 2*d.* a week. We learnt folk dancing and acted little plays and did what we called exercises (P.T.) or just played organized games. I did not join until I was twelve and then was only allowed to because Bern, Bunt, and Betty went to choir practice on that night and I could go and come back with them.

12

Characters and Neighbours

APART from the two-day annual fair, and Christmas, Harvest Festivals and the Parish Tea, nothing spectacular happened in Ducklington. But the place was full of lively characters who brought colour and sometimes excitement into our otherwise quiet rural lives.

There was Edna—poor Edna—subject to fits and 'the drink'. She was tall and thin and had a pile of black hair above her blotchy purple face. Her eyes were wild and bulbous and we kids were all scared stiff of her, and squittered* past the tall stone wall that circled the house where she lived.

She would career round the village on her old bicycle, searching for anyone who would get her a bottle of spirit. From somewhere she would get the money. The landlords of the two pubs had been warned not to serve her but she'd hang about till she found a willing passer-by. Sometimes Edna would wait in vain for her bottle while one of the villagers sat in the ale bar of The Bell, supping away at Edna's expense.

We came upon her one hot sunny day; she was sprawled out under one of Pudney Wilsdon's sweet-smelling hayricks—tight as a tick† she was. Her shiny black straw hat askew, her face more purple than ever and her loose red mouth wide open. Perhaps she was dead; we stood and stared at her. Then she started to grunt and snore like a pig.

Suddenly she opened her eyes and saw four ragged children staring at her. With one movement of her long thin body she was

---

* Running away quickly and quietly.　　† Drunk.

up. Swinging her empty bottle high above her head she chased us over the meadow. Her blood-curdling screams brought a farm worker to our rescue.

'I'll drown myself,' Edna shouted, 'I'll jump in the river.'

'Go on then, jump!' Carter Temple said, but she didn't. This was an old trick of Edna's to threaten drowning when she was caught drunk.

Someone sent for her father and Edna slunk home, shame-faced. At other times she would let down her hair and ride round and round the village on her bicycle, shouting at anyone who went by, and only go back home when she was utterly exhausted.

The old man who lived next door to us, in the thatched house, was always known as 'e in the corner. Go out on any starlight night and 'e in the corner would be standing by the gate, one eye shut tight and the other pressed to an ancient telescope.

'Venus is clear tonight,' he would say if we happened by. 'She won't be as near again for a thousand years.' We should have listened more intelligently to him.

One night 'e in the corner spied something special in his telescope. Excitedly he shouted, as if he were greeting the heavenly body, 'Jupiter, Jupiter!' and a small voice from the darkened roadway replied, 'No it isn't, Mr Horne, it's me, Claudie, Claudie Collis.'

By trade 'e in the corner cut and carved names on tombstones. Lying abed we could hear him chipping away in the outhouse, carving sweet verses to lost villagers.

Whether someone had cancelled an order or whether 'e in the corner laid in a stock at some time I don't know, but for months a plain tombstone was propped up against our gate (the three cottages used the same). On the tombstone was fixed a notice that read 'For Sale for Four Pounds', but who on earth in our village had four pounds!

When 'e in the corner fell ill, our mother used to pop in and do his housework for him or take him some hot pudding or stew.

One day in early summer it was, he said to her, 'Missus, stop they dratted birds a-singing, they gets on me nerves, chirp, chirp chirping away all day long.' The thick thatch of his snug cottage was full of sparrows and the garden full of blackbirds and thrushes greedily gorging his fruit. 'Poor old fellow,' our mother said. 'He's complaining about the birds singing—where he's going there'll be no bird song.' The next day 'e in the corner died.

Everybody liked Dick Clarke. Dick would have been called a spastic these days. Poor devil!—legs mis-shapen, bent inwards at the knees, and hands and fingers all knotted up. He shuffled about somehow on two sticks, dragging his feet along the ground. He lived with his brother and sister. The brother was our postman and he also kept a few cows. And each day Dick would prop himself up in their little shed which they used as a dairy and turn the handle of the milk-separating machine; this would take him about a couple of hours to do.

But he was cheerful and chatty, and he would tease us girls about boys. There wasn't much that went on that Dick didn't know about.

Young lads of the village were always on the lookout to make a few coppers, my brothers amongst them.

Some of them would make themselves a little wooden truck by using the wheels off an old pram and a box cadged from one of the shops in the town. Then they would go round the village roads picking up horse manure.

All you needed for this job was a truck, a small shovel and a good left foot. The foot was placed behind the heap of muck, and with the shovel in the right hand you had to take a sharp shove at the heap so that you collected all the muck at one go without scattering it all over the place. This the lads would sell for about sixpence for a full truck. Those who hadn't a truck did their collecting in an old bucket. And gathering up the horse manure as they did helped our roadman Charlie Hickman who had a long length of road to keep clean and tidy—nearly seven miles, which included Ducklington. To me Charlie had always seemed aged, a weather-beaten, gnarled old fellow who rode an old black tricycle. He used to carry his tools tied on the back of his trike and these included a broom, shovel, scythe, sickle, fagging hook, and sharpening stone, besides his dinner bag and an old coat. He always wore thick brown cord trousers yorked up below the knee with leather straps, and his face was the colour of a bit of old leather.

When we went back to school on some days Charlie would be sitting on the side of the road eating his victuals—usually a great hunk of bread and fat bacon. This was always swilled down with a bottle of cold tea, winter and summer. We used to kick at the neat little piles of dust that he had carefully swept up. 'Drat your eyes on you, you little devils. I'll swipe you with me broom handle if I catch you,' he'd yell as we ran away.

Besides doing the hard road-work Charlie kept bees and pigs at home and hand-planted three of his allotments each year with barley, tilling the soil with a breast plough.* Then he would cut the corn with a scythe and take it to the flour mill in the village to be ground. This barley meal was to feed and fatten up his pigs. Then Charlie was given notice to quit his job, just a month off his eightieth birthday. We had other road-men but Ducklington never seemed quite the same without the old man's familiar figure.

There was a family of eight who lived fairly near us. They all grew up great strapping people, yet when they were tiny their furniture consisted of orange boxes to sit on, and one big deal table to eat from. When the Rector went to visit them he was asked to take a seat—on the stairs.

Yet no one thought them any the worse for this. They were clean and healthy and lived mostly on 'taters, bacon and greenstuff. The father worked hard and his allotments were a picture, and woe betide anyone who put a foot near them. He was a strong, red-faced, giant of a man who could push a breast plough as easily as most men push a wheelbarrow. Rabbits in-

---

* An early plough which a man pushed by hand and his chest.

vaded his allotments from the surrounding fields, sneaking his precious greenstuff. But he would set traps for them and made a fair bit on the side. Most of the housewives gladly gave him ninepence for a rabbit.

A man we were scared stiff of was called Peter Painter, who lived in the town near by. He was an expert at biting off puppies' tails. He was never seen without a pail with a lid attached, always shut too. As kids we thought this was full of bitten-off tails. Mothers would say to disobedient children, at least to the little boys, 'If you be naughty I'll sent for Peter, an' 'e'll do the same fer you as 'e does to they puppy dogs.' And for a while the boys would behave and look very solemn at the prospect of their 'belongings' being whipped off and carted away in Peter's lidded pail. We found out when we were older that his pail contained pigs' chitterlings, probably given him in lieu of payment for biting off the puppies' tails.

Another man we were frightened of was Joey the Flag. He pushed a little old truck round the town filled with something mysterious, all wet and wriggling. The truck was partly covered with a sack which dripped and made a trail in the road as he went by. We were almost afraid to look as he scuffled along—you could hear the contents of the truck, flip-flop, flip-flop, as he passed, Mothers used to threaten naughty children by saying that they would get Joey to push them under the sack and take them away. We found out that he, like Peter, was carrying pigs' chitterlings around. Joey used to collect them from a slaughter-house and take them to a large piggery on the other side of the town, where, people said, they were fed back to the pigs.

There was never any real tragedy in the village. The worst thing that happened was when foot and mouth disease struck Wilsdon's farm. One morning we went to school to find disinfectant pouring over the road. The farm buildings happened to be on both sides of the village street.

The slaughter of the animals came first. All the farmers' men were sent out into Gooseham field where they had to hand-dig a great deep pit. The bottom was lined with cartloads of faggots and paper. Then the bodies of the cattle were thrown in—I still remember seeing that huge pile—stacks of legs, tails, heads and bodies piled up against the sky line. They set fire to the lot and the awful smell of burning flesh floated over our village for days. After the fire had done its job the workmen poured sacks and sacks of quicklime on the remains, and the hole was covered over with turf. And although there were two other farms very close, the outbreak was confined to Wilsdon's.

At the back of the row of cottages where we lived there was another row of three or four. Joe Hill and his wife lived 'up the back'. They were very old; Mrs Hill died there. Old Joe must have been well over seventy. He lived on there for a while longer, then he fell ill. Neighbours did what they could but in the end old Joe was taken off to the nearest workhouse.

And one fine morning someone came and put their bits of furniture out into the yard, and along came a man and sold it. There was a white scrubbed table, and a few kitchen chairs and odds and ends. Most of the items were bought by the nearest neighbours. Our mother paid four shillings for what was probably the most prized possession in the cottage, Joe's wooden armchair.

At some time Mrs Hill had crocheted the red woolly cover that was fixed over the spars at the back to stop the draught getting on Joe's shoulders. We used 'Joe Hill', the name we gave the chair, for years at home. I have it now; the wooden arms are almost white with wear—the crocheted cover has long since worn out and has been replaced by a bright red cushion, and we still call it 'Joe Hill'.

In those days the workhouse was the only place for the very old, especially if they were ill and had no relations. By selling the bits of furniture these unfortunate souls could at least have a decent burial—to have to end one's days in the workhouse was dreadful, but to have a pauper's grave was much worse.

What some of the really old folks suffered from was semi-starvation. One dear old lady that our mother used to go to see almost lived on what she called 'tea-kettle broth'. This was a piece of dry toast soaked in hot water—no wonder some of them folded up like flowers at eventide and died.

13

Growing Pains

I can remember the excitement and indeed the sadness, when our sister Betty went off to service*—somewhere in Hampshire it was, but it seemed like the other side of the world to us. When girls went to be servants in big houses, their future mistresses would send a list of clothes that the young girls needed. Mothers had to find two of everything, and all had to be marked with the owner's name.

Our mother had such a list and wondered how on earth she was going to get together the necessary items. But the neighbours were wonderful; one made a morning apron, another made two white cambric nightgowns, lace-edged and feather-stitched. And dear, deaf-and-dumb Sally Castle made a morning and afternoon dress and never charged a penny for the making.

They came to fetch our sister in a car. This was wonderful because at that time only two or three people in the village had such a luxury. This one was chauffeur-driven, so we knew that the family must have pots of money. But we all cried when she rode away—a forlorn figure she made. This was the first time any member of the family had gone away to work. But one fourteen-year-old out of the house left a bit more room for those that were left.

With her leaving, my elder sister's jobs became mine, and those that I had done became my step-sister's. So now, before I went to school, ashes had to be taken up and sifted, and the black grate given a bit of a shine. One of my brother's daily tasks was to get

* To be a maid in a big house.

the morning's wood. Every night found him up the hedgerows gleaning dry twigs and little pieces of rotten wood at the base of the hedge; box wood was unheard of. In winter time he would slip the kindling wood into the fire-oven so it was nice and dry by morning. Then it would light easily and boil a kettle so that he might have a cup of tea before he went off to work.

But our mother was rather extravagant with wood and loved to have what she called a 'blizzy'. Many times Bunt, stumbling from sleep about six o'clock on a winter's morning, came downstairs to find his precious kindling wood had gone. Our Mother had burnt the lot. 'Had one of my blizzies, boy, had to warm myself up a bit before I went to bed,' she would say when Bunt chided her. And he would have to go and get some more sticks, probably damp ones. Then he would kneel in front of the grate and blow himself red in the face in an effort to get the wood to catch.

My Saturday job was to scrub the stone-flagged back kitchen, a job I detested. Once, at Christmas-time, our stepfather brought home a couple of ducks, and our Mother quickly made a bargain with me. 'I'll do your scrubbing,' she said, 'if you'll go and pick the ducks.' I was out in that old wash-house for hours and hours; those ducks had half-a-dozen coats on, I'm sure. The trouble was I did not know that the art of picking ducks is to plunge the thumb and finger right into the thick down as near to the skin as possible. After being out in that freezing wash-house for about three hours, cold and miserable, crying, and covered in feathers, I gave up, though the ducks still had quite a bit of fluff on them, but I didn't care. The weekly scrubbing of the back kitchen never seemed so bad after that.

Bunt, the more enterprising of my real brothers, used to earn himself a bit extra by catching moles. He would set his traps in Pudney's field, and early every morning he would go out to collect those he had caught. Then he would skin them and carefully tin-tack the velvet-like skins on a board to dry. When he had got a dozen or more he would take them up to Warburtons in the town, where he would get sixpence each for them.

Both Bern and Bunt helped on a milk round before they went to school. In the very cold weather they wore old socks on their hands in an effort to keep them warm. Handling a steel can on a frosty morning could be murder. They got sixpence each a week for this, a seven-day week at that. But they got a few 'perks' as well: housewives would give them hunks of cake and apples, or perhaps a copper or two at the end of the week.

When Bunt left school he worked for a few months for the milkman, his wages being half-a-crown a week, but he used to wear out that amount in shoe leather. So, as soon as he could, our step-father got him a job at the brewery where he worked and Bunt stayed there, rising to the job of yard foreman until he was called up during the war.

Bern, the eldest, was already holding down quite a good job at one of the big warehouses in the town, where they finished off and packed the blankets and dispatched them all over the world. He was lucky to get a job like this because during the 1920s good jobs were few and far between. When he had first left school he worked on the farm for Mr Parker, walking up to Barley Park Farm at seven in the mornings, taking a short cut across the forty-acre field. Then our mother heard of this job going at the warehouse and walked up to Witney and got it for him.

Some Sunday mornings after he started work, Bern would say, 'Pop up to Smith's and get a few sweets.' Mrs Smith was a widow who lived in one of the cottages 'up the back' and she sold sherbet dabs, cheap toffees, and liquorice pipes in her front room. Armed with sixpence we would rush up there with strict instructions on how to spend it. Two penn'orth of toffees at two ounces a penny—hard as a brick but very welcome. Six ha'penny gob-stoppers, one each for us younger ones and one each for Bern and Bunt. We loved gob-stoppers; they were so big you could hardly move them from one side of your mouth to the other, and as you sucked away at them they kept changing colour—we would fetch them out of our mouths, saying 'mine's pink now, mine's yellow'. Then we had to get two penny bars of Cadbury's chocolate for our parents and a ha'penny bag of popcorn with the last copper. We would hang round Bern until he had shared the popcorn with us and had doled out each a toffee. And that was that—everybody had had a treat but the remaining toffees were his.

We loved it when our Auntie Emily came home for her annual holiday. She was a lady's maid to someone very wealthy, and she nearly always gave us some money to spend. Once she met Mick and I in the square at Ducklington and gave us sixpence each— sixpence each!—we were practically millionaires.

We went into the village shop and spent thre'pence each. I bought two sherbet fountains and forty aniseed balls (twenty a penny). Instead of sucking up the white powder through the liquorice tube I just emptied the whole packet down my throat. Suddenly the sherbet started to fizz and bubble and pour out of my mouth and down my nose. Red-faced, eyes watering, I coughed, spluttered and nearly choked to death outside Stranges' farm. 'Greedy guts', were the only words of sympathy that I got from Mick who had her mouth chock-full of nougat.

We had planned to tell our mother that Auntie Emily had in fact only given us thre'pence each. We went home and told our tale and handed over the money. Then, wallop! we were punished for telling lies. Our *dear* aunt, in the meanwhile, had called at our house and told our mother what she had so *generously* given us. We were sent off to bed for the rest of the day, but I didn't mind so much because I still had the remaining aniseed balls stuck up my knicker leg.

14

Pig Killing

Our parents, like many of the village folk, kept a couple of pigs—'ran a couple of pigs' was the expression. Much of the food they ate was 'come by', apart from the toppings (pig meal). After school in summertime we would go off with hessian sacks and fill them with sow thistles, dandelion leaves, keck (cow parsley) and waywind. The pigs loved this fresh-picked food.

Little pig 'taters were boiled up in an old saucepan over the living-room fire every day. These were mixed with a little toppings and the water our own vegetables had been cooked in, to make a good evening meal for the animals. Keeping pigs meant there was no waste at all for they cleared up cabbage leaves, rotten apples, and garden weeds, and provided a good supply of manure for gardens and allotments.

In the autumn we paid an annual visit to a field a couple of miles away called 'The Devil's Nutting Ground' where there were several giant oak trees in the field and in the hedge. Here we collected acorns by the peck. When these were fed to the pigs it was almost guaranteed to put a couple of extra inches of fat on their backs before it was time to kill them.

Then, about the middle of October when the weather had turned colder, our stepfather would go down to the village and ask Piggy Humphries to come and kill them. One we would have indoors for eating, the other Mr Humphries would buy, and the money we got for it paid Baker Collis what we owed him for toppings and bought us a few warm clothes for the coming winter.

The pig killing now seems to have been a gory affair, but it was such a common occurrence in the village that we took no notice at all.

Mr Humphries would arrive on his bicycle with his tools carefully wrapped in a sack: a pig sticker, a very long sharp knife, and a sharpening stone. The poor animals seemed to sense that something was wrong and while the men struggled to slip a noose over each snout to help drag them out of the sty ready for the killing, they would set up such a squealing that could be heard all over the top end of the village.

Once the animal was outside, the men would lift it on to the rough bench; then Mr Humphries would plunge his pig sticker down the animal's throat, cutting an artery; the blood used to ooze out. Some people made a point of catching the blood in a basin. This, mixed with other ingredients, makes very good black puddings.

Once the pig was dead the carcass was placed on a pile of smouldering straw to burn off the bristles. Then, re-sharpening his already sharp knife, Mr Humphries skilfully cut up the carcass. Our mother would be standing close by with a couple of dishes and a clean bucket for the chitterlings. Onto the dishes went the heart, liver, kidney, and head. And my elder brothers waited patiently for the bladder which they used for ages afterwards as a football—the only sort they ever possessed.

Then the flear—that's the piece from which the home-made lard is produced, was hung up in the cool wash-house along with the lights. Then the 'sperib' (spare rib), hams, and backbones were cut out, leaving two sides. After treatment these sides would be our winter's bacon.

The first night's supper after a pig had been killed was the best treat in the world. That was when we had the pig's fry: the liver and fat fried in plenty of lard. Two loaves of bread we would eat with this, wiping our plates round so as not to leave a morsel on them.

All the offal and the 'sperib' had to be eaten quickly in case it went off. Sometimes the weather would suddenly turn very mild. Then we had to gorge like mad so as not to waste a thing, and for about a week we all lived like fighting cocks, stuffing ourselves with great boiled heart and kidney puddings and wonderful faggots that our mother made from the lights, tongue and sweet herbs. She would cover each faggot with a small piece of the caul, the lacy portion of fat that protects the intestines.

Another thing we would have was 'Boney Pie' made from the backbones that Piggy Humphries cut out when he carved up the carcass. The 'sperib' we always had on pig-killing Sunday, baked in the coal fire oven along with huge, crisp, fatty potatoes.

After soaking the head and trotters in salt water for a couple of days our mother would set about making the most wonderful tasty brawn. 'Collared head' is the real country name for brawn. She would boil the head and trotters in fresh water along with half-a-dozen good-sized onions, a few peppercorns and a blade of mace, until the meat fell off the bone. The meat was then put on to a large dish and chopped very finely, and to this was added a cup of chopped sage, pepper to taste and a teaspoon of nutmeg, and some of the liquor which the meat had been boiled in, making the mixture quite wet and floppy—wetter than cake mix. While it was still warm it was put into greased basins with a plate on the top and something very heavy on the plate to press the brawn well down. When it was cold and turned out it was all set firm and could be cut into slices.

Then there were the chitterlings to clean. First they were turned inside out on a stick to get them clear of any waste matter. This was quite a hard job and messy, too, with no tap-water available. Then they were left to soak in salt water for three days. Our mother would plait the tiny ones and simmer them all until they were tender. We would either eat them cold or frizzled up in the frying pan.

The day after the pig killing we kids would sit round the table and help to cut up the flear into pieces about as big as a meat cube.

This was put into saucepans over a gentle heat. As soon as the fat started to run it had to be poured into basins so as not to let it boil away; you had to keep at it all the while. 'Pop out and pick me a sprig of rosemary,' Mother would say to one of us. This gave the lard a wonderful flavour. (She always put rosemary in milk puddings too.) After melting down all the flear we would have four or five basins of snow-white lard. This would last us on our bread for weeks and weeks.

Then the little bits of shrivelled-up cooked fat which was over from the lard-making made us another tasty meal. We called them 'crutlings' though in some counties they are known as 'scratchings'. We ate these piping hot, straight from the pot—it was a sort of reward for helping to cut up the flear.

Another job that had to be done quickly was the salting and pickling of the sides and the hams. Out in the back kitchen where it was cool our stepfather would set up his salting trough by standing it on a couple of trestles. He would place the sides in the trough and rub salt and saltpetre well into the meat, turning it over in the brine every day so that it was all well-salted. After several days of this treatment the bacon was taken out of the brine and hung up to dry off, either on racks near the ceiling or behind a door, carefully covered with a bit of butter muslin. Then in a little while it was ready for eating.

Sometimes our stepfather would salt the hams like the bacon, but at other times he pickled them in a mixture of old beer, brown sugar, juniper berries, and salt. He would boil these up together and when the mixture was cold it was rubbed into the hams every day for a month. Then the hams, like the bacon, were hung up to dry off. 'Best pictures we got in the house,' Mother would say to visitors.

The flavour of ham pickled like this was wonderful and something I have never tasted since. While it lasted we used to have a slice each on Saturday nights for supper, cut thick and fried in plenty of lard. They were such great slices that one filled a good-sized dinner plate.

Pigs were often twenty score and over—the 'fatter the better' the women would say; the meat was more flavoursome and satisfying anyhow. During the winters we had the bacon cooked all sorts of ways—fried, great lumps boiled and eaten hot or cold, and about once a week we had a great big bacon and onion clanger. That's what we called the huge roly-poly that our mother made from flour paste, butcher's suet, chunks of bacon and thickly sliced onions, all rolled up and sewn into a floured cloth. It was about a foot long and bubbled and boiled in the oval saucepan for about five hours.

One very large family in the village had one of these bacon and onion clangers every day—while the children were all small—and because of this they earned themselves the nickname of 'Clanger' Browns, to distinguish them from several other families of the same name.

15

Good Times and Bad

OUR mother's temperament blew hot and cold according to the weather or the domestic situation. Sunny days found her full of the joys of spring, light-hearted and loving, taking us for miles, pushing a pram full of kids on wooding jaunts, blackberrying, or mushrooming, or just out in God's good air. No doubt there were occasions when she was very hard up, or maybe just fed up with everything in general. At times like this you had to watch out—slap bang!—you would be smacked for the most trifling thing.

Once I called a boy a 'guts', and she rubbed carbolic soap in my mouth—to wash out the filth, she said—and I sat on the stairs for ages picking that soap out of my teeth. One thing she could not abide was any sort of swearing, or rough words, and although we were surrounded by people who spoke what she termed as 'a bit on the rough side', we were all encouraged to speak properly.

When we became too big for hidings our mother punished us by sending us up to bed without any tea. In the summer, when all the other children were out at play, this was a worse punishment than a good hiding. I don't think any other members of the family were sent off to bed as often as I was, but then none of them happened to be as wilful and cheeky.

But one of our mother's favourite sayings (and she had got one for most occasions) was: 'Never let the sun go down on your anger', and often when I had been sent to bed early she would bring me up a plate of bread and dripping just as it was getting dark, and sit on the bed and talk to me while I ate it. Then she would give me a goodnight kiss and ask me to try to be a good girl the next day. 'And don't forget to say your prayers,' she would call as she went back downstairs, 'and ask the dear Lord if He can make you behave, because I can't.'

Every night in wintertime our mother would fill the oil lamp and trim the wick. Then she would clean the glass chimney by pushing her duster up the fine clear glass, blowing on it and then polishing it to make it shine so that it would give out a better light.

After we had all had a good hot meal and the crocks were washed up and stacked away, the big table was left clear for us to play for a while before going off to bed. For hours we girls would make doll's furniture from conkers—the lovely shiny horse chestnuts made a good base for chairs and tables. Carefully selecting the squat ones we would stick them with pins or spent matches to act as legs, using some as frames for the backs of the chairs and sofas, weaving wool in and out to give a nice upholstered effect. Sometimes a table could be made from a good big fat conker.

Empty match boxes were carefully saved and by glueing them together, three high and two across, we made a lovely chest of drawers using big-headed pins to act as handles to open each box-like drawer.

Other winter evenings were spent doing french knitting. For this you needed an empty cotton reel with four tin-tacks nailed on to one end. These tin-tacks acted as needles really, on which were set four stitches. Any odd bits of wool were used. Then, holding the reel in the left hand and a pin in the right, you kept slipping the stitches over the tin-tacks, gradually pulling the knitting, which was tubular, through the cotton reel hole. Yards and yards of this we did, sewing it up afterwards to make pretty mats for our mothers to stand pot plants on. Some girls even made fronts of cushion covers with it.

Another indoor game that we played for hours was 'I spy with my little eye'. Once my brothers and some village lads were playing this game when a fellow called Sid said he spied something beginning with L.L. They tried for ages to guess what began with L.L. and finally all the gang said 'Give it up'. Then Sid announced very proudly 'Lectric Light'—it was a battery torch one of the lads had on his bicycle. He was never allowed to forget this and is still referred to as 'Old Lectric Light' by fellows who were there.

We often got hold of the wrong end of the stick because we didn't speak or pronounce our words properly. 'Our Father Giraffe in heaven,' I said for years when repeating the Lord's Prayer, and 'God in heaven save my "soup"' instead of my 'soul'. And for years I puzzled my brains as to where the Darden Hills were. I knew the Aston Hills were just outside the village on the way to Aston, but the Darden Hills I'd never heard of except in the song we bellowed:

> *Charlie Chaplin, his shoes are crackin',*
> *And his old baggy trousers, they want mending,*
> *Before descending to the Darden Hills.*

But I found out when I got older that the last line should have been— *'Before they send him to the Dardanelles'.*

With Bern and Bunt at work, Betty away in service and the rest of us at school, life began to be a little easier for our mother, and she gradually refurnished the home by going to house sales, often picking up good bargains. She would career off on her old push-bike and come struggling home hours later with her purchases. Once she bought a carpet for five shillings—about fifty years old it was. 'Waste of good money,' our stepfather said when he saw the faded bundle.

'I can cut a lot of good bits out of that,' she told him. 'There's pieces in that carpet that's never seen daylight—been stuck under some sideboard for years—real Axminster it is—look—it's stamped on the back.' And she cut and joined the not-so-worn pieces together and made a carpet to cover our living-room.

Sometimes she would linger at the sales too long and come puffing down the road about half an hour before our stepfather was due in for tea. With her hat and coat on she would start cooking, with us children rushing about like mad things helping her. 'Quick Mollie—go and find some dry sticks to jostle the fire up and bring a shovel of little knobs of coal too.' Mick would be sent up the garden to pick sprouts, while she herself hurriedly peeled the potatoes, cutting the skins off thick and rough. For a while pandemonium raged.

'Ben,' Mother would shout, 'pop out to the gate and see if your father's coming,' and Ben would come rushing back crying:

'He's just up by the milkman's.'

'Then you and Denis get off up the road to meet him,' she'd yell. 'It'll give me an extra five minutes.'

Our stepfather would get off his bicycle and sit Ben on the saddle and Denis on the carrier and slowly walk the rest of the way home. When he finally got indoors all was calm. Our mother in a clean pinafore would just be in the act of pouring him out a cup of tea. Potatoes and sprouts in separate string nets would be boiling away on the bright fire, and the home-cured bacon was sizzling in a pan on the hob.

She was generous to a fault, often giving away things we could do with ourselves. Once she gave a tramp half a bread pudding meant for our stepfather's tea. When he grumbled at her for it she said, 'Half of them aren't roaders, just poor devils who can't get work. Surely you don't begrudge them a mouthful of food.'

Next day one of the neighbours sent us a bucket of chitterlings as a gift. 'There you are!' she cried. 'Cast your bread upon the water and it'll come back to you with butter on.' And she rolled up her sleeves and set about cleaning the messy innards.

When there were smelly jobs to do, like chitterlings-cleaning or drawing the insides from rabbits and fowls, our mother used to sweeten the air indoors by burning a few sprigs of dried lavender. She would light the stalks and whirl them round and round, filling the room with a sweet summer smell. When our precious Axminster needed sweeping she would lay damp tea-leaves, straight from the tea-pot, onto the edge of the carpet and sweep them right across it to pick up the dust.

As we got older our mother did all she could to encourage us to broaden our outlook, and would cycle miles with us. We explored Roman Villas, churches in fields miles from anywhere, holy wells and ancient moats, cruck houses, and old preaching crosses.

When we got back from these expeditions she would send us down to the lending library to get books on the things we had seen or on the locality. She taught us to find pleasure from simple country things—to appreciate sunsets and sunrises and each season in turn. To her, everything had a golden glow; even the common dandelion was a thing of beauty in her eyes.

I never see the sun breaking through the leaves without remembering the simple way she instilled in our minds that beauty was ours for the looking. I have heard her say that, after living in the same cottage for over fifteen years, she could still look out of the window and see something different every morning.

Walking back from Witney, sometimes with the east wind roaring against us, she would quote George Borrow's—'There's the wind on the heath, brother'. She never minded being out in all weathers; the only thing she objected to was fog—horrible and unhealthy was her opinion of it, and it blocked her vision of the outside world which she loved so much.

Much of her time in later years was spent 'catching up' on all the books she had not had time to read when we were small.

She taught us to respect our fellow men, saying, 'If you can't say anything good about anybody, don't say anything bad.'

And as each of us started work she gave us a bit of useful advice: 'Keep your job by working hard. Don't try to keep it by telling tales.'

One thing she never did was to tell anyone how old she was. And we children never dared ask her. But when friends and relations brought up the subject she would smilingly answer, 'As old as me tongue and a little bit older than me teeth,' which was perfectly true anyway. And when she died we found out that she was, in fact, eight years older than any of us had imagined.

16

A Time to Remember

BY the end of the 1920s a gradual change had come over all our lives. We older ones had begun to spread our wings like a brood of young fledglings, gradually breaking away from the old ways, leaving the elderly to sing at church and camp meetings.

Bern had saved hard and bought himself a fine racing bike. He joined the Oxford Cycling Club and on Sundays he would go along with dozens of other young men, smartly plus-foured, tearing through the countryside, heads down, behinds in the air. A hundred miles or more they would go sometimes! Bunt was courting strong and saving every penny so that he and his Sylvia could marry.

Betty, fed up with service, had come back home to the crowded cottage and had got herself a job at a laundry in the town. She stood ironing all day long with a couple of dozen other girls. The work was hard but quite well paid, and they laughed and sang as they smoothed the creases from the gentry's clothes.

She went dancing on Saturday nights; she wore fancy garters, cami-knickers, and French knickers, and curled her already wavy hair with a pair of curling tongs, thrusting them into the fire, then twirling her hair up with the hot irons to make it frizzy. She used lipstick, and strange boys used to wait outside our gate for her, sometimes coming on their push-bikes from other villages to see her. She was beautiful.

When I left school she 'spoke for me' at the laundry, asking Mrs Cameron if she could find me a job. I was put in the sorting- and packing-room. For a while I had to walk backwards and forwards to work until our stepfather picked up a second-hand bicycle cheaply for me. But I was rather a misfit at the laundry: big and clumsy and a bit of a tomboy. Mrs Cameron used to swear at me and say, 'You'll never be the lady your sister is, why can't you behave nicely like Betty?' But my sister had the advantage over me—that year away in service had taught her a lot, whereas I had come raw, straight from a village school.

I stuck the job as long as I could. Our mother kept saying how lucky I was to be working at such a nice place, but it was no good. One bright Saturday morning the rebel in me surged up. Mrs Cameron called me 'a black-headed bugger' for some trifling thing. I gave her a mouthful of cheek that for once left her speechless and ran out of the laundry—and got another job within the next hour.

It was around this time that Alice Spindlow and I used to pretend to go down to church on Sunday nights. Then we would slip back over 'The Moors' and up to Witney, to walk up and down The Causeway or 'Bunny Run' as some called it, in an effort to 'get off' with boys. One night Alice bought some liquorice allsorts. In them we found a nice round red one and we smeared the red all over our lips, trying in vain to look grown-up. 'They 'ad thur mouths made up, they looked as if they'd cut thur throats,' one of the villagers told our mother. And that put an end to our walking up the Bunny Run for a while.

As we lay lazily abed on summer mornings, loath to get up for work, we could hear Walter Weaver go plodding over 'The Moors' on his way to work. He always wore great heavy boots. His father was a farm labourer and they lived up in the fields somewhere. Walter had to walk down muddy lanes leading to Ducklington, then on to Witney, so heavy boots were essential. He had the steady gait of the ploughman following the furrow and he always sang loudly as he went—for weeks it was: 'I'm Goin' Back to 'im as 'as, 'im as 'as a Pub Next Door.' When he got tired of that one it was 'Tiptoe Through the Tulips' for weeks on end. Other tunes followed—'All by Yourself in the Moonlight', 'Springtime in the Rockies', and 'The Old Kitchen Kettle'.

Bet and I used to stay in bed until the last minute. With sleep still in our eyes we would stand and gulp down hot tea, our mother would shove our lunch into our hands, and then we were away up the town to work.

We began to join clothing clubs—The Great Universal Stores was the favourite. By doing this we could order a new coat or shoes, and then it would take weeks to pay the bill.

The GWR* started to run cheap trips to the seaside. You could go to Brighton or Southsea for about 4s. 6d. When we could afford it some of us would go, taking sandwiches, enough for the day, for nobody had money to spend on food. We used to start eating them almost as soon as the train pulled out.

Soon boys began waiting outside the gate for me as well as for Betty; shy lads they were, too—sometimes bringing bunches of flowers with them, carefully tied on to the handlebars of their bicycles—violets and primroses, cowslips and dog roses. Some of the lads wore a great big buttonhole, as big as a saucer, in their lapels, and a nice swank handkerchief in their top pocket.

The lanes and fields that had been our playground for so long now became our courting places. I used to have dreadful crushes on some of these boys—for weeks I would have lain down and died for them; then suddenly it was off with the old and on with the new, until our mother thought that I would never take anyone seriously for any length of time. 'You're not bringing any more fellows home,' she would say, 'making fools of them—you'll go round the orchard and pick up a crab if you're not careful.'

In the village, too, things were changing. Mick did not have to stay at Ducklington school until she was fourteen as we older ones did, but went along with the other kids of the village up to Witney for the last couple of years of her education.

Collis's bought a van to deliver their bread in. They also became owners of a couple of sleek black cars that were used for local weddings and funerals and general taxi-ing, with one of Mr

* The Great Western Railway.

Collis's daughters doing the driving. Benny Clements, the old oil man, no longer came round on Saturdays. Hog Puddin' Walker and Spetter King passed away too.

Now each week on Fridays a pretty ginger-haired girl called, driving a green motor van. She sold all sorts of things to eat, including cold fried fish which our mother used to buy and warm up for our tea.

Betty found a cheap gramophone in Jacky Brooke's second-hand shop in the town and almost every week she bought a new record—songs by Layton and Johnston, Hutch, and Gracie Fields.

The talkies came to The People's Palace at Witney and we began to use slang expressions like 'Sez You', 'Oh Yeah', and 'Sez Me', as the great spectaculars flashed across the screen. Waites' ha'p'nny leg dangle paid their annual visit to the town but hardly anyone went—the talkies were much more exciting and we never heard of the Waites travelling theatre again.

Times were changing even faster now. Boys came a-courting us on motor-bikes and in cars. We went dancing night after night—sometimes to real big dances, Police Balls, Fat-Stock Dances with red-faced farmers for partners—Twelfth Night and the annual Conservative Ball.

Bet and I made most of our own dance dresses, running them up on the old hand sewing-machine. One day our mother went to a jumble sale in the village, bringing back a most lovely dance dress which she had bought for one shilling. Flame georgette it was, with a fringe of real fine ostrich feathers round the bottom. Betty looked like a Queen in it. 'I shall wear it to the Corn Exchange Dance tonight,' she said, ripping off the lovely ostrich feather fringe.

'But that makes the dress,' Mother protested.

'And how do you think I can explain such luxury to the laundry girls?' Betty cried. 'I shall go up to Witney and buy a bit of lampshade fringe from Georgie Wickham's and sew it on in place of the feathers and then they'll think I made it myself.'

'I see the Witney Ladies' Hockey Club want some new members,' Mother said to me one day. 'Why don't you join? Funny,' she went on, 'I saw a second-hand hockey stick in the town yesterday, 'twas only three and six!'

So, without knowing one end of a hockey stick from another, I joined the club, greenly explaining that I could not play. One of the older members took me to her home, and after telling me how the game was played, taught me all the rules—she even had to tell me how to hold the stick! I stayed with the Club for years. Mick joined later.

We took up tennis and continued to swim in the Windrush from the first of May till the end of September, and all the time thoroughly enjoying ourselves, although we were always perpetually hard up.

Our stepfather bought a series of old motor-cycles—he was clever with engines, and soon had them ticking over like new. He used to go off early some Sunday mornings to see his ageing Mother, often taking one of his children on the pillion. Other Sundays his brothers and sisters used to visit us. They came on motor-bikes, too—great roaring things they were.

Bunt and Sylvia got married and Bet and I were bridesmaids for the first and last time in our lives.

It was around this time that we moved from 'Wayside' to a new bungalow about a mile away from Ducklington, but well outside the town. For our mother, especially, the move must have been wonderful after the crowded years at Wayside. At last we girls had a bedroom of our own, instead of sharing a curtained-off one with our brothers. We had a wardrobe and a drawer each, in a newly acquired chest of drawers.

Bern, Ben, and Denis shared a second bedroom and our parents the other. We had a front room (for courting), a living-room, kitchen, and bathroom.

Water was pumped from a spring by a rotary pump and was heated in the copper in the kitchen, and the bath-water had to be carried through into the bathroom, but at least the water ran away on its own into a cesspool in the huge garden. The lavatory, too, was indoors but we still used oil lamps and candles for lighting.

We had a summer-house and a greenhouse, and kept pigs and chickens and bees.

But I missed the cosiness of the cottage and the nearness of the big family, and I longed to return to the crowded living-room at Wayside and the cheese box under the bed where I kept my few clothes.

I became restless, walking for miles on my own. I fell out with my boy friends and began to write both poetry and prose. As I walked along the twisty leafy lanes I knew that the magic of my youth was gradually fading away. The funny, familiar things that had happened during those green years were already half-forgotten memories. I was trying desperately to hang on to a world that would never come back again, but it was months before I realized this.

The writing became less now—my sisters teased the life out of me about it, anyhow. But one poem, the only one that finally emerged from that time, and yet was not completed until after our mother died, explains the heartbreak on leaving the cottage at Ducklington.

> Wild roses of my home,
> you climb and circle round my brain,
> stirring my aching heart
> with your festooned loveliness,
> taunting me with your delicate perfume.
>
> Let me return
> to those sun-drenched lanes
> to press my face
> in your bee-kissed blossom,
> brush my cheek
> as the gentle breeze
> loosens your pale blooms,
> spilling your fragrance

over the dew-wet grass,
speckling my path
with confettied profusion,
your thorns
stabbing the memory,
flooding the mind's pool
with nostalgic dreams
of half-forgotten childhood.

Let me return
where the wild rose blooms,
drowning my empty heart
in your summer glory,
cooling my fevered brow
in the lost fields of home.

The Green Years

To my brothers and sisters
. . . the whole and the half

Ducklington

To Ducklington, the signpost read
And that's the way for me I said
For that, I thought, must surely be
A pleasant kind of place to see,
Where downy and delightful things
With yellow feet and cherubs' wings
And busy bills, and bobbing heads
Will dip and dive in osier beds,
Or dabble by the brooklet edge
And hunt for tadpoles in the sedge,
Or heedless of the careful clucks
Of such poor 'hens' as mother ducks
Put out, true infant 'Drakes', to sea,
On the broad ponds immensity.

Alas the dream, the year was old,
The rickyards brimmed with Autumn's gold
Low bowed the weighted fruit tree's down
The green was parched and bare and brown
And all the ducks that quacked beside
The pond, that drought had all but dried,
Were old and sober, staid and sage
Forgetful in their riper age
That they, in some sweet April gone
Were ducklings once in Ducklington.

But time will come and time will go
And this year follow last year's snow,
And spring come back to Windrush side
With swallows flight and mating tide,

With fleeting sun and flying shower
The coltsfoot and the cuckoo flower
With bloom in spate on orchard trees
And faint frail scent of primroses
And running brooks, and ponds abrim
Where downy ducks shall dive and swim
As broods like them since time began
And grass grew green and water ran
From year to year have surely done
At duckling time in Ducklington.

by C. F. S.
Reproduced by permission of *Punch*

I

Come Summer

'COME SUMMER', our Mother said, 'I'll get Uncle Ted Mid-winter to drive us over to see Auntie Maggie and Uncle Amos.' They lived in a farm cottage away in a field about twenty miles from us, and as no trains went anywhere near the hamlet where they lived, we had to rely on Uncle Ted Midwinter to take us.

We children looked forward to the long-promised trip to Robinsgrove, counting the days, almost the hours, till it seemed that the magical day would never come. Then suddenly, one misty June morning, Uncle Ted Midwinter was outside our gate with his pony and trap. He smelt strongly of polish and horses, his smart brown gaiters and boots shone like glass bottles, and on his thin, wiry frame hung a peat-smelling tweed coat. The trap too was polished to perfection and its yellow painted wheels looked for all the world like giant sunflowers. Pete the pony must have been brushed for hours, for his chestnut coat gleamed healthy and shiny.

We were wildly excited about the journey and rushed in and out of the cottage urging our Mother to hurry.

'It's no good you tryin' to rush me,' she shouted, 'I shall be all the longer if you keeps on.' And she calmly went about her preparations for the journey, stowing away a loaf of bread and a pot of jam for us to eat on the way, and a jar of her apple chutney for Auntie Maggie into a rush basket. 'And don't you dare get dirty,' she yelled to us, as we kicked dust and pebbles in the garden while we waited impatiently for her. The night before we had all been scrubbed clean in the old tin bath, and changed our clothes, like we usually did on Saturday nights; we had no such thing as Sunday best clothes, but just clean ones each week.

After a while we piled into the trap, Uncle Ted Midwinter sitting up front one side and our Mother the other for balance, and we kids behind.

'Ready then?' Uncle Ted said. Then with the flick of his whip and a click of his tongue we were off through the deep Oxfordshire countryside.

'My goodness,' our Mother cried, turning round and eyeing us, 'you all looks that clean and tidy, I wonder how long it'll last.' She too looked fresh and pink in her print cotton frock; she had picked a small posy of bright blue cornflowers from our garden and had pinned them to the brim of her old straw hat, and I thought that she looked quite lovely.

The first hour of the journey passed quickly. It was still early for we had set out just after six o'clock, and the morning mist hung over the valleys like drifts of cotton wool. Then suddenly it gave way to brilliant sunshine.

'Goin' to be a sweater,' Uncle Ted remarked as we jogged along. The verge sides were banked with summer flowers and grasses and the air was filled with the sharp tangy smell of elderflowers.

'Ah,' our Mother said, when Uncle Ted remarked on their profusion. 'Do you know what my old Dad used to say about 'um? He said that summer was never fully established till the elderflower was in bloom, and that it ended when the berries was ripe.'

We waved excitedly to old Charley the roadman, he was just putting his trike in the shade before starting his day's work.

Just after we left the village of Westford we pulled up at the edge of a small wood. We were all frantic to go to the lavatory and squittered off to find a convenient bush.

'If a beans a bean, wass a pea?' one of my brothers called.

'A relief,' giggled the other one.

'You 'ent 'alf awful,' Betty said, 'our Mum 'ud clout you if she heard you say that!'

We ran back to find our Mother getting the food ready. A feast of doorsteps followed. 'Doorsteps' we called the thick hunks of bread that she hacked off the loaf, hugging it to her chest as she clumsily cut the bread. 'Never a sharp knife in our house,' she cried, excusing herself for the thickness of the slices.

Uncle Ted had wandered off to a nearby cottage to get water for us and the pony, then he returned to eat his own neatly cut sandwiches. 'We shall be thur be half-past 'leven I reckon,' he said, as we all climbed back into the trap.

Three of Auntie Maggie's children were waiting for us at the top of the lane. Our Mother got down and walked up to the cottage while the children climbed into the trap with us.

Auntie Maggie was massive, she was over seventeen stone, red-faced and jolly. Uncle Amos was just the reverse, tall and as thin as a whipstick, and very quiet. Still his wife made up for that, she was always chattering and laughing: ''erd laugh tu see a puddin' crawl' was one of her husband's expressions of his buxom wife. She was sitting in the warm kitchen waiting for us; she was so big that she completely filled the chair, in fact some of her fat body hung over the sides. She flung back her head and laughed as we entered, her numerous chins wobbling pink and wrinkled. Her legs, like huge cider bottles, were wide apart, revealing a great expanse of bare leg and pink stockinet bloomers.

'My blessed Kate' she said to our Mother, 'I should think that you was up before the crow piddled this morning wasn't you?' And they laughed, glad to see each other again.

Leaving the grown-ups to chatter, we children all went outside and played for a while, charging round the cottage like mad things; then we shut the boys in the pigsty and when they got out they chased us down to the field pond where we all played ducks and drakes with flat stones. Then young Ernie fell in and we dragged him out—covered in green slime and water weed he was. He went crying back to the cottage. Auntie Maggie stripped off his clothes. 'I shall have to wash 'um straight away,' she cried. 'He got no more tu wear, good job 'tis a fine day, they'll soon dry,' and she had them washed and out on the line in no time, while Ernie was packed off to bed where he had to stay till his clothes were fit to wear again.

We all sat round the big table for dinner, eight of them and six of us. We had oxtail stew, thick and lovely and swimming with onions, carrots, and haricot beans, which Auntie Maggie doled out from the biggest saucepan I'd ever seen. Afterwards she fetched two piping hot gooseberry tarts from the oven and from the back kitchen she brought a huge jug of runny custard made from milk that Uncle Amos had brought from the farm where he worked as a cowman.

As she collected the piles of dirty plates, Auntie Maggie chanted good-humouredly:

> Thank the Lord for what I've had
> If 'twas more I should be glad,
> But as the times they be so bad
> I thanks the Lord for what I've had.

'Go on, outside, all the lot of you,' she cried, 'while we gets on with the washing up,' and we staggered out to the field and lay fattening, like pigs, in the cool grass.

After a while, one of the boys said, 'Let's go and play on the trucks,' so we trailed off to the edge of a wood where, during the week, gangs of workmen cut down some of the great oak trees and loaded them onto the trucks on the small-gauge railway. The engine pulled them along from the wood to the roadway where they were re-loaded onto horse-drawn wagons. The track ran through four of the farmer's fields, so each time the train went along, the gates had to be opened and shut, so that the cattle did not get out. But on Saturday afternoons and Sundays the little engine was silent, so that it was quite safe for us to play on the track. Auntie Maggie had asked us to pick up some wood chips, which burned well in her big grate, and we all worked quickly to fill the hessian sack that we had brought with us. Then we clambered onto one of the trucks while the boys tried hard to push it up a small incline, but the truck was too heavy for them so we girls got down and helped them and we gradually moved it back up the hill, then we all climbed on and had a ride as the truck slipped back down. But I soon got tired of this and said that I wanted to ride both up and down, so they gave in and said that I could sit on the front. It was fun for a while and then a sudden burst of energy sent the truck over the ridge. It careered helter skelter down the other side and crashed into a closed farm gate. I was knocked clean off my perch, my face smashing into the spars, the truck continued madly on for a hundred yards or more. The boys ran and picked me up, blood was streaming from my nose, my sister Betty rushed up to my side, up went her frock as she swiftly ripped off the bottom of her white cotton petticoat to hold my nose, then she shouted to the others to grab handfuls of cool grass which she stuffed down the back of my neck to try and stop the bleeding.

Back in the cottage I sat on Auntie Maggie's lap while she washed away the blood, my nose was throbbing and swollen. ''Er'll have two black eyes be morning, I'll be bound,' she cried, and my brothers began singing:

> Two black eyes and a broken nose
> And a little bit off of her topknot.

That set me off crying again. 'Don't you take no notice of um, my lamb,' she said, 'you stop your crying and I'll let you swill out a jam-jar.'

The swillings of a jam-jar were indeed a great treat. Auntie Maggie had left a bit of jam in the bottom too. I filled the jar full of water swishing it round to get all the jam off. The others stood and watched me enviously as I sipped my lovely drink, but there was none for them; anyhow they had not hurt themselves. Then I nestled down against Auntie Maggie's ample bosom, her huge pink arms enveloped me and I wished that I could stay there for ever pillowed in her warm, comfortable embrace.

Then Uncle Amos came home from work smelling of cows and hay. He tweaked my ear as he passed, 'Hey, can you do this?' he said, trying to cheer me up, and keeping his outstretched arm stiff he swung the can full of milk that he had brought, round and round like a great wheel, without spilling a drop.

'Don't you be so daft,' his wife cried, ''er'll be tryin' to do that when her Mother sends her for the milk and you know where it'll end up, don't you?' She went on, 'when you've had a cup of tea take her to see Daisy's new calf, that'll cheer her up no end,' and I did not give him a minute's peace until he took me up to the farm.

The calf had been parted from its mother and was shut in a small pen, and it looked at us with its huge sorrowful eyes.

'Put your fingers in its mouth,' Uncle Amos said; the calf sucked away at my fingers, it had such a rough tongue too.

'What shall we call her?' Uncle Amos asked.

I thought for a few moments. 'What about Alice?' I said, thinking of the girl next door.

'That'll do fine,' Uncle Amos said. 'We'll call her Alice then.'

When we got back our Mother and Auntie Maggie had got the tea ready; there was a mountain of new bread, cut thick and spread with home-cured lard, and flycake, as Auntie Maggie called it. It was what we called 'seedy cake', but then our Mother explained that Auntie Maggie came from a different county from us, where they had different names for many things.

Soon it was time to go home. Our Mother collected up some flower plants, a new pattern for boys' trousers, and Auntie Maggie's own recipe for oxtail stew.

We clambered back into the trap. 'Try and come again next year,' Auntie Maggie called, ''tis bin lovely to see you again,' she said as we turned into the lane.

It was a much quieter journey than the outward one had been and we were all sleepily tired. My nose had a distinct bump on it, which I have to this day. Our Mother was not sure if it was broken or not, and I cuddled up to her for comfort. She sang softly to us most of the way home, but the only thing I can recall is:

> The day is done
> O God the son
> Look down upon
> Thy little one

And that was because I thought she was singing it specially for me.

Uncle Ted pulled up outside our cottage, we got down from the trap, stretching our stiff limbs and yawning loudly.

'Shan't want much rocking tonight,' our Mother called to a neighbour, and the cat rubbed itself round our legs, welcoming us home.

'Go on, hop off to bed all of you,' our Mother cried. 'I'll come and kiss you goodnight when I've made some cocoa.' But the day had been long and exciting and we tumbled quietly into bed. I remember starting to say my prayers, 'Gentle Jesus meek and mild . . .' that is all.

2

Cotswold Days

SOMETIME after our Father had died, our Mother married again. Our stepfather was a handsome, hard-working fellow, who had been a dispatch rider during the war and at sometime had emigrated to Canada, but then settled down with us at Ducklington.

Our Mother was very keen to show him off to her ageing parents and to her brother and his wife and family, who all lived in the village of Sherbourne in the Cotswolds, about sixteen miles away.

So, with our stepfather driving this time instead of Mr Midwinter, we set out in his pony and trap that he had kindly lent to us. There was our Mother, stepfather, Bern, Bunt, Betty, and me.

It was summer time and, as we bowled along the roads, we met other folk also travelling in traps, wagons and carts, all of course were horsedrawn.

Our stepfather, a jolly, laughing man, sang most of the time, wartime songs like 'Take me back to dear old Blighty' and 'Mademoiselle from Armentieres' with we children joining in, not singing the right words—'Inky Pinky Parlez Vous, Charlie Chaplin's got the 'flu, Inky Pinky Parlez Vous' we bellowed, thinking that we were ever so clever to be able to sing some French words. Along the Cheltenham Road, some way from Burford, we came to The New Inn pub. It was to this same pub years before that my grandfather used to walk every Friday night from the lodge where they lived a couple of miles away, to have a weekly pint of beer, always taken in half pints so that it would last all evening. He looked forward to this outing, the only one he had apart from a day off once a year to go to Stow on the Wold sheep fair. At the pub he met a few of the village men and picked up the local gossip and news.

One hot summer evening he arrived at the inn. There were two or three of his old cronies there and a couple of strangers. My Gramp went up to the bar and called for his first half pint. He put his hard-earned florin down, then turned round to say 'How be 'e?' to Fred Ashcomb.

'That'll be one penny then, Joe,' the innkeeper said.

'But I put me money on the counter,' my Grandfather replied bewildered. But there was no sign of the precious florin. Nobody would own up as to who had taken it. My Gramp turned on his heel, walked out of the inn and never went in one again.

Anyhow, our stepfather tied the pony up under a tree and went inside the pub for a drink. We sat out in the trap and drank ginger beer that our Mother had made from a ginger-beer plant that she kept in a jam-jar on the window sill at home. The liquid had to be fed every day with a teaspoon of sugar and one of ground ginger. If you forgot for one day the plant died, and then it meant that you had to start all over again. And our Mother was always letting hers die. Then she would shout, 'Go on, take a jam-jar and call at Mrs Tremlins and ask her if she has got a ginger-beer plant that she could let me have.' And Betty and I would go squittering off down the village to Tremlins' house and make our request to the old lady.

'What?' she would cry. 'I never see such a person as your mother for letting her ginger beer plants die, I gave her one only last week. And tell her to look after it proper this time,' she called to us as we slunk back up her garden path.

But sometimes she did remember to feed the demanding plant and then she made the most lovely drink from it. It was sweet and strong and fizzy, and once one of the full bottles exploded in our kitchen, shooting glass and ginger beer all over the place.

Our stepfather came out of the inn, smacking his lips and wiping his mouth; he had enjoyed his pint—all that he could really afford with his ready-made family to keep.

We set off again arriving at our grandparents home about mid-day. They lived at one of the lodge cottages at the entrance to Sherbourne House and park. The cottages were situated on the main road, but the great house was down an avenue of trees.

Our Gran had prepared a meal for us, lovely rabbit pie it was, but I cannot remember what vegetables we had. For pudding there was a huge dish of lovely red plums and a jug of custard.

We piled into the trap again and made the short journey down into the village to the house of our Mother's brother Uncle Will, his wife Auntie Sarah, and their three children, cousins Will, Arnold and Mabel. The boys were busy cleaning out the cowshed and Mabel, the youngest, was helping her mother in the small dairy.

We all settled in the living-room, chattering nineteen to the dozen, then I realized that our Mother was talking about me.

'The trouble is,' she went on, 'I suppose we all spoilt her a bit, her being the youngest and the fact that she never even saw her father.' (He died two months before I was born.)

'Ah, I expect she's had her nose put out of joint a bit lately,' my Auntie said, looking at our stepfather. 'You let her stay here a bit Kitty, a change might do the little maid a bit of good.'

Instead of feeling happy at the thought of staying at their little farm for a few weeks, I felt jealous and angry, that was my trouble, I was jealous of our laughing, jolly stepfather, and my parents thought that a short break away from the family might cure me.

I watched them go trotting off down the dusty road, they all waved goodbye and our Mother called 'Now you just be a good girl and we will come back for you very soon.'

Once they were out of sight I stormed and raged and then shut myself in the lavatory down the bottom of the garden and refused to come out. I whiled away the time by looking at a seed book that was hung up behind the door, then I killed several blue bottles that came buzzing in on that hot, sultry afternoon. After a while my cousin Mabel, who was about four years older than I, came to see if she could entice me out.

'Come on,' she cried, 'come out and I'll take you for a walk, I know a secret way to reach the old windmill. We won't let on to nobody where we are going,' she said.

I had never even heard of a windmill, let alone seen one. The offer sounded so tempting and I eagerly left my sanctuary.

She took my hand and we walked over hundreds and hundreds of fields, at least it seemed like hundreds to me. But the windmill, standing up there on the skyline seemed further away than ever.

'How much further?' I cried.

'We shall soon be there,' my cousin said.

But I was hot and tired and I sat down in the middle of a field and bawled my head off. I took off my boots, threw my bunch of wild flowers away and refused to walk another step.

We were lost and nobody would ever find us. My cousin sat down beside me, she was crying quietly, wiping her hot, streaming face on her white lace-edged petticoat.

Suddenly we heard voices shouting our names urgently, there were men running across the fields towards us. It was my uncle and cousins who had been searching for us for hours.

'Thank God you're safe,' I heard Uncle Will cry as he gathered me up in his hot, sweaty, sunburnt arms.

We had walked over six miles across those fields, crossing Sherbourne brook over a narrow footbridge, we had been gone five hours and we still had not reached the windmill.

Later that night as I lay in the coolest, nicest, lavender smelling sheets that I had ever slept in, my cousin whispered, 'Never mind, you and I will go to the windmill one day, when you are bigger,' but we never did make it. I walked with my cousins backwards and forward, to and from the village school and hated it and was a naughty, disobedient girl.

One day, after school I was running back up the tree-lined road, crying as usual, when I saw someone coming towards me on a pushbike. In a moment I was in my Mother's arms, being smothered with kisses and hugged very tightly. She had borrowed a pushbike and then she had cycled from Ducklington to fetch me home.

I remember the long, uncomfortable ride home on the hard metal carrier on the back of the bicycle, but at least I was going home.

There was a wonderful surprise waiting for me when I got there. In my absence my Mother had produced a new baby, my stepsister Kathleen (Mick), a fat, curly-headed bundle that looked more like a doll. Suddenly my jealousy disappeared. I was a big girl now, I had been miles and miles away from home for almost a year and I felt quite grown-up.

But from then on, until I left school, I continued to go to stay at my Auntie Sarah and Uncle Will's home for my summer holidays. No other members of the family ever stayed for weeks as I did.

And gradually, over the years, the form of transport that took me to that lovely Cotswold village changed. First of all, I travelled several times in the carrier's cart, then in Mr Midwinter's pony and trap. But the last few years I travelled in a grocery van. It happened that a Mr and Mrs Caswell and their family came to live next door to us at Ducklington in the little thatched cottage at the end of the row. Mr Caswell was employed by a wholesale grocer in the town, where it was his job to drive his van round to many of the small villages within forty miles radius of the town delivering groceries to the shops. And every fortnight his journey took him to Taylor's shop in Sherbourne. So without his firm knowing anything about it, Mr Caswell used to take me there, drop me at Taylor's shop down the bottom end of the village, then I used to walk to my Auntie's cottage up at the top end of Sherbourne. Sometimes I stopped for a fortnight, sometimes for a month. On the return journey Mr Caswell would pick me up at my Auntie's because he could never be quite sure just what time he would get to the shop. Years and years later, during the Second World War,

I worked for the same wholesalers and drove a three-ton van all around those same country villages, delivering two hundredweight sacks of sugar, one-and-a-half hundredweight sacks of flour, great double cheeses in crates, and great heavy boxes and cartons filled with goods that wholesale grocers sell.

I even called regularly at Taylor's shop and Post Office at Sherbourne, where we would sometimes reminisce about the days when I went there with Mr Caswell. A snotty-nosed, tousle-headed, wild thing, someone said I was, but with very winning ways.

Apart from once when Bern took me on the back of his motor-bike, the last few journeys that I made to Sherbourne were made in a very different way than in those early days. In the late 1920s, I think it was, the Black and White coaches began to run from Oxford to Cheltenham. The coach used to drop me on the top road and I would walk down the long, narrow lane which lead to the village, skirting the great Cotswold stone wall which surrounded Sherbourne House and park, which at that time was still the home of Lord Sherbourne. Now the great house is a boys' school, my Auntie and Uncle are long since dead and my cousins scattered. But the tree-lined road through the village is still reasonably quiet and the clear waters of Sherbourne brook flow on swiftly and silently to join my beloved river Windrush.

3

Wireless Sets and Home-Made Wine

DURING the early '20s, only a few families in the village owned a crystal set: we were one of these because our stepfather was clever with his hands and had made one. He had bought copper wire, ebonite, and a magic thing, a crystal in a glass tube, which, I believe was called a 'cat's whisker', because of its fineness. This cat's whisker had to be twiddled very carefully so that it contacted some other part of the wonderful contraption which then transmitted words and music all the way from London. Mind you, you also needed to have a tall wireless pole, which had to be erected at the bottom of the garden, and the higher and further away from the house the pole was, the better the reception. A wire was then attached to the top of the pole, and brought into the house where it was connected to the wireless set. You had to have an earth wire as well, and this, after being attached to the set, was then taken out of the house via the window, in our case, and then the earth wire was plunged into the soil in the garden.

To be able to listen to this wonderful invention you also needed a pair of headphones or earphones, so really only one person at a time, could listen. Sometimes our stepfather would call us, 'Come quick, and hear this, it's wonderful.' He would swivel the headphones round so that we each had one earpiece pressed against our young pink ears, we would sit there absolutely transfixed listening to this magic contraption, which brought, in some mysterious way, music and words from a distance of sixty miles or more.

One particularly windy day our stepfather met old Fred Bones pushing his bike. 'What's up then Fred?' our stepfather called to him.

'That old wind's too strong fer I to ride me bike,' he said, 'but I'll bet you can hear London well today on that wireless thing of yourn, with this yer east wind a-blowin', thur yent nothin' to stop it.'

Fred had been into our house and listened to our wireless set and had talked of nothing else since, but he was a bit too old in the head to ever understand how it worked.

Almost every week another family in the village would acquire a wireless set. 'Ah missus,' Bertha Botherum said to our Mother one day. 'Guess who got one now? Them Arnolds, I see 'um puttin' the pole up, and Mrs Simmonds next door was looking that envious, I'll bet they be the next to have one.'

Bertha was the village gossip, there was nothing that escaped her eagle eye or ears. If you wanted to know what was going on, all you had to do was to ask Bertha. She was always sweeping the path in the front of her cottage, waiting for someone to come along to chatter to. She told her mother that is what she did it for.

'Ah, Mrs B,' she said one day, 'you don't know what loneliness is, when I gets fed up with me own company I just gets me broom and goes out to me front and starts sweeping, and before long somebody comes along for I to have a word with.' Poor Bertha, she was her own worst enemy: some village folk would go the long way home just so that they would miss passing her cottage.

But apart from the pleasure that our wireless set brought us we still relied very much on the annual village activities for much of our enjoyment, and the highlight of the year was the parish tea always held on the Tuesday nearest Twelfth Night, a night when we tirelessly galloped round the parish room, joining in with the Lancers and Roger-de-Coverly. But to me the highlight of the evening was when Mr Franlin the M.C. announced, 'And the next dance will be a Paul Jones,' when I, as a fat fourteen year old, had the chance to dance with grown-up men, real good dancers some of them were too. Somehow I nearly always got fat Mr Spink; mind you, he waltzed beautifully and I seemed to ride round the room on his fat stomach, my feet just skimming the ground. We took up a lot of room, Mr Spinks and I, for as he twirled me round and round, his left arm, which lightly held my right was held outstretched, his eyes closed dreamily as we glided round and round to the strains of the Blue Danube. 'Make a good dancer one day I shouldn't wonder,' he puffed at me as the dance ended.

It was after one such parish tea that fate brought widower George Stokes and spinster Mary Ellen Brown together. Both of them lived in one of the nearby villages, but they did no more than pass the time of day with each other. George was a blacksmith by trade, though now retired; his wife had been dead for about ten years. Mary Ellen had never married. Most of her life had been taken up by looking after her ailing mother and father. But after they died she surprised everyone by opening up a little shop in the front room of her house, where she sold the most delicious assortment of home-made sweets which she made in her kitchen. The small window in the front of the house was filled with dishes and bottles of Mary Ellen's sweets, and the wonderful smell that floated across the green when she was 'boiling up', tickled the nostrils of everyone who happened by.

She also made a goodly supply of rhubarb wine every year and some folks reckoned that she had got some stored away that was ten years old. Rhubarb was all that grew in her overgrown garden, which, folk said, looked like a forest of elephants' ears. The wine, Mary Ellen said, was 'for medical purposes only'. Occasionally she would give a bottle of it away, and those who had the privilege of sampling it said that it was some very potent stuff.

On this particularly cold frosty January night, George Stokes had stopped to chatter with some of his cronies after the parish tea festivities before cycling home, and when he did reach the village he noticed the light was still on in Mary Ellen's home. Coo, he thought, what wouldn't I give for a drop of Mary Ellen's celebrated rhubarb wine to warm me up! While these thoughts were running through his head, the light in the cottage went out and the village street seemed darker and colder than ever.

Whether it was the excitement of the evening, or the fact that Sam Finch had sent George on his way with a glass of his special parsnip wine, but we shall probably never know what made George act the way he did. He had heard that the famous rhubarb wine was kept locked up in the shed, next to the cottage. So he propped his bicycle up against Mary Ellen's gate and crept quietly into the yard. After a good deal of pulling and pushing, shoving and grunting, he managed to remove a couple of the wooden panels from the side of the shed. He squeezed himself through the opening and his eyes popped out like chapel hat pegs. There, neatly laid on their sides, were dozens and dozens of bottles, filled with the pale pink nectar. He struck a match, all the bottles were labelled and dated. He went along the neat rows striking match after match, reading as he went—1921, 1920, 1919. 'Ah,' he exclaimed. 'This is the one, made May 1918, bottled July 1918, I'll try this one for a start,' George muttered to himself. He pulled the cork, took a sniff, and then a long, long drink. This, thought George Stokes, is the wine of the gods, wine of a long-forgotten summer, heady and sweet.

By mid-morning the next day it was all round the village that George Stokes had spent the night with Mary Ellen Brown. At five o'clock that morning postman Tempest had seen George's bicycle propped up outside Mary Ellen's cottage and it was still there at midday when the baker went by.

'I don't believe it,' the postman's wife said when her husband told her the news. 'Mary Ellen wouldn't do such a thing.'

'Well, why don't you go down to her shop and buy yerself two penneth of clove sweets,' her husband retorted. 'You will see for yerself then.'

'You'd a thought he'd a had the decency to have took his bicycle round the back, out of the way, wouldn't you?' Bertha

Botherum said. 'Downright disgraceful I calls it,' she went on, 'and at 'er age too, 'er's sixty if 'er's a day.'

Poor Mary Ellen knew nothing about these tales that were flashing round the village like wildfire. Mind you, she had had two or three customers in for sweets that morning who had seemed highly amused about something. There was Mrs Crook, usually so friendly and chattery, but on this morning she had a job to even pass the time of day with Mary Ellen. Mrs Crook always came in on a Wednesday morning to buy her weekly half pound of humbugs which she took to her old mother who lived at Aston, and she fair flounced out of the shop with a very curt 'good-morning'. Then there was Jimmy Drake, he had actually winked at Mary Ellen as he went out.

About three o'clock that afternoon she went to the shed to get a few dry logs for the fire, and she noticed that some of the wooden panels had been forced from the side of it. 'Now I wonder who did that,' she thought. 'Best to unlock the door first to see if anything has been stolen, then I must see if I can fix the wood back where it belongs.'

Mary Ellen unlocked the door and pushed it open, then she let out a terrific scream, there, sprawled on the floor, surrounded by empty wine bottles, his mouth wide open, was George Stokes, and he looked as if he was dead.

Postman Tempest who was just going past on his afternoon rounds, heard the screaming, he threw his bicycle on to the grass verge and went running up the path to see what on earth was happening. He found Mary Ellen bending over the prostrate form of George Stokes, she was almost hysterical, crying over and over again, 'He's dead, he's dead.'

The postman bent down and touched the body, and sniffed, 'He's dead all right Miss, dead drunk that's all. Come on,' he said. 'We had best get him into the house.' Mary Ellen opened her mouth to protest but no words came out.

'Ah, thas wur 'e spent the night then,' the postman said as they half carried, half dragged George into the cottage.

'We had best take him into the front parlour,' Mary Ellen cried. 'It's more comfortable in there.' They managed to get him onto the horse-hair sofa where he stayed, in a kind of stupor for the best part of two days.

When she heard what the village had been saying about her and Mr Stokes, as she insisted on calling him, Mary Ellen blushed, in fact she went on blushing every time a villager dropped in to see how the patient was getting on. And although George was very ashamed of what he had done, he quite enjoyed the care and attention that Mary Ellen gave him during the next few days. Then it was back to his blacksmith's cottage, where, he admitted, he felt quite lonely.

On the following Sunday afternoon he knocked at Mary Ellen's door. 'I've come to thank you again,' he blurted out. 'And to say how very sorry I am to have caused you so much trouble.'

'You had better step inside out of the cold wind,' she said. 'I'm just going to make a cup of tea, you are welcome to join me, and I should push your bicycle round the back this time,' she added, blushing shyly. 'We don't want to start the villagers on again.'

'I've brought you a bit of greenstuff from me garden,' George said. 'I've got that much I can't keep upsides with it.' He handed her the bag of brussel sprouts and cabbages, and said, 'I noticed that you hadn't got any in your garden.'

When they spoke about it afterwards, neither of them could recall which of them it was who had suggested that George should give up his blacksmith's cottage and come and settle with Mary Ellen.

Within a few weeks George had sold his cottage and blacksmith's shop to Ern Brooks, a young man to whom he had taught the trade. It would do young Ern a treat, he and his wife were very keen to start up on their own.

Mary Ellen and George were married a few weeks later on St Valentine's Day, and they enjoyed several years of happy married bliss. Mary Ellen still made and sold her home-made sweets in the front room, while George spent most of his time cultivating the garden. But he left no room for rhubarb, for although the wine drinking episode had brought them together, he vowed he would never touch another drop of the stuff as long as he lived, and strangely enough Mary Ellen did not seem to need any for medicinal purposes either.

'But what happened to all the wine that Mary Ellen had already made?' we asked our Mother who knew much more about the affair than we children.

'Well, come the following summer there was a special fête in the village to raise money for the church funds, so Mary Ellen and George offered the bottles of wine to be used in a raffle. My blessed, didn't they raffle tickets sell well, when folks knew that they stood a chance of winning a bottle of that wine. You see,' our Mother went on, 'that wine was a sort of symbol of revitalizing, giving the men back their youth and all that, at least thas what some people thought, and 'twas that wine as was blamed for a lot of things that followed in the villages around during the next year. Forty-year-old Mrs Snaith had twins, fifteen years after her last was born, Harry Patson went off with a housemaid from Lord B's estate, leaving his wife and seven children to fend for thurselves, and thur was ten weddings in as many months. And they reckons that all these parties had won bottles of Mary Ellen's wine.

'Of course,' our Mother went on, 'it was just a coincidence really, at least that's what I told Mary Ellen, cos her got quite perturbed about it. Folks be quick to make excuses for thur wrongdoings, that's what I always says. Mind you, I had a very small glass of it one day, down at Mrs Adnuts, and I have never tasted anything quite like it, it sort of lifted you up as it were. I got on my bicycle and I kind of floated home in a dream, but I soon came down to earth with a bump, for young Bunt had been digging up some potatoes and he had put the garden fork straight through his boot and into his big toe, so it was out with the carbolic soap and a good bowl of hot water. His toe came up like a balloon and he couldn't get his boot back on for a week, but it cleared up all right in the end. Mind you that boot of his let the wet in after that, and he hadn't had 'um long either. And do you know,' she went on, 'for years folks plagued the life out of Mary Ellen for the recipe for her rhubarb wine but she would never divulge how she made it, just as well, I suppose, if it was as potent as folks said it was.'

4

Hatching and Dispatching

ONE person who I was particularly fond of was Auntie Liza.

I can never remember anyone else living at 60 The Causeway except her; I suppose at some time or other there had been a Mr Green, but I do not remember him; no doubt the faded photograph on the chiffonier of the man with the droopy moustache was the man in Auntie Liza's life, though I never did hear her mention him.

Auntie Liza was not related to us, but just a very good friend of our Mother. She was the local midwife and had brought us all into the world; the youngest of our family, Denis, was the one to be most thankful to her. On a freezing cold night, with the roads covered with ice-packed snow, she half walked, half crawled, down to our cottage, to find that our Mother had already given birth to Denis, she was too ill to try and break the umbilical cord which had almost strangled him. He was blue and purple when Auntie Liza, with her coat still on, rushed over and did whatever was necessary, but it was touch and go with young Denis for a while.

She was certainly a very handy person to have in the district, and the doctors had great respect for her. She used to say that she was in the 'hatching and dispatching' department of life, for as well as attending almost every birth in the area, she also laid folks out after they had died. But that was not all she did. People would come running to her when both children and grown-ups were ill. The latter services were all given freely, as most of her 'customers' were very poor, and even some of the mothers she attended had not any money to pay her for her services. 'But,' she used to say to our Mother, 'it don't matter about a few shillings, as long as I've helped somebody, cos that's what we be here for right enough.'

To me she always seemed rather old-fashioned, long-skirted, small-waisted and with a fat round chest; she reminded me of a rather large cottage loaf. Her grey hair was scraped back into a tight, tidy bun, and she had big soft brown eyes, and, to use our Mother's expression, 'A heart as big as a bucket'.

Auntie Liza's living-room was very small and she had quite a big table in the centre; this along with the rest of the furniture made it difficult for her to get round the room, so that she had to squeeze herself between things, shuffling sideways as she went.

'That boy wants holding over a tar barrel,' she cried one day when she heard Ben, the youngest but one, coughing a croupy sort of cough.

'But they haven't started tarmac-ing the roads anywhere round here yet,' our Mother replied. 'As soon as I knows that they've started I shall be off, don't you worry. None of our others ever had the croup as bad as he, he's on night and day, we don't get hardly a minute's peace with him.' It was widely believed that if a child could inhale the fumes that came from a boiling hot tar barrel it would help to break the phlegm and, of course, ease the cough or croup. And it was quite a common sight to see a red-faced coughing child, held by its equally red-faced mother, over a tar barrel when the workmen were re-surfacing the road.

I remember being suspended over one of those fearsome-looking things when I was about seven, kicking and screaming with fright in case I fell into that black boiling mass, but I proved too much for our Mother, strong as she was, and was handed over to a huge, red-faced roadman. 'Come on, young Mollie,' he said as he lifted me up: his arms were as strong and brown as tree-trunks. 'Come and spit it up, it might be a tanner,'* he went on goodhumouredly, as I coughed and spluttered. But I went on

* Slang word for sixpence.

crying, longer and louder, when I found that, try as I may, I could not produce a sixpence. 'Yer be,' he said, grinning, handing me tuppence. ''Tis all I got till pay day.'

One day Auntie Liza said to our Mother, 'I reckon 'tis going to rain, my corn's playing me up summut dreadful, do you think you could remember to ask shepherd Spindlow fer a bit of sheep's wool, that do soothe my old corns, and soften um too, and then they'll drop awf after a while, 'tis the oil in the wool what does it you know.' She knew lots of old-fashioned cures for many ordinary ailments.

'I got hold of this nice coat the other day, Kitty,' she prattled on as they sipped their tea. 'I thought that it might fit you a treat, you deserves one Lord knows.' She brought out the soft, brown coat. Our Mother looked at it lovingly, 'Ah, much as I'd love it, I'd better have it altered for Bet, she's growing that fast the one she's wearing fits her so tight you'd think she'd been poured into it. Mollie can have hers and I'll get Sally Castle to alter this one for Bet, that 'ull do her nicely for a couple of years then.'

The better-off people that Auntie Liza attended often gave her their cast-offs, and although she did not need much for herself she never refused, knowing that we would be glad of almost anything.

'And this,' she went on, 'might make them two youngest a pair of trousers each.' She held up a long navy blue serge skirt.

'Aah, that it will,' Mother cried joyfully. 'I got a very easy pattern that Auntie Maggie let me have, I'll cut them out tonight when they've all gone to bed, that won't take me long to run um up.'

'Don't ferget to line um,' Auntie Liza said. 'Else you'll have um with sore bums first time they wears um.'

Round the fire-guard was an assortment of beautifully laundered baby clothes. Hard-up mothers knew that if they could not afford all the needs of their new-born babies, Liza Green would see that the newcomer was properly clothed, at least during the period that she was attending the mother and child. This was done out of the kindness of her own heart. Over the years she had collected day-gowns, night-gowns, back-flannels, and minute vests. As soon as the clothes were finished with, Auntie Liza had them back, laundered them and stowed them away in the rush basket ready for the next time.

Our Mother looked at the tiny garments, 'Still finding plenty of customers then, Liza?' she asked.

'Ah, poor devils, some of um are too,' she replied, 'not a penny in the house to buy a bit of bread and three or four hungry mites already to feed, there's more poverty in this town than anybody realizes,' she went on. 'I does what I can for um, but half the mothers ent had a decent meal for weeks, so how can you expect the babies to be strong and healthy. I was along at Mrs Smith's yesterday,' she went on, 'just had her ninth she have.'

'You means Mrs Quaker Oats Smith?' our Mother asked.

'Ah, that's the one,' Auntie Liza said smilingly.

We all knew the story about the Quaker Oats, but at that tender age I wondered what they found to laugh at. Apparently during the war this Mrs Smith went to the Doctor; she explained to him that she was feeling bad and getting quite fat. The Doctor examined her and said, 'You know what's wrong with you, don't you? You're going to have a baby, quite soon by the look of things.'

'But I can't,' she cried. 'My husband's bin in France for a twelve-month or more and I've never been out with another man. Could you be mistaken, doctor?' she asked, 'perhaps it's summat as I've ett as makes I feel so bad.'

'What have you been eating?' the doctor asked, humouring her.

'Well, I have been eating a lot of Quaker Oats,' the weeping woman told him.

'Well then,' the doctor replied, 'it must have been the little man on the packet, cos you're having a baby all right.'

Just then there was a hammering on the door and a neighbour poked her head inside, 'Oh, Auntie Liza Green, could you come quick, our Freddy's caught his fingers in my mangle, and I don't know what to do, he's crying summut terrible.'

'Shan't be long, Kitty,' she called to our Mother as she went out the door. 'Just pour yourself another cup of tea,' and she went rushing down the path with the tearful woman.

In about ten minutes Auntie Liza was back. 'The boy's fingers ent badly hurt,' she said, 'there's nothing broken, no skin cracked or anything, I think the poor little chap was more frightened than anything. I got his mother to hold his hand down in a bowl of cold water, that u'll ease it and fetch the swelling down. I told his mother to make a nice cup of tea, it would do her and the boy good, but she hadn't a bit of tea in the house. Here,' she said to me, 'just pop along to the cottage, fifth one from here, with this screw of tea,' and she came to the door to make sure that I took it to the right place.

'I promised you some drunken husbands* next time you called,' Auntie Liza said, 'I'll just pop out and get some while I thinks of it.' She returned in a few minutes with some green plants. 'Here you are, Kitty, just push 'um in the wall anywhere and they'll grow a treat, and flower next year if you leaves 'um be, course you knows the old saying, don't you, that these plants u'll only survive in a home where the woman wears the trousers,' she said laughingly.

'Oh, I must just tell you about old Jim Paine,' Auntie Liza prattled on. 'At last I've persuaded him to get some false teeth, 'e bin suffering summut dreadful with indigestion fer years, I told him 'twas because he couldn't chew his food properly. Well, he's fitted up with some now, but they be taking a bit of getting used to by all accounts. He was in the garden planting his "sharlots" as he calls shallots, when I went by on me bike, so I jumps awf and goes back and asked him how he was getting on with his "artificials" and he said the funniest thing, he said, "Well they be no good fer ettin' but champion fer 'oldin' me pipe."'

It was nice to listen to Auntie Liza and our Mother chattering and laughing over a cup of tea; we visited her quite often, for

* Drunken husbands—house leeks.

she only lived in the town a couple of miles away. Whenever we called she always found us children a biscuit apiece, always the same sort, digestive, which she kept in a pretty china biscuit barrel that stood on the chiffonier next to the photo of the man with the droopy moustache. The biscuit barrel was white with delicate pink and blue flowers on and pale green leaves.

'Ah, old Mrs Wafler gave me that,' Auntie Liza told our Mother when she remarked on its beauty. 'That's a band of silver round the edge,' she went on. 'You shall have that, Kitty, when anything happens to me, cos I knows you'd appreciate it.' But when the time came our Mother did not mention it to the tighted-lipped niece who quickly cleared out the crowded cottage after Auntie Liza had been laid to rest in the nearby cemetery.

'After all, they'd have thought I was cadging,' our Mother said. 'But never mind,' she went on, 'I got some lovely memories of her, I shall miss her and so will a lot of folk. Ah, if anybody have earned their harp and crown, she have,' she said tearfully.

Quite often before we went into the town, our Mother would pick a bunch of flowers from our garden and take them and lay them on the otherwise deserted grave. We all missed Auntie Liza very much, and it did not seem right to pass the cottage, where the window had always been packed tight with ferns and the little room stuffed with furniture, and not go in.

Each Christmas time, when we were all living at home, our Mother used to receive a Christmas card simply signed 'Flora'. She would open the card, and read the signature, smile sadly and say, 'poor dear', then promptly throw the card on the fire. She never said who the mysterious Flora was, and we knew, the way she looked when she read it, that we were not supposed to probe either. And so the years went by, Christmases came and went and the cards kept coming. Then one Christmas she did not get one. I asked her why. 'I knew I shouldn't receive one this year, neither shall I ever get one again,' she replied sadly. 'But then, maybe it's all for the best.'

Whatever 'the best' was I did not learn until many years afterwards. I do not think any other member of our family ever knew, maybe because none of them were ever as inquisitive as me.

One year I was helping our Mother to get her Christmas cards away, for in her later years with her memory failing, she was never quite sure who she had sent to. I happened to mention the card that she used to have each Christmas time signed Flora, and the fact that she had never told us about it.

She thought for a moment and then said, 'Well, I can tell you about it now, because there is nobody alive today that was involved.' She went on, 'I hated having secrets from the family, but a promise is a promise and I've kept that for nearly fifty years.'

'It all happened before you was born, before we came to live in Ducklington,' she said. 'We had rather a nice house in Witney. I'd only got young Bern and Bunt at the time. There was only thirteen months between them, so they were babies together as you might say. I used to push them for miles; every day I used to take them out for a long walk. Well, on this particular day that I'm telling you about, I had planned to walk four miles to visit a tiny church away in the fields. By the time I reached the village both the boys were fast asleep, so I pushed the pram in to the shade, making sure that Bern was safely strapped in. Bunt of course was still at the lying down stage, so he was safe enough. Then I tiptoed into the church. Oh, it was so small and beautiful. Then I heard the sound of giggling and scuffing coming from the vestry and I thought, "If that was my children messing about in church they would get a good hiding." So I went up to the door, which was ajar, about to tell the children off for larking about in God's house. But it wasn't children larking about, it was the churchwarden, a married man with two children, and the vicar's daughter, in the act of love making.

'I turned on my heel and walked quickly out of the church and stood for a moment in the warm sunshine absolutely numbed with shock. Then I caught hold of the pram and was just about to rush out of the churchyard gate, when a young and very beautiful girl came out.

'"Oh please, please don't go. Please stop and talk to me for a moment," she called to me.

'"If you want to do that sort of thing" I said to her, "I would have thought you would have had the decency to have chosen somewhere different, that's all. Anyway where's *he* gone?" I asked her. I knew the man by sight and had heard of his amorous goings on. "Gone sculking off home I suppose, leaving you to face the music," I cried.

'Then the girl broke out sobbing. "Please sit down, I must talk to someone." So we made our way to the old wooden seat set against the church.

'I put my arm round the young girl's shoulders which shook with sobs as she told me her story. She had just finished three years at college and after the summer vacation she was going to Scotland where she had taken the post to tutor three sons of a wealthy family who lived in the Highlands. Her mother had died two years ago, she was an only child, and it would break her father's heart if he found out about her and Mr Brookson. The affair, she said, had gone on all the summer. She met him every day, always in the church where the love making took place.

'"But," I said to her, "you must have been out of your mind to have started such a thing, and why don't you put a stop to it now?"

'Then the girl went on to say that Mr Brookson had threatened to tell her father that it was her who was pestering him if she didn't turn up every day.

'So I said to her, "What happens if he puts you in the family way?"

'"Well," she said, "I think he already has, it's only a matter of two weeks, but I've never been late before. What am I going to do? I dare not tell my father or Mr Brookson."

'Well, I talked to the girl for ages, imploring her to tell her father, but she said that she would rather kill herself than bring shame to him in the village where he was so respected. In the end she decided, and I agreed with her, that she should go to Scotland and take the job, at least until Christmas. Then leave saying that she had another post to go to. She could find some quiet place to stay until the baby was born, and then arrange to have it adopted and no one, at least in this part of the country, would ever know any different.

'Then the girl said, "But what about the Christmas holiday, my father would expect me home for that."

'Well, I told her, she could probably just about make it without suspicion if she bundled herself up in woollies and furs, but she would have to tell him she was changing jobs. You see, he might have begun to get worried if the postmark on her letters to him was different.

'Fortunately the girl had plenty of money. Her mother had left her some, so too had an aunt, on her mother's side.

'Well, the hot day wore on, the boys woke up hungry. I was breast feeding Bunt and this simply horrified the girl. "Don't worry," I told her "there will be no need for you to do this, there's plenty of patent baby food on the market for those who have the money to pay for it."

'We talked for hours in that quiet churchyard about the girl's future. Of course she wanted to write to me regular like. But I said to her, "Oh no, you mustn't do that." No, that would have never done. You see, I would have had to explain her letters to your father and the rest of the family. So I suggested that she should just send me a card every Christmas and I should know that she was all right.

'Mind you, she was a bit worried about Mr Brookson, you know, that he might talk.

'"My dear child," I said to her "you must forget you ever met the man, if that's possible. Don't you think that you are the first young girl that he's led astray because you are not. He's got a terrible reputation, and him pretending to be a good churchman too." Evidently the stories of his conquests had not reached her

154

father's ears but everybody else knew. It was his wife and children that I felt so sorry for, and the girl of course.

'The warm sunny afternoon wore on, the clock on the church tower struck three and I said that I would have to make tracks for home. I'd got a meal to cook and have on the table ready for when your father got home. I left the tearful, beautiful, young girl in the churchyard, after making her promise that she would do nothing foolish, and that every year she would send a card at Christmas time to assure me that all was well.'

'But what did happen to her?' I asked.

'Well, she had a child, a little girl, but it only lived for two days, which was just as well I suppose. She might not have wanted to have parted with it and then the truth would have had to come out.

'But Flora never married,' she went on. 'She continued her governessing, and taught the children of several wealthy families. She came home about twice a year to see her father. I met her in Witney once when I was doing a bit of shopping, we chatted for a while but she seemed so sad and lonely. I wondered if I had advised her rightly. Perhaps it would have been best if she had made a clean breast of it, but then there was her father to think of and Mr Brookson's wife and children. The poor girl died some years ago, in a London hospital I think. I suppose she must have been about fifty. Anyway they brought her back to the village. I cycled over to the funeral and the first person I met was that old devil Mr Brookson, and he looked proper foolish when he saw me. He sidled up to me and spoke all smarmsy like. "Hello, Mrs Butler," he said, "a sad day for us all isn't it?" I never answered him, but I just gave him one of my withering looks and he did not know where to put his face. He soon cleared off after that and I never saw him again.

'But mind you,' our Mother went on. 'I heard about his unfortunate family from time to time. He had three children, two girls and a boy, and they all turned out bad, they probably inherited their father's lustful ways. One of his girls had two love children and nobody ever knew who was the father of them. The second girl had a love child too, then she went off and lived with a married man who had put her in the family way. The lad was no better. Twice he was taken to court by young girls who he had got into trouble, then he ended up living with an amorous married woman, years older than himself, and died at forty-eight, a worn-out, lustful man. Ah you know what the good Book says,' our Mother continued. 'The sins of the fathers upon the children, and I reckon that's what that was all right.'

5

China Dogs and China Cups

OUR Auntie Rosie and Uncle Charlie lived in a village about four miles from Ducklington. They always reminded me of a couple of porker pigs because they were both pink and fat with a clean, scrubbed look.

Their snug, warm low-thatched home called 'Walnut Tree Cottage' was like a fairyland to us children. It was filled with china dogs, brasses and copper and brightly coloured antimacassars, and tinkling vases with glass icicles dangling all round them. And the fire grate always shone black and gleaming. Our Mother used to say, 'You could see to comb your hair in Auntie Rosie's grate.' She had a set of shiny brass fire-irons too (we only had steel ones) and when that big old fire was lit, the flames seemed to wink and blink in every piece of brass and copper, glass and china.

Both Auntie Rosie and Uncle Charlie had worked very hard all their lives, but now, in their late sixties they just jogged along happily from one day to the next, and seemed to grow more pink and rounded as the years rolled by.

They were only very slightly related to us on our father's side, and they had always been most kind to us all.

Every year about October time Uncle Charlie would arrive at our house on his creaky, old, upright bicycle. 'We be killing a pig on Saturday, Kitty,' he would say to our Mother. 'You will be a-coming over as usual, won't you?'

We knew that we should come back from their house simply loaded with the pig's chitterlings, its head and trotters and some spare-rib. We always invited them to our pig killing, but they would never take much of ours. 'No, Kitty,' Auntie Rosie would say, when our Mother tried to press her into taking some of the fresh meat, 'You got more mouths to feed than we have, I'll just take a little bit of the pig's fry for our tea tonight, that will do we just fine.'

We in Ducklington had Mr Humphries who came and killed our pigs, but Auntie Rosie and Uncle Charlie used to have an old fellow called Tom Arthurs to kill theirs. Old Tom repeated everything twice. We thought that he did it 'a purpuss', as Auntie Rosie called it, but Uncle Charlie said that it was just a silly habit that he had got into. Habit or not we used to laugh at him, not unkindly, but just because he was such a cheerful old chap who seemed to delight in making us chuckle.

Uncle Charlie and old Tom were usually just trying to lift the squealing pig onto the wooden bench when we arrived on the scene. They had erected it down at the far end of the garden next to the pigsty, we could hear old Tom's voice above the frightened squeals of the animal shouting, 'Tick t'un Charlie, tick t'un, Charlie.' (Stick to him, Charlie.)

'Damn good pig s'now, damn good pig s'now' (damn good pig you know). 'Ten or twelve score I'll bet, ten or twelve score I'll bet.' The pig was on the bench at last but still struggling, 'Burr on 'is ass a bit, burr on 'is ass a bit' (put a bit more weight on his backside so that the kicking would be useless), old Tom bellowed. Now ready for the killing, he shouted again, 'Hand I that old knife, hand I that old knife,' then old Tom 'stuck' the pig. 'Thas got the old bugger, thas got the old bugger' he shouted triumphantly as the poor lifeless animal lay there.

We jumped about and squealed and laughed all the time old Tom was shouting instructions to Uncle Charlie. 'Dump 'im on 't straw Charlie, dump 'im on 't straw, burn 'is bloody bristles awf, burn 'is bloody bristles awf,' he cried, setting fire to the boulton* of straw where the animal lay. The men straightened their aching backs for a few minutes and the air was filled with the

---

* Boulton or boultings (long bundles of straw tied with string).

smell of burning as smoke wafted across the garden stinging our eyes. Then they lifted the body on to the rough bench so that old Tom could start to cut it up.

We were still giggling an hour later, when Auntie called us into dinner. We had salt belly pork, from their last year's pig. Auntie had baked it in a huge tin in the old fire oven, it was covered with sliced onions and sliced potatoes and simply oozed with fat. Then there was a jam roly poly for afters.

Old Tom had his dinner with us: he was still repeating himself even at the dinner table. 'Damn good cook s'now, damn good cook s'now, fair blowed out I be, fair blowed out I be,' he said patting his drum-like stomach.

'A nice cup of tea before we starts work again will just put us right I reckon,' Auntie Rosie said, as she lifted the kettle on to the fire. 'Let me see,' she said to old Tom, 'if I remembers rightly you likes your tea on the strong side, don't you?'

'Yes missus, I do that, yes missus, I do that,' he replied, 'I likes it so thick, you could trot a mouse across it, I likes it so thick you could trot a mouse across it.' At this remark, we absolutely doubled up helpless with laughter, with childlike visions of har-nessed mice trekking across seas of strong tea, with old Tom holding on to the reins.

Before we left for home Auntie Rosie loaded our old pram up with 'pig's innards, yead and fit', as old Tom called the chitter-lings, head, and feet. There was just room in the pram for Denis, the youngest, to ride with Betty and I lending our Mother a hand in pushing it. We had left the rest of the family at home, for although Auntie Rosie and Uncle Charlie made us very welcome to their cottage, there was not room for us all at the same time, so we took it in turns to visit them.

The next day or two after our visit to them was very busy for our Mother as she made the brawn from the pig's head and feet and cleaned and cooked the chitterlings. She also made some lovely pig's head broth, from the liquor left over after the head had been cooked. Into this she would put plenty of carrots, onions, and turnips and a good bunch of mixed herbs and a couple of meat cubes to give it a bit of colour. 'Look at them lovely pheasants' eyes on top of it,' she would say before she dished it up. She called the glistening minute rings of fat that floated on the top of the broth pheasants' eyes. 'Of course,' our Mother told us one day, 'if you was cooking soup or stew for the gentry, you would have to get rid of every scrattock [scrap] of fat, but we 'ent gentry and it's them pheasants' eyes that keeps us going.'

During all the visits that we made to Auntie Rosie's and Uncle Charlie's home, it never seemed to alter, the warm comfortable living-room always appeared exactly the same to me. On the big, high mantle-shelf over the fireplace there was a wonderful assortment of things. In the centre was a chiming clock, given to Auntie as a wedding present, by The Honourable Elizabeth Hammetly, a lady for whom she worked as a nannie for several years. The clock played hymns at twelve o'clock, and again at three, six and nine o'clock. Two tunes it played: 'Rock of Ages', and 'Fight the Good Fight'. I can still seem to hear Auntie's high-pitched voice singing to the accompaniment of those tunes.

One day when she was singing 'Fight the Good Fight' I burst out crying. 'What's the matter, my little love?' she cried, running to my side.

'I don't want you to go off fighting, Auntie,' I sobbed. 'I wants you to stay here.' You see, the only fighting I had heard about was from snatches of conversation when our stepfather talked about the war and 'trenches full of dead men all piled on top of one another', and I certainly did not want Auntie Rosie to join them.

On the shelf next to the clock was a fat dumpy casket like a tea-caddie, tin it was, and painted on two sides, in colour were the words 'Mazawattee Tea', but on the other two opposite sides was the picture of an old lady dressed in a long skirt, she had a shawl over her shoulders and a mob cap on her head and, sitting on her lap was a little girl, dressed just like the grannie, and the child had the old lady's reading glasses perched on her nose and they were both drinking a large cup of tea. I expect there was a caption written underneath; if there was I have forgotten it.

There were also two tallish vases, black with pink roses on them, these were Uncle's spill jars. These spills were made by folding up thin strips of newspaper. Then, when he wanted to light his pipe or Auntie wanted to light the lamp or candles, they just took a spill from the jar and lit it from the fire, and then lit your pipe, lamp, or candle with it. And in this way a box of matches would last for ages, because the only time you struck one was to light the fire each day. Every cottager reckoned to have a goodly supply of home-made spills on their mantleshelf in those days.

Then at each end of the shelf there was a beautiful china dog, white with reddish patches on them. The reddish patches, Auntie told me, were what made them valuable, because it was a special colour that the makers of the dogs had created.

Some years later when both Auntie Rosie and Uncle Charlie were ailing she told me that when she and Uncle were 'dead and gone' the dogs were to go to our Mother. 'But Auntie,' I said, 'you and Uncle are not going anywhere yet.' I could not seem to use the words 'dead' or 'dying'—they seemed so final.

Yet, in their case the end came quite quickly, quicker than anyone had imagined. One evening they were sitting by the fire chatting away quite happily, then Auntie Rosie asked Uncle a question and when he did not answer she looked up at him and he had gone, died peaceful like, just sitting there. Poor Auntie Rosie never got over the shock, and the very day he was to be buried she had a heart attack and died the next day.

Wisely Auntie had left a note to say that her dear friend Kitty was to have the two china dogs. Unfortunately our Mother was unable to go to the funeral. She had to take young Ben to the Radcliffe Hospital to have his adenoids and tonsils out on that very day.

So our stepfather said that he would ride over and attend Auntie Rosie's funeral and pick up the china dogs afterwards.

He carefully wrapped the dogs up in plenty of newspaper, put them into a bag and strapped them on the carrier of his bicycle and started for Ducklington.

He was about half-way home and coming through a hamlet, when suddenly there was a commotion in the street, the few people about scattered quickly as a runaway horse pulling a cart came careering down the road, the young lad holding the reins was shouting for help at the top of his voice. Quick as a flash our stepfather stood his bicycle up against the wall and took a flying leap at the frightened horse as it passed him, grabbing it by the neck where he hung on tightly until he brought the animal to a standstill.

The driver was only a lad of fourteen and of course not very experienced with horses, especially such a frisky one as this. Our stepfather told the lad that he would drive the animal back to the farm for him if he wished, and he had a few hard words to say to the farmer too for sending a youngster out with such a fresh horse. When our stepfather got back to where he had left his bicycle it had disappeared, china dogs and all. He made enquiries at the cottages near but no one had seen anything. He reported it to the police but we never heard another word about it.

We all thought our Mother would fly into a terrible temper about the loss of the bike and the lovely dogs, but she did not, in fact she was very proud of him for saving the boy's life. Later that evening I crept upstairs to find her crying quietly to herself. I made to comfort her but she brushed me aside. 'Go on,' she said, 'I can't do with anybody's sympathy just now, I shall be all right in the morning,' and come next day she was her old cheerful self again, but it was ages before anyone even mentioned the dogs.

As to the bicycle, our stepfather had to have one to get backwards and forwards to work, and within twenty-four hours he had got all the bits and pieces together and had built himself another one. He found an old bike frame in a ditch that someone had thrown away, some handlebars which he had saved from a previous old bike, and a neighbour gave him an old saddle. Wheels he just could not afford to buy, so Bern and he went off to an old refuse pit and searched over the rubbish until they found some; mind you, some of the spokes were missing so he went off to Witney and bought a few new ones which only cost a few pence which he put in himself, but he just had to buy tubes, tyres, and a chain. I think he had an idea who the thief was, but without proof he was not able to do anything about it.

Years later, long after our stepfather had died and we had all left home, an elderly woman knocked at the door of our Mother's bungalow, thrust a parcel into her hands, and mumbled, 'This is yourn,' and made to rush away. Our Mother called her back and asked her indoors and over a cup of tea the poor frightened woman told her story.

It was her husband, she said, who had died tragically the year before, who had stolen the bicycle and the dogs. Apparently the man had been out of work for eighteen months, they had six children and were near to starving. He had at last got the chance of a job, seventeen miles away and he could earn nearly three pounds a week. The problem was, how was he to get there. He could have walked if he had been properly fed, but the poor man was half starved and would not have been able to hold the job down for long had he had to walk to work. Of course when he got the cycle home and found the china dogs on the back, they just did not know what to do, so they hid them away in a drawer and there they had stayed all these years. As she listened to the old lady's story our Mother took the china dogs out of the very newspaper in which our stepfather had so carefully wrapped them. She stroked them fondly and then re-wrapped them up again. Handing them to the old lady our Mother said, 'You take them my dear, take them and enjoy them, and thank you for having the heart to bring them back after all this time. It's a funny thing,' she went on, 'I don't bear you no ill will. Mind you,' she said with a smile, 'there's no knowing what I might have done a few years back, but we all gets a bit wiser as we gets older, don't we?'

Yes, our Mother had certainly mellowed over the years, and the reappearance of the china dogs reminded me of the time when I lost a cup at a summer school treat—a beautiful china cup it was too, it had a brilliant cock pheasant painted on it and a fancy handle. It had belonged to our Gramp, our Mother's father who had lived at Sherbourne. I think it was a 'fairing', brought back from Stow on the Wold fair, and it was nearly one hundred years old.

When we had a school treat at Ducklington, all the children were asked to bring their own mug or cup. And what an assortment of old cups and mugs turned up on those days. Many families, like ourselves, were very poor and only had a few cracked cups to their name, some handleless too. It was my last but one year at school I remember, I was thirteen at the time. Besides having to find a cup for me our Mother also had to find one for Mick, Ben, and Denis. They went off with their cups, which were carefully labelled with their names written on a piece of tape which was tied on to the handles.

Our Mother looked at the poor assortment of cups left. 'I can't let you go to the treat with any of them,' she cried. 'Look, I'll let you use Gramp's cup if you will promise to bring it back here in one piece.' 'Yes, yes,' I cried excitedly, 'I promise.' I was so pleased to think that I was old enough to be entrusted with Grampy's special cup. It was *never* used for drinking, but kept as an ornament on the shelf. One highlight of the summer school treat was the country dancing on the rectory lawn, in some of them, all the children took part, but the special dances were performed by a select few.

This year I had not been chosen to dance along with the girls of my age, and I was feeling a bit put out about it, and had already threatened to fight one or two of them because of it. But I soon forgot about the dancing when the races began, being 'one a they long legged Woodleys' as we were called, I romped home first in all the races, with the gentle girls who had taken part in the dances looking on enviously at my success.

The shadows had already begun to lengthen on the rectory lawn when we were told to gather up our belongings and make for home. I made a bee-line for the big cedar tree where I had carefully put my Gramp's precious cup—it was gone.

We looked everywhere for it, even the rector joined in the search. 'Perhaps one of your brothers or Micky has taken it home,' they suggested hopefully. But I knew as I crawled home that the cup was lost and I was already crying when I reached our cottage.

Some years after I had lost the cup, I heard that Mrs Compford was bad in bed, so I called to see if I could do an errand for her or maybe a bit of house work. She was very ill, with a bed downstairs in the small living-room. We chatted for a few minutes, then she asked me to get her a drink of water. I reached across to the crowded dresser for a glass, there in the centre was a lovely china cup, it had a brilliant cock pheasant painted on it and a fancy handle. For one split second I was back on the rectory lawn, the day was hot and sunny and I had just threatened to fight Sally Compford because she had been chosen to dance and I had not, the panic when I could not find the cup and the hiding that followed, and besides that I had to go to bed at six o'clock every night during the rest of that summer holiday, and the fact that for years I was never allowed to forget that I had lost the precious cup.

I got the drink for the old lady; her only daughter had married an American and she had gone overseas with him. She had been sent for, but no one knew whether or not she would be back in time to see her old mother alive again. It might *not* have been my Grampy's cup, but I would have bet every penny I had that it was.

ﭭﭭﭭﭭﭭﭭﭭﭭﭭﭭﭭﭭﭭﭭﭭﭭﭭﭭﭭﭭﭭﭭﭭﭭﭭﭭﭭﭭﭭ

6

Where the Windrush Flows

'Smells are surer than sounds or sights
To make your heartstrings crack'

THOSE are the opening lines of one of Rudyard Kipling's poems, and the words are very true. Certain smells do bring back memories of incidents that happened years ago.

The smell of freshly made mint sauce, stewed rhubarb, and pomanders always reminds me of a special trip that we made to our Auntie Mary's, who lived, as our stepfather used to say, 'within spitting distance of us'. Mind you, there would have had to have been a good following wind, for spit to have ever reached her house from ours, because it was at least two miles away. And although we often popped over to see her and she would call and see us on her way back home, after she had been shopping in the town, it is this one special springtime visit that I remember best.

We had never had a meal at Auntie Mary's before. It was usually just a cup of tea and one of her home-made biscuits and sometimes in summer a glass of her special lemonade, made with real lemons.

But it was this super, sunny Sunday morning when we were all invited to dinner that stands out in my mind, for at no other time can I remember having Sunday dinner anywhere else but at home, except when I went to stay with our relations at Sherbourne.

We set out about eleven o'clock, Mother, stepfather, Bern, Bunt, Betty, and myself, with Mick our stepsister in the pram. This was before our stepbrothers Ben and Denis were born.

The reason for this particular invitation was because Auntie Mary had just received the sum of two hundred pounds which had been left to her by a generous employer. She had been in service for several years, and this money was from Lord and Lady Bacters. Auntie Mary had been a lady's maid to her Ladyship. Now both of them had died and all the servants who had been in their employment had received small bequests.

When she heard the news Auntie Mary said to our Mother, 'Kitty I should like to share a bit of the money with you and the family, so I wants you all to come over to Sunday dinner and tea.' She knew this would indeed be a super treat for us, for in those days seldom was a family of seven invited out all together, specially to Sunday dinner.

And it was that smell that welcomed us as we arrived at her house that I shall never forget. Auntie had just finished making the mint sauce; on the table was a wooden chopping board, white as snow from continuous scrubbings and dryings in the sun. There were still some leaves and stalks left on it and the room was filled with the smell of bruised mint and the sharp, contrasting smell of vinegar. And floating through from the kitchen came the unmistakable smell of stewed rhubarb, the first of the season, all pink and tender. She always put a slice of lemon in with her rhubarb while it was cooking, which gave it a lovely flavour.

Pleased to see us, Auntie Mary fussed around us all. We children were each given a glass of her home-made lemonade. For our Mother there was a glass of parsley wine, and our stepfather a bottle of beer that Auntie had bought specially.

'Just hark at that darned bird,' Auntie Mary remarked as we sipped our refreshments, 'he's been on since four o'clock this morning cooing about.'

'Is it a dove or a pigeon?' she asked.

'A collared dove,' our stepfather said.

'Hark at it,' she said again. The bird cooed on regardless, 'Coo oo oo cowee.' 'My toe bleeds, Betty', we said it sang, but Auntie Mary said that it was 'You can't do it, Suzie', while our stepfather said that it was 'not tonight, Lisa'. Whatever it was there was no stopping the courting song of the lovesick bird high up in the old elm tree by the side of her house.

We watched Auntie Mary set the table. The cloth was white and stiff and shiny with starch. Never had we eaten at such a table. Every knife and fork matched as well as the spoons, and even the plates and dishes were all the same pattern, not like in our house. Our cutlery left much to be desired as did our crocks; often you had to get up and swill the plate that you had had your meat and vegetables on, so that you could use it for your pudding, we were that short.

Suddenly it was dinner time. Our stepfather was asked to carve the leg of lamb. Slivers and slivers of pink, tender meat slipped off that sharp carving knife. It was a lovely meal with crispy baked potatoes and fluffy mashed ones, spring cabbage, and that super, succulent lamb, covered with mint sauce. For pudding we had the choice of stewed rhubarb and custard or 'Whitsuntide pie'—a green gooseberry pie.

The meal over and the washing up done we all sat down and had a cup of coffee, a thing unheard of in our house.

Auntie Mary had never married, but she was not the usual prim old maid, she was cheerful and happy and, as she said, she was an old maid from choice, she had had plenty of offers, but was very content as she was. Auntie Mary's mother had worked at Osborne House for a while during the reign of Queen Victoria, and that afternoon Auntie Mary showed us a treasure that was to become mine. When the old Queen died, some of her dresses were cut up, and pieces given to the staff as momentoes. This was a panel from a very lovely dress, black, covered with hundreds of minute beads embroidered on to look like bunches of pink roses. It must have been taken from one of Queen Victoria's earlier dresses, because it is reputed that she wore black for many of her later years.

The reason I was presented with this treasure was because Auntie Mary was my godmother. I suspect too that it was she who gave me the name of Victoria.

It was from Auntie Mary that I learned the art of making pomanders. She always gave our Mother one at Christmas time. I called on her one day when she was busily making some for her Christmas gifts. 'Here,' she said, 'you can make the holes in the oranges with this bodkin and push the cloves into the hole, just leaving the thick end of the clove sticking out.' This done we then rolled the clove-filled oranges in equal quantities of orris root and cinnamon. Then we carefully wrapped each orange separately in greaseproof paper and stacked them in Auntie's spare bedroom, where they stayed for six weeks. By then they were ready to have a bit of pretty ribbon tied on them before being given away.

Before we left Auntie Mary's on that special day she gave us all a small gift. Our Mother had a rather nice blue and silver brooch, our stepfather a tie-pin, Bern and Bunt each had a horn-handled pocket knife, and we three girls a locket and chain apiece. Then it was back home to Ducklington while it was still light.

We met several families out for their Sunday night walk, and some courting couples too. Then we came upon Fred Since, leaning on his bicycle evidently waiting for a someone to come along. We stopped to chatter with him.

'Who is it tonight then, Fred,' our stepfather asked.

'Ah wouldn't you like to know, but I 'ent telling,' he replied, laughing loudly.

Poor Fred, he was a bit on the simple side. Our Mother's description of him was 'that he had got all his buttons on, but they had never been tightened up'. She would only say this at home, never to his face or to other folk.

'I see you got your swank handkerchief showing, Fred,' our Mother remarked. Fred loved it if you noticed things like that.

'Oh yes, missus,' Fred replied in his slow, drawling voice. 'I allus 'as two hankchers when I goes out dressed up like, thas one fer blowin' and one fer showin'.'

'And what's this I hear about you going out regular with a young lady in the town, Fred?' she asked him kindly.

'Well,' Fred replied, blushing to the roots of his hair. 'Well, I can't say as I goo's with 'er mind, I rides round the town a time or two on me bike with 'er, but I can't say as I goo's with 'er, well not to say goo's with 'er like.'

If we kids met Fred down in the village we would tease the life out of him. 'Got yer collar and tie on tonight then, Fred?' we had called knowing darn well what the answer would be. 'I never reckons to wear one all the week, but come Sunday I always puts me collar and hames on.' Fred worked with horses and would never have thought of saying collar and *tie*.

Poor Fred did not have a chance really. Apparently both his mother and father were a bit on the simple side too. And they used to quarrel and fall out very often. One day when they had had a particularly nasty row and Fred's father was a bit more fed up than usual, he went into the local butchers and said, 'I wish somebody 'ud shoot me or something and put me out of my misery.' So the butcher, jokingly, picked up his meat cleaver and made to chop the man's head off. 'Oh don't do it now,' he said, 'wait till I be asleep, it won't hurt so much then.'

And once, when Fred was a youngster, he was apparently very ill and his mother called the doctor in. There was young Fred laid in bed white as a sheet and motionless. The doctor took one look at him and said, 'I think he's dead.'

'That I byent,' Fred said.

But his mother answered, 'Now then Fred, don't argue, Doctor knows best.'

With parents like that Fred could not help getting into all sorts of scrapes, and the lads of the village used to set him up to do all sorts of things, and Fred was simple enough to do them.

One night a gang of boys got hold of an old railway sleeper and dared Fred to push it down old Mr Paine's chimney. They knew that every night the old man, who was as deaf as a post, used to stay up in the evening until every bit of fire had burnt out in his grate. The lads helped Fred to get the sleeper on to the roof and then he slowly let it down the chimney. One fellow was looking through Mr Paine's window, so that he could let Fred know when the end of the sleeper reached the flames. Of course, all railway sleepers are treated with creosote and once the fire got hold of it went like a torch. The villagers helped to quell the fire by forming a human chain of buckets of water, with one man tipping it straight down the chimney, until the fire brigade arrived from the town. But nobody let on who had played the rotten trick on the old man. Even Fred, for once, was fly enough not to own up either.

Another time the lads got hold of an old lemonade bottle, the sort that had a glass marble in, which kept the contents airtight. They filled it with carbide, sealed it up and then got Fred to leave it outside Claggy Weston's cottage. Then they all hurried a safe distance away and waited for the bang. The bottle finally exploded blowing a couple of windows right out.

Mind you, Fred liked to think he was as knowledgeable as the rest of the lads, and he tried to say big words like them, but very rarely got them right. Teasingly we would ask him, 'How's poor Mr Coombs then, Fred?' waiting for him to say, 'You know he's had his leg *amplicated*,' and we would snigger and laugh at him behind our hands.

'And how's your Mother, Fred, still afraid to go out at nights, is she?'

'Well, 'tis like this yu see, 'er reads all them dreadful things in the *News of the World* and then 'ers frit to go out, 'er won't even go up the garden to the lavatory on her own in case 'ers *attached* by one a they *sectional* maniacs.'

Once, when we were teasing Fred, our Mother came along and caught us, and didn't we get a hiding. 'The trouble with you kids,' our eldest brother said, as we licked our wounds, 'is that you wants to learn the eleventh commandment and stick to it. Do you know what tis?' he asked us. 'Thou shalt not be found out. The trouble is,' he went on, 'you be as green as grass, but get another few years behind you, and you'll learn.' And we did, in time.

Mind you, young Ben seemed to be able to get away with murder. He was a jolly good mimic, too, and able to take anyone off. And once when we were in chapel and the congregation were singing, with feeling, 'Wash me in the Blood of the Lamb. And I shall be whiter than snow', a tittering rose above the fine singing. There was Ben taking off one of the visiting lay preachers, one who always shut his eyes when he was singing and rocked backwards and forwards on his heels as he sang. And to add insult to injury Ben was also singing a parody to the hymn:

> Whiter than the whitewash on the wall
> Whiter than the whitewash on the wall,
> Wash me in the water
> That you washed your dirty daughter
> And I shall be whiter than snow

We tried to shush him, but he was that full of himself he just kept on. The audience gradually stopped the singing and Ben was left carolling on his own. Then he looked round sheepishly and burst out laughing.

We were banned from chapel after that. You see we were really church, so the chapel was not actually turning away lost souls and they knew it. But our Mother went down the village and apologized to Mr Ivings who was one of the preachers at the chapel, for Ben's shocking behaviour.

7

Caravans and Kings

LIVING in Little Ducklington, just a few hundred yards away from us was Mr and Mrs Jesse Pratley. Their home was a brightly painted caravan which stood in a field next to the entrance to the moors. I do not know if they were of gypsy origin, but they were both dark and gypsy-like in their looks and dress. He was a big, black-eyed, swarthy type and she was small with jet-black curly hair and sloe-black eyes, and she dressed in the fashion of a gypsy too, with her long, black skirt and blouse and a black, shiny, sateen-like apron, and she had earrings of half-sovereigns in her pierced ears.

Mr Pratley always wore a red, spotted kerchief knotted round his neck, with the ends neatly tied to his braces.

The caravan was always neat and tidy, with its bed at the far end wideways across the van. It had on it a pink, rose-covered quilt, which was covered over by a beautiful hand crocheted lacy bedspread; the small table also had a white, lace-edge cloth on it. All this handwork was done by Mrs Pratley, she used to crochet her own shawls too. There was brass and copper in the caravan in the shape of water carriers, lamps and ornaments.

Mr Pratley was a coal and wood merchant and most days he would journey up to Witney Railway goods yard and load his cart with hundredweight sacks of coal, which he sold, not just to Ducklington housewives, but to many of the surrounding villages. His pony, at least the only one I can remember, was called Nora, and she had hindquarters like a cow.

When trees were being felled in the area, Jesse would buy the tree top wood, leaving the trunk for the timber merchants.

Sometimes our stepfather would go along to the field and help Jesse cut up the wood into blocks. He had a wonderful mechanical saw which sawed through the timber in no time. Mr Pratley did not pay our stepfather, but he would often give him a big sack of blocks which he carried home on his shoulder.

One Saturday afternoon he had gone along to give Jesse a hand, and from our house we could hear the whine as the saw blade cut through the wood. Suddenly our stepfather came stumbling into the house clutching his hand to his chest. He had Jesse's old red kerchief wrapped round his left hand, which was supported by the right one, blood dripping through his fingers onto the ground.

Betty, who was about eighteen at the time, rushed towards him. 'Whatever have you done?' she cried.

'Cut me bloody fingers awf I reckon,' he said, wincing as he did so.

Carefully she took off the blood-soaked kerchief. The top of one of his fingers was all but off—it looked just like the lid of a hinged salt cellar, she told us afterwards. And the other finger was very badly cut too. She plunged his hand into a bowl of water laced with Jeyes fluid. Our stepfather, a very strong man, nearly passed out with the pain. Quickly our Mother ripped up an old sheet, handing Betty a piece so that she could swabble* the injured fingers. When she was sure that all the blood and dirt was washed from the wounds, she started to try to bandage the fingers. She said afterwards that she had, in fact, replaced the finger tip which was completely severed, and the guides on the other one were cut. She bound the two fingers, first separately and then both together, which helped to keep them stiff.

In the middle of all the chaos of sheet tearing and water boiling and general confusion, Mrs Pratley came running down from the caravan. She burst into the house crying, 'I never ast him to do it, I never ast him to do it.' This was in case our stepfather claimed off them for injury, which of course he did not.

* Washing or swilling with water.

He never even went to the doctor for that would have meant that he would have to go on the panel,* which in turn would have meant much less money for us to live on. The accident happened on the Saturday afternoon, but he went off to work as usual on the following Monday, with both fingers still strapped together. He must have been in pretty good fettle, and Betty must have made a very good job of doctoring him because his fingers healed in no time. One, of course, was permanently stiff and the other had a complete ring round the top where the flesh had healed and where Betty had stuck the fingertip back on.

Once, when Mr Pratley was out delivering coal, during a very hot, dry spell, one of the iron rims from one of the cart wheels came off. He was a long way from home, and from a blacksmith, and at first he thought that he would have to drive home without a rim on, which would have been bad for the wooden wheel as the rough roads would have soon cut into it. And Jesse knew that if he wore too much of the wood away, the wheel then would be completely spoilt. So he took hold of a thick rope which he kept in the cart, in case he needed a tow at any time, and wound it round and round the wheel. We heard him coming up the street that night, clump, clump, clump, the old cart went. Jesse said afterwards, 'It nearly shook me guts out, 'twas worse than a ride on the cakewalk—and it lasted longer.'

But back home Jesse soon put his cart to rights. He always had a spare wheel soaking in the water in the ditch that ran alongside the field where the caravan was. Mind you, they did not always match up. When Jesse was a bit pushed, he would fix a wheel on one side of his cart that was bigger than the other side, and this would cause a peculiar noise as he drove down the street. But in those days nobody took much notice of simple things like that.

It was Jesse Pratley who sent me on an errand one day, to get two pennoth of hurdle seed. Green as grass I made my way to the village shop, clutching the tuppence tightly in my hand. I was just

* The National Health. You needed a note from the doctor and you could draw 10s. (50p) per week.

about to open the shop door when I heard someone calling my name over and over again. I turned to see Mrs Pratley running down the street after me. She came up to me, put her arm round me and told me that it was just a joke and Mr Pratley was only teasing me. 'But you have that tuppence and spend it on some sweets, my little love,' she cried. 'That'll teach him not to send little girls on fools' errands.'

I went into the shop. The joy of having tuppence to spend on what *I* wanted was unbelievable. It took me ages to make up my mind. First I thought I would have a sherbet fountain and a gob-stopper and some bulls' eyes, then I decided on some marzipan teacakes and some slab toffee and a halfpenny worth of bright yellow lemonade powder. Poor Mrs Tidball, who kept the shop, lost her usual patience.

'Why not have some of these?' she suggested, pointing to a jar of brightly coloured sweets.

'No, I don't want none of them,' I replied. 'Our Bet had some last week, they makes yu pee green.'

So I settled for some Blue Bird toffees, a liquorish pipe and a sherbet dab.

Mrs Pratley used to accompany her husband round some of the remote Oxfordshire villages. While he was busy selling coal and logs, she would go off calling at the cottages with her wicker basket over her arm. It was filled with all the little odds and ends that the housewife needed, boot and shoelaces, collar studs, needles and pins, hair combs, hair pins, knots of tape and ribbon, elastic and clothes pegs, which she and her husband used to make. They would sit outside the caravan in the evenings, he whittling away skinning the wood and shaping the sticks while she expertly fixed the small tin band on to the top end of the peg, which kept it together.

Later on, when things got a bit better for them, Mrs Pratley acquired a pony and trap of her own, so that she could come and go when and where she wanted to. She also collected rags and rabbit skins as well as selling her wares, and sometimes our

Mother would let me go with her. Mind you, I was not allowed to go with Mrs Pratley as she went from door to door. I used to have to sit on the cart and wait for her. 'You just sit and guard them rags, young Mollie, see as nobody pinches um.'

Often village children would come along and stare at me, sat there in all my glory. 'You be a gippo,' they would call to me. 'You be a gippo, that's what you be.'

'I ent then,' I would cry. 'I ent a gippo, I be just looking after these rags.'

Then they would run off laughing and calling, ''er's looking after they rags, 'er's a gippo.'

And I would poke my tongue out at them and call back, 'Sticks and stones will break my bones but names will never hurt me.'

I was very fond of both Mr and Mrs Pratley and as a child spent many happy hours sitting on the steps of their caravan, while they made clothes pegs for the next day's journey.

I think Mrs Pratley must have had the gift of second sight, because she used to tell me about some of the ghostly things that she used to see, especially in the Minster Lovell area. That village was usually her last call of the day, after she had been round Astall, Swinbrook and Leafield. Well, one autumn evening she said it was getting a bit dimpsy and the mist was already lying low over the water meadows, shrouding the village in a mysterious veil, when suddenly a figure of a white knight rose up in front of her. He was dressed in shining armour and he was astride a huge white charger. Her pony shied, pulling the trap onto the side of the road. In a flash the rider and horse disappeared into the mist. She said she even saw the white breath coming from the animal's nostrils and his long, white tail was stretched out behind him.

It was years afterwards, when I was in my teens in fact, that I heard about the legend of Lord Francis Lovell, one of King Richard III's favourites. But when the King was killed at the battle of Bosworth, Lord Lovell knew that the King's enemies would seek him out and kill him, so he fled from the battlefield.

Later, however, he took part in another battle and this time he fought for Lambert Simnel, a man who claimed to be Richard, Earl of Warwick and therefore lawful King of England. But King Henry VII's men were too good for them, and Lord Lovell, reflecting on the outcome of the battle, left, and the story goes that he was last seen swimming his horse across the river Trent, but owing to the steepness of the opposite bank, was unable to land.

But the story goes that Lord Francis Lovell, now a hunted fugitive, managed to get back to the great Manor House at Minster Lovell, and with the help of a trusty manservant remained there, hidden in a secret room. The servant brought food and drink to his master daily but locked him in the secret room every night. Years passed and the story was regarded as just a legend. But in the year 1708 some workmen were engaged in repairing the manor, and behind a great chimney stack they made a startling discovery. Hidden in a small secret room they found the skeleton of a man seated at a table, with the skeleton of a small dog sitting at his feet. Was this the remains of Lord Lovell? Did his trusty servant die suddenly leaving his master entombed, to die of starvation?

Or was the ghost of the white knight that Mrs Pratley saw that of Lord Lovell trying in vain to reach the safety of his home. Whoever it was Mrs Pratley told me that she saw the same ghost on several occasions along the same stretch of road, but not necessarily in the same place.

And another 'sighting' of hers was that of Old Mother Culpepper, the ghost of a very old lady dressed all in black, with a little poked bonnet on her head, who walked along the tops of the hedges in the Hanborough area. Mrs Pratley used to tell me that as she jogged along in her pony and trap, Mrs Culpepper used to keep up with her until she reached a certain field and then the old lady would disappear as mysteriously as she had appeared.

Years later, during the Second World War, I heard of another 'sighting' of Old Mother Culpepper.

Many people were evacuated to this part of the country, from London, and one family, a mother and her three children, two girls aged twelve and ten and a boy of eight, lived in one of the villages near to Hanborough. The mother used to take the children back to London at the weekends to see their father who had to stay in the city and work. They used to come back on the last train, so that it was around midnight when they reached Hanborough station, and they still had a matter of two miles to walk. They took a well-known short cut along a narrow lane. When they reached the cottage where they lived, on this particular evening the young boy was in a state of shock, white and trembling and he could not speak. The doctor was sent for and he said that the boy must have had a terrific shock to be in the state that he was. When the lad began to recover his mother asked him what had frightened him, and the boy replied, 'It was that queer old lady dressed all in black that walked along the hedge all the way up the lane with us.' Only then did the locals tell them about the ghost of Old Mother Culpepper. But it was only the young lad who had seen her.

8

Poaching Tales and Tall Stories

'I BE JUST GOIN' to take the cows down to the long field,' Fred Paver used to say. A stranger hearing him make this remark would naturally think that he was really going to do this. But we in Ducklington knew darned well that what old Fred meant was, that he was about to take his cows down the road, round Starlum as we called it, from Ducklington to Curbridge, a matter of two miles. Here, along the grass verges he grazed his herd of six cows once every day, and this was what he called 'the long field'. Fred only had a couple of small fields so he found this free grazing a godsend. Goodness only knows how he made a living for after he had milked his cows he spent the rest of the day strolling leisurely along the road with the cows. Of course there was so little traffic about in those days, especially round the Curbridge road. He used to meet a few village people on the way. For most every day wet or fine, poor lame Dick Clarke would be hobbling out for a walk, and he was always glad when folks stopped to have a few words with him. And Fred used to tell the tale that one day a man in a motor car stopped and called out to him, 'I say, do you locals call the town I've just come through Cirencester or Sisister?' 'Well sir,' Fred replied, 'we generally calls it Witney.'

Fred would often meet Brummy Edwards too, not that Brummy wasted much time chatting. If he was not laying a hedge or doing a bit of ditching for a farmer, he would be working away on his allotments. He had two at Ducklington and one in the next village at Curbridge. Sometimes he walked there, over the fields and footpaths, which was a more direct way than the roadway. Someone once asked Brummy why he kept two allotments in the village and another one at Curbridge and his reply was, 'If I didn't grow plenty of vegetables my children would be no bigger than field mice.' As well as cultivating the allotments, Brummy, like many of the village people at that time, used to do a bit of poaching on the side. His keen eyes knew just where the rabbit and hare runs were, and he would set his snares just where the animals made a habit of coming through a hedge or ditch.

As well as setting traps and snares to catch game, he also kept a couple of whippit-type dogs: one used to run along the grass verges while the other sat alongside Brummy in his little cart. He had a whistle hung round his neck, which he blew when he wanted the dogs to 'go', 'fetch', or 'bring'. He had trained them just as a shepherd might train a sheepdog.

The dog which was running would flush out the game and the one on the cart would take a flying leap and bring the bounty back to his master. Brummy's cart was pulled by a mule which he had bred himself, from a he-ass and a mare. In later years when most of his family had grown up and left home, Brummy used to plant the whole of one of his allotments with broad beans which he fed to his old mule by the bucketful.

One day Brummy had been helping with the harvest on one of the nearby farms, and at midday the farmer brought out some home-made cider for the men. A visiting farmer rode into the yard just as Brummy was taking a swig from the jar. 'What's the cider like today then Brummy?' he enquired. And Brummy, the wise old man that he was replied, 'If it was any worse, I couldn't drink it, and if it was any better I shouldn't have the chance!'

I really do not know how some of the families in the village would have managed to survive in those days without a bit of poaching. And although our Mother did not encourage Bern or Bunt to go, she was really quite glad when Denis, the youngest, took it up. He would come back from his escapades with wild ducks, rabbits and hares, and sometimes a pheasant. But she was always uneasy in case he should get caught. When you had got a large hungry family and no money in your purse, you cooked your ill-gotten gains with a song in your heart, but with a prayer on your lips.

One day my eldest brothers Bern and Bunt were over on our allotment digging up the potatoes, when they noticed a man who lived in the village creeping up the side of the hedge in one of Farmer Strange's fields.

'I'll bet that old sod's setting a rabbit trap; we'll go and see when he's gone home,' Bunt said. So they hid behind the huge trunk of one of Druce's elm trees and waited there until the man made off towards the village. Then they both walked over to where he had been crouching. After a bit of searching they found the snare the fellow had cunningly set across a hare run, and decided that they would tell nobody about it, but they would get up early the next morning to see if there was anything caught in it.

They crept out of the house at half-past five in the morning, across the green and up the Curbridge road they went, cutting across Druce's field and into Strange's to where the snare was set. In it was a beautiful hare, dead of course. Very carefully they lifted the body out and re-set the trap, in hopes that the man would never know that it had been tampered with. Then they cut off home as fast as their legs would carry them. Our Mother was amazed to see the boys coming through the gate carrying a sack at that time in the morning.

'Guess what we've got?' Bunt asked her excitedly. Then Bern thrust his hand into the sack and brought out the lovely, sandy-haired, long-eared hare. He held it at arm's length and it was nearly as big as he.

Our Mother gave a loud whoop of joy which was probably heard a quarter of a mile away. 'Where on earth did you get that?' she cried, almost beside herself with excitement.

Bern and Bunt, both talking at the same time, told her how they had watched the man the day before, then found where he had set the trap, and how they sneaked off before anyone was up to see what was caught in it.

'Well,' she said, 'I'd best get it skinned just as quick as I can, then I'll put it to soak in some salt water for a while, and cook it for tea tonight. We'll have it jugged,' she gabbled on. 'I'll cook it in that big brown stone jar that belonged to Granny Broad, and then we will all sit down tonight and have a meal fit for a king. Let me see,' she went on, 'if I can get it in that old fire oven by eleven o'clock, that will have seven hours slow cooking. When you have had your breakfast, one of you can pop up to Mrs Adams and ask her for three or four bay leaves, jugged hare 'ent nothing without a few bay leaves in.'

She made the boys some porridge, then went out into the back kitchen and started to skin the hare. She had not been out there very long when there was a loud banging on the door. She went to answer it, wiping her bloody hands on her coarse apron as she went.

The man who had set the trap stood there, his eyes blazing with temper. 'Oh yes,' he shouted eyeing her blood stained hands, 'Oh yes, it *was* your Bern and Bunt that stole my hare, wasn't it? I followed thur tracks in the wet grass you see Missus, come on, it's no good trying to deny it; 'and it over quick, or I'll go and fetch the police.'

'You'll go and do what?' our Mother shouted indignantly. 'You'll go and do what?'

'I'll go up to Witney, thas what I'll do and fetch a policeman,' he bellowed.

'Go on then, fetch one if you dare,' our Mother cried, 'you haven't got permission from Mr Strange to set snares in his field. We've got just as much right to the hare as you, you'd be frightened to death to go anywhere near the police station, they'd soon put you inside with your reputation. Go on, clear off with you,' she went on, 'and I hope Bern and Bunt finds some more of your traps that you've set, and don't you dare let me hear that you've said anything to my boys about this either, or you'll have me to answer to.'

'You haven't heard the last of this,' he shouted as he stamped out of the yard. 'I'll get my own back one of these days, you mark my words if I don't.'

Of course he knew that legally he had not got a leg to stand on and, as far as we knew, he never told another soul about the incident.

He knew that our Mother was a lot more knowledgeable than he was, and what she had said was right. Had the affair happened to a simpler sort of person, he would have probably bullied them into handing over the animal.

In those hard-up days there was much rivalry between the men who did a bit of poaching; everyone knew that it went on, and occasionally a landowner would take some poor devil to court, having been caught with pheasants on him. But hungry men with hungry families grew very cunning and very rarely got caught. And once when Shirty Calcutt and another local man called Denole started arguing about the ownership of a rabbit which had been caught in a trap, the local policeman acted as referee when they decided to fight each other for the rabbit.

'Righto, off you go,' the policeman said. 'And remember the winner takes the rabbit,' and at once the two men fell upon each other, fighting and wrestling and rolling over in the road. They fought for nearly an hour, tearing at each other like mad things. When both of the men were absolutely exhausted, the policeman said, 'Well, I declare the result of this fight a draw, so I'll take the rabbit,' and he promptly got on his bicycle and rode away, leaving the men speechless.

Not only did we feed off the fat of the land, but from the rivers too. Proper fishing tackle was unheard of, so the lads of the village used to use their own methods to catch fish. They would cut themselves a good long withy stick and fix a rabbit wire on the end of it. Mind you, you also needed a steady hand, and a good eye to be able to see the fish laying on the bottom of the river. Then all you had to do was slip the wire over the fish's head, then give a sharp tug and yank it out of the water. Our Mother

was not all that keen on fresh-water fish, but she used to jolly
them up with herbs and things and it used to make quite a tasty
dish.

Some of the older men could even catch fish with their hands.
You needed the patience of a saint, lying there on your stomach
with your hand in the water waiting for a fish to come along
and settle, before you began to tiggle its stomach. Crayfishing
was a very popular sport too; crayfish bred well in our limestone river. And I remember once our cousins, who also lived
in Ducklington, Harry Del and Pete Woodley, had been
crayfishing one evening and they had caught dozens and dozens
of the little fellows. But their parents were cross with them because they were late getting home and said that they would not
cook them that night, but they would have to wait until the
next day. So they put the live crayfish (they have to be cooked
alive) in a bucket of water and stood them in the larder. When
their father, our Uncle Harry, got up the next morning the
crayfish had all disappeared. Apparently they had crawled out of
the full backet and were all over the house, in the furniture, in
the ashes that were left in the firegrate, even in the coalbox. So
the boys did not have their treat after all, because most of the
crayfish were dead, as they can only live a certain time out of
fresh water.

I suppose you could call egg pinching sort of poaching too. I
mean pheasant, partridge, and duck eggs all of which our boys
used to find and bring home. And one day a gang of the village
lads were walking in the plantations at Cokethorpe and one of the
Godfrey boys stumbled on a pheasant's nest absolutely full of
eggs. At once he threw his great arms around the nest, shouting
'They're mine, they're mine, none of you others 'ent going to
have any of 'um.' The rest of the lads crowded round protesting
loudly when a stern voice over the other side of the hedge said,
'Whose eggs did you say they were?' It was the voice of the head-
keeper. Scared out of their wits the lads all took to their heels and
ran home as if Old Nick was after them.

And a man who farmed at Coursehill, which was about a mile from Ducklington, had his suspicions that there was a fair bit of rabbit poaching going on on his land, but he could not seem to catch the culprits. Night after night he lay in wait at different places around the farm, at points where he thought they might enter his fields. Then one evening he was just making for home when he heard voices coming from the Great Western Railway line which skirted his land. The poachers were just off home—to Witney—and he had been thinking all along that the men netting his rabbits had come from Ducklington.

The next night he let the men come into the fields and saw them creeping along the hedges, frightening the rabbits and sending them into the long nets, from which, once they were in, there was no escape: Then one of the men said, 'All right, pass the word along, thas enough for one night.'

Then the farmer stood up and shouted, 'All right fellows, we've got 'um,' making out that he had plenty of help. 'Come on,' he went on, shouting at the poachers, 'come on out you thieving buggers, there's more of us than there is of you.' But no one came out; the poachers must have shot off in all directions back to Witney, leaving their long nets full of rabbits. The farmer collected them up, and the next morning took three sacks of rabbits into White's shop in Oxford, and got ninepence a-piece for them.

Another story of poaching that is told around Ducklington happened at the beginning of six weeks' terribly hard weather. The tale is about two men who had come to live in one of the nearby villages, town fellows they were. They had heard the locals talking about their poaching conquests, so they thought that they would have a go at it. It did not seem that difficult, and they might get a few good meals out of it. So without telling anyone of their plans, they set off. One of the men had a motor-bike and sidecar, they would go on this, but leave it at a fair distance away from where they hoped to catch, or rather, pick off the branches, some roosting pheasants. It was a freezing cold night and trying to snow as the men made their way down to the wood. But nothing went the way they planned: the men, not used to creeping about woods in the dark, made far too much noise as they trod on rotten wood, which snapped and crackled in the quiet air. Suddenly someone shouted, 'All right, I've got you covered, walk towards the sound of my voice with your hands above your head, or I'll blast your bloody legs from under you.' Both men turned and fled, running for their lives, stumbling and falling, as they tripped over fallen trees. At last they emerged from the wood, breathless and bleeding where they had run blindly into brambles and branches. They reached the safety of the motor-bike, and Bill the driver threw himself on the machine and started it up, while Fred jumped on to the top of the sidecar, where he sat perched, too breathless to get right in.

Their journey home took them through Ducklington, and they tore round by the pond at a rare pace and then on up towards the Aston Hills towards home. Bill pulled up at the house where Fred his passenger lived, and said, 'All right, mate, 'op out quick, and make yourself scarce,' but there was no reply, because there was no one in the sidecar. Bill was worried sick about his mate, but he dare not go looking for him in case he ran into the keeper. Well, Fred did not turn up the next day, or the next, so the police were notified, and a lot of questions were asked but they still could not find out what had happened to him.

Now the story goes that when Bill was driving home that night and was rounding the pond at Ducklington at speed, Fred, who was still only perched on the top of the sidecar, rolled off, striking his head on the road as he fell, rolling into the pond as he did so. The terrible hard frost that night froze the pond over solid, and the severe weather lasted for six long weeks, and it was only when the thaw came that Fred's body was found.

But there were many different ways of eking out a living. One old fellow who did not seem to do anything else in the way of work, used to make walking sticks from ash wood, cutting the straight sticks low at the base from where they were growing, and here, there was always a sort of knobble. He used to carve dog's faces on this knobbly piece which also formed the handle of the walking stick. Then he would take them up to Witney and get one of the barbers to sell them to his customers when they came in for a haircut.

Even the choir boys used to earn themselves a bit of pocket money now and then. Once our rector, the Revd Tristram, thought he would get the boys to clear the weed plantain from the churchyard. He offered the choir boys a penny a dozen for all the roots they brought him. He even got Mr Barratt the village blacksmith to make each boy a special little two-pronged tool, which helped to lift the long rooted weed out of the ground. All went well, the boys were doing fine, earning themselves quite a lot of pocket money. But after a few weeks, the rector realized that the weeds in the churchyard were not getting less. Then he discovered, that after he had carefully counted out the plantain roots, and paid over the money, and told his gardener to tip them on the rubbish heap at the bottom of the rectory garden, the choir boys were simply picking them off the heap and offering them again to the Rector for payment.

9

Come Day, Go Day,
God Send Sunday

SOMETIMES in the summer time there was a bit of excitement in the village when some of the farmers' hayricks caught on fire. Because, if the grass had not been allowed to dry and make good hay, the ricks were inclined to 'heat', often with disastrous results. If a farmer spotted a rick steaming he would ask a couple of his men to try and cut the offending hay out, and it was nothing to see a two or more farmer workers, stripped to the waist, cutting away at the centre of a rick with a huge hay knife. They would throw the damp hay out on to the grass below where the cows soon ate it up. When they were sure that the danger of fire was past, they would emerge from the rick looking like fugitives from a minstrel concert party.

But sometimes the ricks were left too long 'heating' and that would cause them to set on fire. The only thing left then was to send for the Fire Brigade.

I remember winter mornings too, waking up to hear the great lumbering threshing tackle going by, puffing and snorting its way down the village street, to set up at Wilsdon's or Strange's farms. They would be in the village for a week or more threshing the corn ricks and puffing chaff and coal smoke all over the place. The men, swarthy and strong, mostly wore navy blue boiler suits, and their faces were as black as tinkers from the dust which came from the cornricks. From any part of the village you could hear the engine that drove the threshing machine, start up at about seven o'clock in the mornings and it went on all day until half-past four or five o'clock at night. We used to stop and watch the men at work, when we came out of school.

'Stand well back, you children,' the farmer would shout to us, 'unless you wants your head 'ett off with a rat.'

When they had nearly reached the bottom of a rick, the big boys and the farmer would stand round it with stout sticks in their hands, because this was when the rats, who had been living happily in the ricks since harvest time, made a run for their lives. As they ran out the waiting boys whacked them on the head and killed them; the few they missed the dogs made short work of.

Another thing I remember about the winter times of our young days in Ducklington, was when my elder brothers Bern and Bunt used to go beating for the local farmers and gentry. The boys started to go beating when they were about thirteen. Sometimes on a Friday Mr Salmon, one of the head gamekeepers, used to go into the school and ask the headmaster if he would enquire if any of the older boys would like to go beating the next day. Of course nearly all the lads said yes, because it meant they would get a shilling, a good midday dinner and a rabbit for their day's work.

Later on, when they were older, my brothers used to receive two shillings and sixpence and a good dinner and a rabbit. This was in the days before wellington boots, and the only protection against the wet and mud was a pair of strong, leather boots and putties. Most men and boys wore these putties, a remnant from the First World War. You could purchase them from Cook & Boggis's shop in Witney for threepence a pair, but I expect the ones Bern and Bunt wore were some that our stepfather had himself worn during the 1914–18 war. Mind you, there were lads who had not even got putties to wear because they could not afford to buy any, then old sacking was wound round and round the legs to try and stave off some of the wet.

The variation of the midday meal that the beaters had depended on which farmer they were working for. At one place they had lashings of rabbit pie, great big ones they were, made in huge cream pans, about two foot across oozing with meat and lovely thick, brown gravy, topped up with potatoes and greens, with a great big slab of bread and butter pudding for afters and as much cocoa as you wanted. At another farm a bucketful of stew and chunks of bread was brought into the room where the men and boys had their food, they were handed basins and spoons and simply helped themselves to as much stew as they could manage. And at another they had super beef sandwiches and a mug of hot soup.

At one of the places they went to, Brummy Edwards was in charge of the beaters. He was a wise old fellow and taught my brothers quite a few wrinkles about beating. 'You go and poke they brambles,' Brummy would say, 'I'll bet thurs a rabbit in thur,' and sure enough two or three rabbits would rush out. 'You lay one a they in the ditch, my lad,' he said to Bern one day, who was struggling along with three or four hares. 'You can always come back fer him tomorrow.'

So Bern did this on several occasions, but sometimes the hare that he had carefully hidden was gone, already found by someone else. And one day Bunt acquired an extra rabbit. In the early afternoon they were beating through a small spinney when a couple of rabbits ran out. Someone took a shot at them and killed one. Nobody wanted to start loading themselves up with game that early in the afternoon, so Bunt threw the dead rabbit in the hedge, thinking that he could pick it up for the farmer when they all made their way back to the farm at night. Somehow the rabbit was forgotten. At the end of the day the men and boys lined up for their pay and a rabbit, and only then did Bunt remember the one in the hedge. Later when he was walking home along with Bern and a fellow called Skeecher, Bunt made out that he wanted to go to the lavatory and that he would catch them up. In a few minutes he found the rabbit, tied its legs with string, let the rabbit down inside his trouser leg then tied the string to his braces. He ran and caught Bern and Skeecher up. Of course neither of them realized what he had got, and he did not let on until Bern and he were safely indoors. There was great jubilation in our house that night. We were rich, we had three rabbits and an extra five shillings that the boys had earned. 'I wouldn't call the King me aunt,' our Mother remarked happily. This was a favourite expression of hers when she was very pleased about something.

A great event in our lives was when you got hold of *two* two-pound golden syrup tins and a fair piece of string; then you could set about making yourself a pair of stilts. You see golden syrup was a luxury in our house so you had to wait ages before you got two tins. Besides that, you had to take your turn with the rest of the family. But once you had got your tins all you had to do was to turn them upside down and pierce two holes in each tin, in the bottom sides opposite each other. You didn't need a lid. After cutting the string in two, one for each stilt, you simply pushed one end of the string through one hole and tied a knot in the end, so that it would not pull through the hole. This knot must be on the inside of the tin, and then you would poke the other end of the string in the other hole and tie the end in a knot just as you did the other side. This gave you a loop of string which acted as a sort of rein. So now the original bottom of the tin was the top of your stilt. To use them you simply placed your feet on the top of the tins, then you just lifted the string up and down as you walked along.

'You looks as 'ockered as a pig in pattens,' Dick Clarke called to me when I met him down the village as I hobbled along on my newly acquired stilts.

Dick was always glad when anyone stopped to have a chatter to him. Being a cripple he did not get much further than just up and down the village street a little way, and that was quite an effort for him. But he nearly always had a little tale to tell or a bit of village gossip.

'Have you heard the story about the milestone inspector [tramp] that called at Witney workhouse one day then, young Mollie?'

'No,' I said, glad to slip my feet from the stilts and sit down on the dirt path for a rest.

'Well,' Dick said, 'this is supposed to be gospel truth and I'm relaying it just as I heard it. One cold night a man was admitted to the Witney workhouse, but the only place they could find for him to sleep was in the mortuary. Not very inviting and perishing cold, and thur was already a corpse thur in an open coffin. After looking round, the man decided that the warmest place [in the burra] would be in the coffin, so he moved the corpse onto the bench he had been given, and got in. In the morning somebody came in with his breakfast, and tried without success to rouse the corpse. The man watched this for a minute and then sitting up slowly in the coffin and said, "Well if 'e won't 'ett it I 'ull." The attendant fled from the room frightened out of his wits.'

'That 'ent true is it, Dick?' I asked, as we laughed over his story.

'Of course it is,' he replied, 'coo, I'll bet he wasent half cold staying the night in that old morgue, I should think the only place he sweat was at the nose end. Which is more than can be said about I,' Dick went on, 'I be maggled to death, I be that sweaty.'

I expect it was the fact that Dick could not walk without the aid of two walking sticks; even so he could only just shuffle along, and it was indeed a beautiful day. The hot sun bore down on us as we made our way slowly down the road. Then we stopped to lean on Holton's wall and watched the shepherd at work while Dick got his breath back.

The shepherd was busy rubbing something into the sheeps' woolly backs.

'What's up with 'um?' Dick enquired.

'Ah, they got the maggot summut dreadful,' he replied. 'I've had to treat every one of 'um, but this is some pretty good stuff as I rubs into 'um. I done some of the sheep 'issday [yesterday] and within a couple of hours they maggots was fallin' out like rice through a cullendar, so I've done the rest today. Course the gaffer was a bit upset about it, but I told 'im it was nothin' to get upstrapluss about, wus things 'appens at sea.'

'Ah!' Dick said, 'I got summut to ask you. Now a man was telling I that on the farm wur he works they always puts some geese and a gander in the same field wur the sheep be lambing, to keep the foxes away, cos one year the farmer lost a lot of his lambs, that old fox used to pick um up like picking up stones. Did you ever hear of anybody doing that before?' Dick asked him.

'Ah, I have hear tell as folks does that, they do say the geese and ganders in a farmyard be as good as a dog any day.'

'Ah,' Dick went on. 'What about all they flies as we've been plagued with fer weeks. I hopes they'll soon get shot of um. They do say as a council man from Witney come to Ducklington yesday and had a talk about um with Frankie the chairman of the parish council. Course they goes and sends a lad-di-dah chap, the sort as don't understand our lingo. Because when this man said to Frankie "What sort of flies are they?" and Frankie replied, "Ah, they be they blue *asst uns*," and this yer fellow ses "Do you mean to tell me that this plague of flies you've got in Ducklington come from *Aston*?"' (A village two miles away.)

Then Dick got on to a more serious subject.

'Did you hear what happened to "bomber Claridge" then, damn near got hisself killed he did. He was jogging along with his old horse and cart on his way to Witney. And you knows that horse is usually as quiet as a lamb, well, summut must have upset him cos all of a sudden he pricked up his ears and took off up that road like a wild thing. It took old Bomber by surprise and as the horse bolted the reins was flung out of his hands, then the cart hit the grass verge and over the lot went into the ditch with poor old Bomber underneath the lot. Well, 'twas your Uncle Harry, Mollie, as see it all 'appening as he was coming home from work on his bike. With his body he eased the cart up so as he could get to Bomber who had got all the reins sort of wound round his body. He gets out his pocket knife and cut the leather reins and dragged old Bomber out, wet as a toad he was, and the first words that the ungrateful old beggar said was, "Now I shall have to buy some new reins".'

Leaving Dick and the old shepherd still chattering, I mounted my stilts and went on my way further down the village.

First, I met Sally Saunders; she had her hair done up in rag curlers, like a heap of conkers her head looked and I told her so.

'Ah, you be only jealous,' she replied, 'cos you haven't got nothing new to wear at Whitsun [Whitsunday was in fact the next day]. You know what they ses if you 'ent got nothing new fer Whitsun don't you?' She went on, 'They ses the birds 'ull shit on you, ha ha they'll shit on you all right,' she shouted as she ran indoors.

Then I made my way down to Gooseham by the river. In a field down there that backed on to one of the farms were some stone buildings, where Mick and Ben and some of the other kids had built themselves a den. They had pulled one or two of the stones from the side of one of the smaller buildings and poked elder branches to make a sort of roof, then pushed some on the ground for the upright of their den. It was quite big inside and they were having great fun. It was their sort of summer camp, with large stones that they had found acting as stools. Apparently they had just been reinforcing the roof and young Ben, who was about nine at the time, was sitting inside. Suddenly the side of the building began to fall in and part of it came crashing down around Ben's ears. He crawled out of the rubble, miraculously not a stone had hit him, but he was crying and very frightened. We knew that our Mother would go mad if she found out. First of all the danger that Ben had been put in, and secondly to think that it was because they had been pulling stones from the building, that the side had caved in, and this was damaging the farmer's property.

We dared Ben and all the other kids that they were never to breathe a word to a soul. I forget what we threatened them with but it must have been pretty drastic, because no one ever knew a word about it. But for months, every night young Ben woke up in bed screaming and had awful nightmares, and our Mother could not understand what was causing them. Always there was something falling on him, Ben cried, but he never let on, and in time the nightmares ceased.

Even now when I open a tin of syrup I am back in the meadow on that hot summer day, my stilts slung over my shoulder because I could not walk on them in the grass. The acrid smell of bruised elder leaves and the dragonflies—we called them devil's darning needles, darting and flying over the river, and young Ben screaming and the other kids crying because they were frightened.

10

Uncle Jesse and Pigsty Passion

UNCLE JESSE was not anybody's Uncle really, but all the
children called him uncle. He lived in a hut at the far end of the
village. A bit of a mystery was Uncle Jesse. No one really knew
from where he had originated, but to me he always seemed to
have lived in his hut. In fact when I grew up I found that he
had come to settle in the village just after the First World War. He
had a sort of nasal twang, picked up, we discovered, from his
numerous visits to Canada.

He was a tall, bronzed, freckly man with sandy hair and a
waxed military moustache and a distinct military bearing; he
marched rather than walked, striding out, arms swinging, with a
back as straight as a ramrod, and although his hut was small and
cramped, he was always clean and tidy with a freshly sponged
celluloid collar round his tanned neck—a striped shirt, khaki
trousers, and an army greatcoat.

He was a 'Jack of all trades' having the ability to do almost
anything. He worked mostly on the farms in the neighbourhood,
never at one for long, just 'jobbing' from one to the other. He
could shear sheep quicker than anyone in the district, lay a hedge,
or plough a furrow as straight as the next man. Engines he was
very clever with, and when the first steam ploughs and tractors
came grunting into the village Uncle Jesse was the only one who
knew anything about them.

We were watching him repair an old threshing drum one day
and he started to tell us about when he was in Canada.

'Thur ent no fields out there,' he told us. 'Well, not fields like
we got here any road. One farmer would have acres and acres of

land stretching as far as the eye could see, thur's no hedges, just miles and miles of golden corn, and at harvest time there might be anything up to eight horse-drawn binder machines working alongside one another. Then gradually most of the farmers bought steam ploughs and then tractors, which still pulled the old type cutters and binders behind us. My word, that was a sight too, a dozen or more tractors driving across the prairies, all in line, like an army on the move they looked, except that they was cutting thousands of acres of corn.

'Well, one scorching hot day twenty of us started work, ten driving tractors and the others sitting on the back of the binder where 'twas their job to see that each sheaf was tied and flung out in straight lines. We was getting on quite well when suddenly the tractor that was working next to we caught fire; the other drivers quickly drove theirs out of the way of the one that was burning— but then the corn caught fire, thur was a bit of a breeze a-blowing, and it looked as if the whole corn harvest for miles would be going up in flames.

'Quick as a flash I could see what I had to do. I shouted to Bert Atkins, my buddy, who was set on the binder at the back, "Bert be you game, boy? Shall we try and cut round it?" "Yes," he hollered back, "but get a move on before it all goes up like tinder."

'So I drove round the outside of the spreading fire in a huge circle cutting the corn as we went. Round and round we drove sealing off the rest of the prairie. The other lads, seeing what we was doing, armed thurselves with anything they could lay hands on and began to beat out the fire that tried to spread on to the stubble. After half an hour the fire was out and old Bert and I was heroes—well, in the boss's eyes we was, we had saved the corn, with little more than four or five acres spoilt which was nothing really.

'Now go off home to tea, you kids,' he said to us, 'that's enough story-telling for today.'

But if we knew that Uncle Jesse was working at any of the farms, we children would make a bee-line for the farmyard in the hope that we might see him. Sometimes it was too wet for him to work outside, then we would all make for one of the old barns where we would perch ourselves on straw bales and there we would sit, wide-eyed, listening to his tales of travel and excitement.

'How many times have you been over the water?' Jack Everet asked him one day.

'Oh, six er seven times,' Uncle Jesse replied, 'but I shan't be goin' no more now, me travelling days are over,' he said. 'I shall stay here till the good Lord calls me home to his golden acres in the sky.'

'Tell us about the things you done when you was young, before you went to Canada,' one of the boys said.

'Well, we was a big family,' Uncle Jesse told us. 'Ten of us, six boys and four gels, and my father was a farm labourer bringing home twenty-five shillings a week. So when we boys got older we used to go off poaching to get a bit of extra grub; worried our poor old mother to death it did. She knew as we would be sent to prison if we was caught—but we never was. Mind you we had some near goes I can tell you, and some damn good dinners too.

'Rabbits we could catch with a snare, and hares too sometimes. But it was them long-tailed uns [pheasants] as we liked to catch. Thur was several different ways of poaching um without the noise and expense of a gun.

'One way we used to do it was to get hold of some nice plump winey raisins; our mother made a lot of home-made wine you see. Well, we would fix one or two raisins on a fishing hook, using an old fishing line that our mother had bought for threepence from a jumble sale. Then we would lay the hook and line in the grass where we knew some pheasants usually fed. Then we would lie in the hedge holding the fishing line tightly, and wait for the birds to come along. Sure enough, they soon found the winey raisins and with a fish-hook down their throat they couldn't squawk—then before you could say "Jack Robinson" we had their old necks wrung and they was stowed away in the sack.

'Back home, our Mother used to worry and grumble—she didn't know what to do with the feathers, somebody was sure to see um. So we carefully collected every one up and chucked them on the back of the fire—coo didn't they stink too! "If anybody smells them feathers burning they'll know we be up to something," our Mother would cry. "Tell um you emptied your feather bed and what they smelt was the ones that you swept up afterwards," our Father told her.

'But thur's more than one way of killing a cat,' Uncle Jesse went on, 'and pheasants too for that matter. Another way we used to catch um was by tying up some flowers of sulphur in a piece of flannel, tie the flannel on to a piece of wire and hang it up in a tree just underneath where we knew the birds roosted. Then we'd sit and wait till the pheasants had settled for the night, then we'd set fire to the flannel—talk about pong—the fumes was that strong the birds was soon overcome and would fall off the tree like ripe apples in autumn. Ah, we had more pheasants than you've had hot dinners,' Uncle Jesse said, bragging a little.

'Ah, 'tis an ill wind as blows nobody good,' he went on. 'Take the flooding as we allus get in February, cos in my young days that month allus lived up to the saying "February fill dyke", and although the village where we lived was very low-lying and some of the houses flooded summut dreadful, the rains brought some compensation. Our Mother would call us and say "the floods be up boys", and when we looked out of the cottage window and saw the great expanse of water we knew 'twas time to go rabbit catching.

'You see, as the water gradually flooded the fields the rabbits would come out of their burrows and run up the withy trees, and sit there to keep dry, and thur they had to stay, trapped, either till the floods subsided or we went and grabbed 'um: 'twas as easy as picking cherries. Some days we've had as many as twenty rabbits; our Mother used to keep four or five for us, then we'd take a couple down the village and give to Ted Carter and his Missus— they was an old couple who was very poor and they loved to get hold of a rabbit or two. "Best take one to your Auntie Florrie as well," our Mother would say, "not that she deserves one," she would add, but we boys never asked why.

'The rest we sold cheaply to the folk in the village, giving our Mother the money. "You're good boys to me," she would say with tears in her eyes, "I don't like to take it, but I must get Margie's boots mended for school on Monday."

'Ah,' Uncle Jesse went on, 'and other times we used to get hold of the long-tailed un's, was either when we'd had a good sharp hoar frost or perhaps arter that had been snowing all night. Well, we lads would get up early and pick the roosting pheasants awf the trees like picking pears. You see, when they a-bin perching all night and the snow 'ad settled on 'um, specially on their tails, thur was no warmth to melt it, and then along would come Jack Frost and freeze that snow hard—well, in the morning, the poor devils couldn't take off. Mind you, if we hadn't bin up to all them sort of games we should never 'ave made it, grub was that short and money was shorter.

'Course a lot of the credit should go to our Mother, for the wonderful meals as 'er cooked fer us. I reckon her was just about the best cook in the world, talk about make your mouth water, I regler froths at the mouth just thinking of they lovely meals.

'Course the gentry in them days, well most of um anyroad, thought as everything belonged to them and that nobody else should have anything. The lord of the manor in our village was Lord Boverton, owned a lot of land he did. Well, he was out one morning, riding round his estate on his horse when he came to his boundary where his land joined a small farmer's few acres, and the small farmer whose name was Parker was very busy cutting and laying a hedge. "Morning, squire," Jack Parker said politely, "Good morning, Parker," his lordship replied, "I'll bet you get hold of some of my pheasants when they stray on to your land don't you?" "Well," Parker replied, "if they strays on to my land they byent yours any longer be 'um, and I take a perticular notice as they don't stray back neither."'

'Uncle Jesse's mother used to put mushrooms in their rabbit pudding,' I said to our Mother, after we had been listening to him telling us tales of his youth.

'Ah well, perhaps his mother hadn't got seven hungry mouths to feed like I have. Besides,' she went on, 'I never seems to find any mushrooms at the same time as I gets hold of rabbits and vice versa, and don't forget,' she said, shouting at me, 'no going out until you've cleaned the knives and forks.' How I hated that chore, one which I had to do each week.

'I can't find the Monkey brand,'* I said, trying to get out of doing the job.

'There's none left and I got no money to buy any, you'll have to use elbow grease and ashes instead,' she cried.

Young as I was I knew what she meant by using ashes, but elbow grease I had never heard of before. I searched around in the back kitchen, amongst the old rag dusters and half tins of brasso and boot polish that had gone hard because someone had left the lid off. Then Betty came in, 'I can't find the elbow grease,' I said, and she burst out laughing.

'She can't find the elbow grease,' she cried going into the living-room, telling the rest of the family, and they all hooted with laughter and I burst out crying. Then Bunt came up to me.

'Don't take any notice of 'um, look this is elbow grease,' he said, 'just rubbing hard till you polishes it,' and he started to clean the knives. 'You just go and rout some fine ash from the grate and I'll help you.' So we cleaned the knives and forks together, spitting first on the rag, then dipping it in the ash and then rubbing very hard, with 'elbow grease'. Mind you, we only thought that it worked with spit; no doubt plain water would have worked just as well. One of the knives still smelt violently of onions (our Mother had been peeling some for dinner) and they must have been rather strong.

* Monkey brand was a block of sort of solid vim; you simply rubbed knives and forks across it and it made them shiny. Of course, they were made of steel in those days.

'You'd better go and put him in the garden,' Bunt said, 'that'll start her off again if you don't.' So I went outside and plunged the knife blade down into the earth several times, until all trace of the onion smell had gone. Then I wiped the knife, put it in the box with the others and was soon off out again. If our Mother was in a bad mood, the best thing was to keep well out of the way until whatever was causing it had passed. But mostly I think it was because half the time she did not know where the next shilling was coming from.

I went in search of Uncle Jesse, but could not find him. He had not seemed too well lately, he would tell us one story and then say 'that's all for today you kids, I got a bit of a head, I shall have to go and lie down'.

A few weeks later when we came home from school our Mother said, 'They took Uncle Jesse away last night to Woodstock work-house, he's pretty bad I think.'

Two days later we heard that he had died, but I cannot remember what he died from. Poor old Uncle Jesse. He had fought for his country and had saved a prairie in Canada, and now he was gone. We children missed him and his cheery stories, but the rest of the villagers went on as if nothing had happened.

In my childhood the seasons seemed to dominate our lives. In winter we did not go far afield, perhaps into the next village or into town, but when the spring sunshine broke through and there were violets down the lane our Mother would say, 'Ah, if 'tis like this come Saturday, we'll walk over to see Auntie May.' She lived about four miles away in the next village but one to us and she and Uncle Patrick were distantly related to us. 'Their cat walked across our garden,' was the expression Mother used when people asked what the relationship to our family was.

But come Saturday, most likely the east wind was rushing down from Siberia or wherever it came from and the trip to Auntie May's would be put off time and time again.

Then we would wake up one morning to find that spring had really arrived, the air was soft and balmy, birds were tearing about the sky like rockets, courting and building nests, and the wall-flowers smelling sweet underneath the window.

'I've sent Auntie May a card,' Mother would announce, 'to ask if it's all right for us to go over on Saturday.'

Back came a message to say 'be sure and come in time for dinner'. So we set off, our Mother, Betty, Mick, Ben, and me. My two elder brothers, Bern and Bunt, were old enough to do a job of work on Saturdays and they did not think much of it when they knew that we were going off for the day. Ben and Mick rode in the pram while Betty and I trailed behind. Before we had gone far I started to cry—I wanted to have a ride too. In the end our Mother gave in, she shoved Mick up nearer Ben and then balanced me on the end of the pram. My weight almost tipped it up. It was not long before Mick started wailing 'our Mollie's sitting on my legs, they be gone to sleep'. Protesting strongly I was dumped down again.

'Catch hold of her hand, Bet,' our Mother shouted, 'and help her along. If there's going to be crying I shan't bring you next time,' she threatened, so I wiped my eyes and nose on the sleeve of my coat and strode along as fast as I could. I certainly did not ever want to miss the treat that we knew awaited us at Auntie May's. You see, Uncle Patrick worked in a grocer's shop in the town a couple of miles away, and one of his perks was that he was able to buy odd bits of bacon, and for three pence he could get enough to make a big pudding. And always when we visited them Auntie May would make the loveliest boiled bacon and onion clanger that I have ever tasted. It slipped out of the wet pudding cloth onto a great oval dish, a big damp, shiny, steaming, succulent pudding. Then with her hand raised high in the air Auntie May would plunge the knife into it, revealing slivers of pink bacon and releasing a luscious smell which made our nostrils twitch and our mouths water.

'You certainly makes a good pudding,' our Mother remarked, as we all tucked into the feast, 'and just look at the bacon!'—indeed there was more bacon than onion.

'Well, it's nice to see you all enjoying it,' Auntie May said, 'our little Marion wun't touch it.' White-faced Marion sat at the end of the table, toying with a boiled egg that she had insisted on having. But to us the meal was a feast of the gods.

Auntie May was comfortably rounded; she had wispy grey hair and a complexion like an orange, and false teeth that clicked and clacked as she spoke. Uncle Patrick was as lean as a greyhound in training, a quiet solitary man who liked nothing better than to work in the peace of his potting shed or sit in their stuffy front parlour and read. 'Read hisself silly, thas what he'll do,' Auntie May would cry, 'dun't know how I ever come to marry such a mouse, that I dun't.'

But we all knew. One hot summer, after the First World War, she had cornered him in her father's pigsty and seduced him. Every night young Auntie May, a slip of a girl of seventeen, lured young Patrick Day into the pigsty. For two whole weeks the passionate love affair lasted. He had never been known to even look at a girl before. 'Didn't know what he'd got it for,' Auntie May told her friends afterwards. At the end of the fortnight Patrick emerged, a wiser, sadder young man, and a few weeks after Auntie May's mother made arrangements for them to marry as quickly as possible, 'to make an honest girl of our little May', she told the villagers. And twenty years on, history repeated itself. But instead of a pigsty it was an air-raid shelter at the bottom of their garden. There their only child Marion, blonde and as pretty as her mother had been, fell in love with an American soldier.

'Our poor innocent little Marion,' Auntie May cried when she discovered that her daughter was pregnant. After the war Marion and her husband Jake went off to the USA where they helped to populate an already over-populated country, producing eight boys in as many years.

But during those uncertain years between the wars Auntie May and Uncle Patrick were very kind to us. We often walked over to see them or they came over to visit us. Whenever we called, Auntie May would produce a piece of home-made cake or a few sweets tucked away in an old tin. If we called on a Sunday then Uncle Patrick would be home and he would always find something interesting to show us. One year it would be a robin who had built her nest in his old gardening jacket as it hung behind the potting shed door. Another time a pair of blackbirds built their nest in his pea sticks that were propped up against the wall.

'Can't disturb 'um,' he told us. 'I shall have to go awf on my bike presently and cut some more sticks, thur's plenty down Ham Lane.' And the blackbird sat there, bright-eyed and trusting, as Uncle Patrick showed us the beautifully made nest.

Another thing we enjoyed was playing with Marion's toys; she seemed to have so many, more than we ever dreamed of. But we were a bit too boisterous and rowdy for her really, and I got into awful trouble once for teaching her cheeky rhymes. Of course she had to go and say one in front of the vicar when he had called to see her father one day about the local fête. She went dancing into the room and swinging her knickers in her hand she chanted:

> What's the time?
> Half-past nine,
> Hang your knickers
> On the line,
> When the soldiers come along
> Hurry up and put them on.

At that time it seemed strange to us children that Auntie May and Uncle Patrick did not seem to be the least bit interested in one another, and only spoke to each other when it was absolutely necessary. Auntie May used to tell everybody that he'd 'never touched her' since the pigsty affair; she would say, 'reckon he's all dried up, 'tis a wonder I ent gone off with somebody else affor now.'

Then one day, soon after Marion had sailed off to America for good, Uncle Pat was missing. He had set off on his bike for work as usual with no more than a flask of tea and his dinner tin in an imitation leather bag, and his old raincoat strapped on the carrier where he always carried it in case of rain. But he never arrived at the grocer's shop where he had boned bacon and skinned cheeses and patted butter into half-pound slabs for the last twenty-five years. Rivers were dragged and hospitals phoned but no trace of him could be found. And the village gossips reckoned that he had probably gone off because he could not stand the sight of Auntie May any more. Which was what *had* happened, but it was over two years before we really knew the details.

Poor Auntie May was furious when it finally dawned on her that Uncle Pat had just walked out on her, and after waiting over a year without a word from him she sold up their little home and went off to America to live with Marion and Jake and their children, only to die of a heart attack within three months of settling there.

Then about a year after her death a curious thing happened. Back came Uncle Patrick, now a changed man. There was a jaunty air about him and he had got the merriest twinkle in his eye. And he had brought with him a small gentle woman—the new Mrs Day in fact, and it was obvious that they worshipped each other. The villagers accepted them at once, and only then did we learn what had happened to him since he had ridden away on that lovely May morning over two years ago.

He told our Mother, 'It was such a perfect morning, Kate, and I thought to myself as I rode along that life was too short and too precious to waste any longer, and I asked myself, what had I done? What had I seen in all those years? It wasn't until I got within a hundred yards of the International Stores that I made up me mind that I'd ride off, away from everything. So instead of gettin' awf me bike when I got to the shop, I just kept on going. I didn't really mean to hurt May, I should have told her I was going awf, but honest, I only made me mind up on the spur of the moment. Well, I rode and rode for miles, only stopping to have a bit of food and drink, then when evening come I was miles away and I thought, ah, Pat me boy, you can't go back now, so I slept agen an old hayrick, must have slept like a babe too, for the next thing

207

I knew was that a farm worker was prodding me and asking me what the hell I was doing. Well, we had a little chinwag, seemed an understanding sort of chap and he said that his gaffer would most likely take me on, casual like. They were a bit short-handed and there was plenty of hoeing and beet singling to be done. By golly, Kitty, I don't think I've ever bin so tired before; them first days hoeing nearly creased me. I was that weary at night I went straight off to sleep. Ah, I had lodgings with the fellow who'd found me under the rick, nice couple they was, he and his wife, so I stayed with um all that summer.

'Then come autumn I moved on, I'd saved quite a bit of my earnings so felt that I could now see some of the countryside, before winter set in. Oh, I did enjoy that autumn; I rode through the Lake District, through the industrial north and on again through Yorkshire, where the sheep graze over the mountains. One day, in November, I was riding through a biggish town, so I stopped at a provision shop to stock up my supplies, always carried some food with me I did. Well, I went into the shop and talk about chaos. Apparently that morning the manager and two assistants had all gone down with 'flu, the undermanager had been taken off to the local infirmary after being involved in an accident, that only left two young girls in the rather big grocers. I asked for cheese, there was no one to skin one they said. I asked for bacon, there was none boned. Neither of the girls had been there long enough to learn either of these jobs, people were coming into the shop and going out again pretty quick when they found they couldn't get what they wanted.

'So I said to one of the girls, "Could I help you, miss? I used to work in a shop like this. I could skin a cheese or bone a side of bacon for you." The girl looked at me a bit hard, didn't know what to say, poor devil, she'd never been in charge before. And besides, I expect she thought I'd make off with the takings when her back was turned. So I said, "It's all right my dear, you can keep your cash desk locked. I shouldn't blame you, you've never set eyes on me before."

'Well, three weeks later I was still there, ah and I got on well with the staff and customers. When the manager come back he offered me a permanent job, but I turned it down. 'Twas time I set out over the hills again. Well, I spent most of the winter in Scotland. Think of it, Kitty, I'd hardly been out of the village before. I done mostly farm work, there was plenty of threshing work and potato sorting on a big farm where they grew special seed spuds. As I come back down the country I called at a Post Office in Leeds where I'd written and asked our vicar to write to me. There were four letters from him, course they was months old, and in one he told me about May's sudden death.

'I felt quite sick for days, guilty conscience I suppose, walking out on her like that, but there hadn't been a shred of real love between us.

''Twas a beautiful spring that year, the countryside was so green and fresh and new and I thought that it was a sort of omen, maybe, it was a sign of a fresh start for me. Again I done all sorts of jobs, sometimes I even called back on farmers that I'd worked for the year before; they was all pleased to see me and would set me to work if there was any extra hands needed. Then I got a job near to Rotherham. I felt quite excited. but didn't know why, it was in this town that I'd worked in the grocer's shop. So I called to see how they all were and was given such a welcome. Then the girl who'd been scared for me to help them came into the shop. She'd been out to the storeroom, she blushed when she saw me, and that was that. We just fell in love there and then I reckon. Course I know I was eighteen years older than her, but it didn't matter. So I got a job in another shop in the same town and lodged with her folks. We never got married till just before I came back here. Somehow I wanted to come back home, course I didn't know how the people would be, me riding off like that, but I thinks most of them understood.'

'Well, as the years went by Uncle Pat became a parish councillor and a church warden and both he and his wife took an active part in the life of the village. They died within a week of one another; she went first, then Uncle Patrick just slipped away having nothing left to live for. They are buried together in the little overgrown churchyard; a simple tombstone reads

'Lucy and Patrick Day
died June 1963
Servants of God'

At Uncle Patrick's wish their ages were not carved on the stone for, as he told the vicar once, 'In my eyes my Lucy is still a young girl and I'm her young man, the only pity is that we didn't meet years ago.'

II

Dumble Dads and Foster Mums

IT was just a turn of fate that Clarrie Ford became our Auntie. For Clarrie was already 'bespoke' to a young man in the next village where she came from, when she met our Uncle Fred, and he, at that particular time, already had an 'understanding' with eighteen-year-old Daisy Simms, who lived next door to him and his widowed mother. Daisy was away in service and Uncle Fred only saw her about twice a year. But they were saving up to get married; Daisy already had a fair-sized bottom drawer, filled with embroidered cushion covers, crochet-edged tablecloths and beautifully made chemises, knickers and camisoles, lace-edged and feather stitched.

Fred was saving all he could; he had an old tea caddie, which he kept for safety under the bed. The caddie was filled with florins and half-crowns, along with several silver threepenny bits.

He was under-gardener up at the big house. There were four gardeners employed there and his wages were eighteen shillings a week, but it was a good steady job and there was a chance that he might become head-gardener in time.

But one day in early summer, about two months after Clarrie Ford had arrived at the big house, where she held the post as under parlourmaid, a strange thing happened that was to alter the lives of Clarrie Ford and our Uncle Fred Brown. Mind you, Fred had noticed that there was a new maid who sat along with the other servants when they attended evensong in the parish church, where he also worshipped. From his pew at the back of the church he noticed that the new maid wore a pretty mauve hat with a sprig of flowers in the front; she was an attractive little thing, neat and perky. Not that she ever glanced in Fred's direction, but each Sunday after the service he would wait by the church gate, along with the other lads of the village to glance shyly at the group of servants as they came out looking very prim and precise, except the kitchen maid who was always at the back of the group; she was a hefty girl and used to turn round and poke out her tongue at the young men standing there awkward and uncomfortable in their best, tight-fitting, navy-blue Sunday suits.

But on this particularly lovely summer evening Clarrie somehow got parted from the little group of servants as they came out of the church gate, so Fred quickly walked alongside her and started to chat, first about the weather, then he asked her about her job.

She started to tell him, then said, 'Really, I should go along with the others, we are supposed to keep together.'

'Well,' Fred replied, 'we'll just follow behind them,' and for a little while they walked along together not speaking a word.

A few minutes later Fred said, 'We could go the field way, it's a lovely walk along by the river, and just as quick as the road way, we shall be at the big house as soon as they,' he said nodding in the direction of the little group walking in front.

Well, Clarrie said that it was a beautiful evening and she had never been along by the river path. As Fred helped her over the stile he noticed that she had dainty small feet and slim ankles. Whatever would Daisy think of him? Fred though, here he was, strolling along the field path on a lovely summer evening with a strange girl, and she was laughing up into his eyes quite friendly like.

Fred showed Clarrie a yellowhammer's nest tucked away in an old willow tree. He was glad that now she seemed in no hurry at all to rejoin the other girls.

Then Fred said, 'Would you like to sit down for a few minutes?' It was pleasant and peaceful with the sun quite warm. He spread his handkerchief on the grass, for Clarrie to sit on, 'Just so you won't get no grass marks on that nice suit,' he added.

Clarrie sat down, carefully smoothing her pale grey skirt so that only her trim ankles peeped underneath. Fred sat stiffly beside her, as she told him about her home back in a small village in Wiltshire.

Suddenly, Fred had the shock of his life.

Up leapt shy, timid Clarrie, screaming and shouting 'Tak um off, take um off.' She was dancing and jumping about on that sunny bank like someone demented.

For a moment Fred did not know what to do. He thought perhaps she was throwing a fit, like one of the boys in his class at school used to. Then she started to pull her skirt up—above her knees—still shouting take um off, take um off, over and over again. Then Fred noticed that her long white drawers and petticoat were covered with small brown objects; poor Clarrie had been sitting on a bumble bees' (dumble Dad's) nest and they were stinging her in the most delicate of places.

'You just hang on,' Fred cried leaping to his feet, then he knelt down beside the poor girl but, short of taking her drawers off he did not know what to do. Then he said, 'I know what, I'll squeeze um dead and you shake um out.' And that was how Bill Bates the head-keeper found them, Fred on his knees finding and squeezing the bees that were inside Clarrie's drawers and Clarrie shaking them down on the ground.

But that was not how Bill Bates *saw* them. Here was young Fred Brown, a good, clean-living fellow, supposedly engaged to Daisy Simms, who was working away in service, gamboling about on the river bank with one of the servants from the big house, and she was letting Fred fondle her thighs and her with her skirt held waist high so that he could do it.

And it was no good them trying to make excuses—he had caught them red-handed and he would report the incident at once to the Master and Mistress.

What followed during the next week or so was almost unbeliev-able; nobody would listen when either of them tried to explain, least of all Lord and Lady Speak for whom they both worked. Her

Ladyship sent for the pair of them the next morning and insisted that they should get married as soon as possible. If this scandalous thing should get to the ear of their friends Lady Speak said they would be the laughing stock of the county.

'You'll make an honest woman of her young man,' she went on, 'not here in the village, oh no, we can't have that, I'll fix it up at Sodbury registry office for next week, the sooner this dreadful business dies down the better. You can have the small cottage at Penn Lodge,' she went on, 'I'll send Dawkins along to see that it's cleaned up, then we'll find some bits and pieces to furnish it until you can buy your own.'

'B—but,' stammered Fred, 'I'm already sort of engaged to be mar . . .', but her Ladyship cut in. 'You should have thought of that last night young man; now off you go the pair of you and get on with your duties. Come and see me at eight o'clock tonight, and by then I shall have fixed up when you can be married. And thank your lucky stars young man that my husband didn't sack you on the spot, and you young woman can leave the day you marry, I don't want anyone fainting and falling about here.'

Poor Clarrie and Fred; they had only known each other for a few hours and, here they were, destined to spend the rest of their life together.

Clarrie wore her best mauve costume to be married in and cook pinned a few flowers on it for her. Fred wore his best navy serge suit that he had had for his father's funeral five years previously. His widowed mother, just as bemused as the unfortunate pair, decided not to act as witness at the wedding.

'I'd not no Sunday go tu meeting clothes, Kitty,' she told our Mother, 'And I was worried tu death, I didn't know how I was going to manage without our Fred's bit of money and, anyhow, I was living in a tied cottage, and I knawed the squire ud ave me out, once our Fred was married.'

But things turned out fine for them all. Fred and Clarrie were as happy as sandboys, with Fred's mother living with them. Clarrie used to help in the fields whenever there was a bit of extra work to do; they had four strapping boys, although it was two years before the first was born.

We did not visit them often, although they only lived a couple of miles away. But if we could get the woman at the lodge gate to let us take a short cut through the park, then it was only about a mile. Each time she said the same thing, ''tis more than my life's worth, to let you through, if ever I was found out my Herbert 'ud get the sack.' But she always gave in, 'go on then, but keep to that little grass path and be quiet'. We thanked her and squittered quickly into the green tunnel of hazel bushes that led to Auntie Clarrie's and Uncle Fred's cottage.

It was ten years since the Dumble Dad incident; Fred's mother had died and Clarrie no longer helped on the farm, but stayed home and looked after their four growing boys and Uncle Fred.

Auntie Clarrie was in a bit of a state the day we called. Her broody hen that had been sitting on thirteen lovely brown eggs had suddenly 'gone off her brood', and had left the eggs, which Auntie Clarrie said were already pipped and should have hatched out the next day.

'I've been all over the place', she cried tearfully, 'to try and borrow a "sitty" hen, but you know how it is at this time of the year, everybody doing the same thing, trying to get a few chicks off so as they gets a good supply of eggs come next winter.'

'Whatever shall I do?' she went on. 'I can't set on um meself, can I?, but if I don't soon do summut about it it'll be too late, they chicks ull be dead affor they be out of the shell.'

'Ent you got a foster moster?' our Mother asked her.

Clarrie looked bewildered, 'A what?' she cried.

'Well have you got a mop head? a new one would be best,' our Mother said. Clarrie rushed out to the back kitchen and came back almost at once clutching a new mop head. 'Bought it only last week', she said, 'when I went into Witney market.'

'I shall want a piece of thickish string,' our Mother said, as she went down the garden path to where the big square box which served as a hatching house was, as was customary, the open front of the box had spars of wood fixed across, so that a broody hen could just get her head and neck through to feed, and later the chicks would be able to get through the slots to the run, but the clucking mother hen would be inside. But there was no broody hen in this box, just a nest of eggs carefully covered with a piece of flannel to help them keep warm.

Our Mother quickly tied the string to the mop head, then lowered it down onto the eggs, covering them with the woolly strands. Then she got a piece of wood, tied the string to it and fixed in on to the top of the box, adjusting it so that all the time the mop head rested on the eggs.

'Now when the chicks begins to hatch out,' our Mother told her, 'you just gently raise the mop head about a couple of inches, that'll keep 'um warm enough and they'll never know the difference.'

Auntie Clarrie was overjoyed. 'God bless you, Auntie Kitty,' she cried, 'I shall never be able to thank you enough.'

After they had had a cup of tea our Mother said we best be getting off home, and anyway it looked like rain. So off we traipsed, creeping stealthily along the grass path. We spoke in whispers lest anyone should hear us, then slipped silently through the little gate at the side of the lodge that the lady had left open for us.

We turned our faces towards home, when suddenly the heavens opened—it did not stop to rain, but came down like stair-rods.

We sheltered for a little while, but we were all drenched anyway, so our Mother said we might as well get off home. 'Come on,' she cried 'best foot forward', and we trudged along wet, cold and miserable.

Suddenly, holding her left foot up Betty cried, 'Look at my sole.' It had almost parted company with the rest of the boot.

'God in Heaven, what shall I do?' our Mother wailed, 'ten shillings and sixpence I paid for them last week and the man said they was leather, it's nothing but cardboard,' she cried. 'We shall have to tie it up with something.' The loose sole looked like a big gaping mouth.

Up went her skirt and she whipped off one of her elastic garters which held up her stockings. Then she twisted it double over the arch of Betty's boot and around the sole. 'Well, at least it won't get any worse,' she said. 'Your father will have to mend it before you wear um again.'

With nothing to keep her bagging stocking up she just took it off and stuffed it in her coat pocket, 'I'm Diddle didle dumpling,' she said laughing at her misfortune, 'only its one stocking off instead of a shoe.'

A couple of days later Uncle Fred arrived unexpectedly, on the back of his bike, he had got a big brown parcel. He handed it to our Mother saying, 'Clarrie hopes you won't be offended, Kitty, but her was that grateful for what you done, we got thirteen lovely strong chicks, ah, every one hatched off and they be doing fine. You see, Kitty,' he went on, 'always at this time of the year her Ladyship gives us a big box of clothes, her 'ave done it ever since our hurried wedding, but some of it ent no good to us and Clarrie thought as you could make use of it.'

'You know what the good Book says,' our Mother cried as she unfolded the parcel of clothes. 'Cast your bread on the waters', she said, as tears of thankfulness trickled down her cheeks.

Although we were quite content to roam the fields and lanes near home, or play games near the cottage, when our Mother did suggest going out, even to the next village, we children would get very excited. We always enjoyed the jaunts we made with her. She made them so interesting that they seemed to be a cross between a nature study and a general knowledge lesson, and lots of fun all rolled into one. She would point out and explain things of interest to us and show us what we could or could not eat when it came to wild berries, fruits and fungus.

'See these,' she cried one day, pointing out a 'death cap' mushroom with its greeny white cap, '*Never, ever* touch one of these or you know what you'll be doing, in very quick time too, pushing up daisy roots.'

'And just look at this,' she would say, pausing for a few minutes to show us bee orchids that we might otherwise have missed, or perhaps a clump of wild thyme, which would start her reciting Shakespeare:

> I know a bank whereon the wild thyme blows
> Where oxlips and the nodding violet grows
> Quite over-canopied with luscious woodbine
> With sweet musk-roses and with eglantine.

'Ah now, there was a clever man, Shakespeare,' she said, 'I've read quite a lot of his works, started when I was at school. The teacher would lend me books of her own, cos I'd read everything in the School Library betime I was eleven. I used to smuggle a bit of candle into my bedroom whenever I could, so that I could read in bed—course I wasn't supposed to and I'd half screen the lighted candle under the bedclothes if I heard my parents about. Course, reading was frowned on in them days, well by ordinary folk anyhow. But,' she went on with a proud tone in her voice, 'I've never forgotten what I read, or regretted it either.'

A trip which we always enjoyed was one that we usually made about twice a year, to the little village of Peasfield, about three miles away and where an old friend of the family, Aunt Annie Edwards as we called her, lived. She had been a great friend of our Mother's for years and was particularly kind to her when our father died, and the friendship continued when our Mother married again, for Aunt Annie Edwards thought that our stepfather was a grand fellow.

She lived on her own in a tiny stone cottage, low-beamed and with small lattice windows whose sills were always crammed with scented geraniums.

'Go on,' she said to me one day, 'just pinch a leaf between your finger and thumb and sniff.' I did as she said and put my hand to my nose savouring that haunting lingering perfume, a smell which to this day still brings back a clear picture of Aunt Annie Edwards and her little stone cottage, with its garden jam-packed with flowers, a colourful crowded patch which she did all herself.

On one of our visits our Mother happened to remark how strong and healthy the plants and flowers in the garden all looked. Aunt Annie admitted that she 'emptied the slops' over her roses, and she went on, 'You must agree, Kitty, they be fine blooms, and the day as they fits we up with water closets u'll be a sad day for we, 'cos the only manure as I ever uses is from my old privvy— well apart from the horse droppings I gets from the road. Oh ah,' she went on laughingly, 'thurs a proper fight between I and my neighbour as to who gyets out with a bucket and shovel first. Bless 'e, I be out there that quick sometimes a-gatherin' it up, that's still steaming when I puts it on the gyarden.'

Bless her heart, she need not have worried about the coming of the water closets for it was the late 1960s before her village was put on the sewer and by that time Aunt Annie had been dead for twenty years.

One of the reasons for our visit to Aunt Annie's in later summer was that, across the fields from her cottage, were the remains of an old orchard where trees bearing small blue early plums, which we called cunigars, grew. These small plums made the most delicious jam—although our stepfather declared that it was 'all stones'.

'Ah,' our Mother would reply, 'them as eats most jam, gets the most stones, and anyway if I was to take um out when I made the jam thur'd be nothing left, so you'll have to put up with um.'

Of course we girls, Betty, Mick, and I, loved to get plenty of stones, so that we could play 'this year, next year, sometime, never' with them, in a vain attempt to find out when, or if, we should get married.

We would wait for a postcard from Aunt Annie telling us that the plums were ripe. Our Mother usually received the card about the last week in August. When we grew up we would go over on our bikes, but while we were young our Mother either pushed the smaller ones in the pram or in Kitty Moore's bath chair, with us older ones tagging on behind.

One hot humid August day our Mother looked at the cloudy sky. We had planned to go to Aunt Annie's straight after our dinner, a make-do meal of bubble-and-squeak and cold bread pudding.

'I don't reckon that it'll rain before night,' she said, as we all went out to view the weather prospects. 'Ah,' she cried excitedly, pointing to a break in the clouds, 'that'll be fine all right; as long as you can see a bit of blue sky up thur big enough to patch "Billy Peglar's britches", that rain will keep off.' This was one of the old weather predictions that her father had passed on to her. He had been a shepherd all his life and was very knowledgeable when it came to weather lore.

As we trudged along the roads we saw several farm wagons as they passed to and from the harvest fields. They were pulled by great sweating cart horses, and the carts were so wide and the country roads so narrow that we had to squeeze ourselves up against the hedge as the big Oxfordshire wagons went by. They were simply overflowing with sheaves of corn, and the hedges were draped with corn stalks where the brambles had caught them.

'Come on,' our Mother shouted to us, 'you leaze* all you can, whatever we gets will feed our hens. Not like when I was young,' she went on, 'then we had to go leazing properly, not for the hens but for us. When we had got a nice lot my dad would take the corn up to old Jack Wheeler the miller and he'd grind it into lovely white flour. Ah,' she went on, 'that flour used to last us all winter fer cakes and puddings and my mother used to make her own bread in the winter if the roads was too bad fer baker Clegg to come our way delivering.'

* Collecting up any ears of wheat left behind after the men had cleared a harvest field of stooks.

The time passed quickly as our Mother told us tales of her youth, so that the journey to Peasfield seemed to take no time at all.

We arrived at Aunt Annie's about two o'clock. She had got the kettle singing away on the hob and soon we were all enjoying a hot cup of tea and a chunk of her dripping cake. Presently she said, 'Who'd like another piece?' Five pairs of hungry eyes faced Aunt Annie as we replied in a chorus, 'I would, please.' It had been a long, hot walk and we were always hungry.

As soon as the teapot had been drained of every drop and our Mother and Aunt Annie had had a good chatter, we made our way up the bumpy cart track, each armed with bags and baskets, and with Aunt Annie striding out as if she was off on a five-mile walk, her walking stick helping her along. But the stick was really for hooking down the high branches. There was always a risk that someone had been to cunigars before us; usually we were lucky, although I remember two or three times when we found very few plums. Then Aunt Annie would make it up to us by stacking the well of the old pram with pots of her home-made jam, and maybe a jar or two of honey, which she took from her own skip that she kept at the end of her long garden. And a bottle of her rhubarb wine for our stepfather.

Sometimes we would walk up the fields beyond the old orchard to gather early blackberries, especially on one occasion when we found no plums at all; Betty had gone on in front and we could see her busily picking blackberries. Then she came running back towards us, she was eager to show our Mother what a lot she had found, when suddenly she caught her foot in a bramble and she, and the almost full basket of blackberries, went flying onto the thick grass.

'Oh, dear,' our Mother cried as she sank down on to her knees, 'we shall have to pick up as many as we can as they're too precious to waste.' Suddenly she grabbed at something in the grass and shouted excitedly to us 'Look what I found!' In her hand she held a struggling leveret, that had been so frightened by the noise of humans that it had crouched petrified in the grass hoping that no one would see it. Quick as a flash our Mother held it up by the back legs and whacked the kicking animal on the back of its neck with the side of her other hand and in a moment the once vibrant body was still.

'Ah, that will make us a good meal,' she said as she knelt down again to retrieve the rest of the spilt fruit, then again there were wild shouts of joy, 'If the Lord don't come he sends,' she shouted, using one of her favourite expressions, and she held out her careworn hands which were full of large, pink mushrooms. She called to Aunt Annie so that she might share her good fortune and they knelt down on the grass together almost as if in prayer. I can see my Mum now kneeling there, her straw hat askew, her face russet red with excitement. I heard her say to Aunt Annie, 'If our Bet hadn't tripped with them blackberries we shouldn't have had neither leveret nor mushrooms, ent we the luckiest people.'

''Tis funny,' Aunt Annie remarked, 'I've lived yer all me life and I've never knowd mushrooms grow in this field affore; still,' she went on, 'now I comes to think of it, old Jack Phipps did have his horses up yer fer a time, back end of last summer I thinks t'was, and they do say as you'll find mushrooms wherever horses have been.'

Content with our finds we wandered back to the cottage. Then another cup of tea and another slice of Aunt Annie's dripping cake and we were off on the road towards home again. We turned to wave to her before we passed round the bend of the road and out of sight of her little stone cottage. She stood there waving to us, a tall, well-built upright woman despite her sixty-odd years.

I must have been about seventeen when I last visited Aunt Annie, but by then she was 'too ett up wi rheumatism' to make the journey up the rough cart track to the cunigars. I was wearing a pair of my eldest brother's trousers (I had borrowed them unbeknown to him), and Aunt Annie was disgusted. 'Making yourself look like a fellow' she said, 'I don't know what the world's coming to.'

But my brother found that I had worn his only good pair of flannels, for they were covered in green where I had brushed against the old tree trunks as I gathered the plums; and to make matters worse I had got oil on the turn-ups off my old bike chain, which I had carefully oiled to make the bike ride easier.

My brothers and step-brothers continue to go to cunigars each year up until the outbreak of the Second World War, but by then I had found other paths to tread.

12

Rhymes and Relations

THINKING back, I am sure that our Mother was the inventor of occupational therapy.

When we got too big for hidings, or when she realized that they ceased to have the right effect on us, she thought up jobs for us to do that were far more effective than a good clout behind the ear. Sometimes she found us jobs to do just so that we would not get bored and consequently into mischief, and sometimes because she did not want us to play with the children who happened to be out in the street, and sometimes just out of plain cussedness.

One day Mick and I had to take the two youngest, Ben and Denis, for a walk: our instructions were to keep them out of our Mother's way until dinner-time, a matter of about three hours.

'And take them up the Curbridge Road,' she called to us as we pushed the old pram out of the gate.

All went well for the first hour, then the boys began to get restless, so we stopped by one of Strange's fields. I lifted them out of the pram and we all went into the field and sat down by an old pond. When we got tired of throwing stones in the boys started chasing each other round it, while Mick and I gathered up some kindling wood. I had just turned round to put the wood in the pram when there was a yell from Denis who had fallen into the green, slimy pond and was floundering about in the middle. I waded in and dragged him out: he had swallowed some of the stinking water and was coughing and spluttering and very wet.

'We'd best get him home quick,' I yelled. Denis was very prone to chesty colds. If we left him to dry it would be tempting providence. So we packed the boys into the pram and started to push like mad, running and careering down the road as if we were being chased by the old nick himself. But we had forgotten about the great potholes, we hit one at speed and over went the pram, boys, wood, and us. Ben and Denis began to yell at the tops of their voices. Ben had a nasty cut over his left eye and was bleeding like a stuck pig. Denis, thankfully, had landed on the wood, which had saved him from hitting the rough road, and seemed none the worse for the fall. We picked up the wood, piled it back in the pram, carefully sitting the boys on top and crept slowly home.

Our Mother was furious, 'You'll go without your dinner, both of you,' she cried as she bathed Ben's cut eye, 'you shan't go out any more today, you can spend the rest of your time ravelling.'

Mick and I looked at the sack in the corner of the room, it was full to the brim with bits of cloth, mostly of the looser woven type. All this had to be unravelled. First we had to cut the cloth into smallish squares, then each thread could be pulled out in short strands. Our Mother used it to fill cushions and pillows, and sometimes she would even add some to an old mattress to help make it a little more comfortable. Ravelling was a long, boring job and one that often fell to Mick and me. To make the time pass quicker we would tell each other rhymes and jingles, laughing and giggling into the piles of unwoven threads. Even so, if she thought that we were enjoying the job, our Mother would shout, 'And shut up that gigglin' or I'll knock your two heads together.' As soon as she was out of earshot we would start again.

'You heard this 'un?' Mick asked. 'Teddy Simpson told it me yesterday, it's a good 'un.'

> In days of old
> When knights were bold
> And paper wasn't invented,
> They used blades of grass
> To wipe their ass
> And went away contented.

We nearly exploded as we tried to stifle our laughter, getting redder and redder in the face as we did so.

Suddenly I wanted to go to the lavatory. I shot off down to the bottom of the garden. The day was hot and sultry and I had to shoo dozens of wasps and flies out of the privy before I could sit down and do 'me bounden duty' as Missus-next-door called it. There was a good supply of torn-up newspapers and magazines hung up behind the door. This was another of our Mother's occupational jobs. If you were a bit cheeky to her she would soon have you tearing paper into sizeable squares, then you had to pierce a hole through each piece with an old steel meat skewer and thread the lot into a piece of string and hang it up behind the door—for the use of.

It made good reading material too. You could pull off a couple of sheets and sit there in comfort then, just as you got to an interesting piece, there would be a hurried search through the thick pad hoping to find the rest of the story. I reckon I did most of my reading down there. Living in a crowded cottage as we did, the lavatory was the one place where you could find a bit of peace—apart from the flies. But even if there wasn't much to read, it was nice to sit there with the door open at about forty-five degrees, with one foot on either side of the door, one to keep it open and one to stop it from shutting. Then if you heard somebody coming down the path, all you did was to move your left foot out of the way, give a quick shove with your right one and the door would shut.

But, undisturbed, you could sit down there for ages with the sunshine pouring in, relaxed, comfortable, and dreaming. Or maybe watch a spider catch and eat a fly that he had caught in the huge cobweb which always seemed to fill the far corner, or count the leaves of a piece of waywind (bindweed) that had forced its way through the wooden sides of the lavatory and was winding its way up to the low ceiling, or just sit there and sing, as Missus-next-door did sometimes. There was only a wooden partition between our privy and theirs, so you could hear everything that was going on. Once when Bern, the eldest, was in ours and Missus-next-door was in theirs, she started to sing in a high piping voice, 'I be fer ever Blowing Bubbles' and my cheeky brother called out, 'Ah and that ent the only thing you be blowing, Missus.'

When she told our Mother that Bern had been cheeky to her, he had to either go and dig the garden all day or spend the whole of Saturday and Sunday wooding, as a punishment.

Suddenly the quiet air was shattered, our Mother in full voice hollered from the house, 'Come on out of there, Mollie, you've been down there half an hour already. If there's anything wrong with you, you can have an extra dose of senna pods tonight.' At that threat I dragged my knickers up quickly and was soon back indoors, back to the eternal ravelling.

Dinner time came and went, but our Mother kept her word and we remained in the corner, our fingers automatically pulling out threads, our eyes and minds on other things. About half-past three she said, 'All right, I think you've been punished enough, here, take this,' she said handing us each a huge chunk of bread and treacle, 'and go on out to play for an hour.' We grabbed the food and were out of the gate as fast as our legs would carry us.

'Wur yu bin all day?' Sally Parker said. 'We've had some lovely fun, you should a bin here.'

'Well, we are here now,' I said, 'what shall us play at?'

'Let's go and see if Perrit's plums be ripe, shall us, they be gone walking up to Witney, so they wunt be home yet.'

We ran off down to the village. 'Come on, let's go the back way,' I cried. So we made our way down Coltham which would bring us right at the bottom of Perrit's garden.

The plums hung fat, ripe, and pregnant, luscious red and gold in the quiet orchard. They were Mrs Perrit's pride and joy. She always won first prize at the annual flower show with her bottled Victorias and her lovely red plum jam.

A few wasps and blue-bottles buzzed about on the tops of the trees, sampling the over-ripe fruit: the afternoon was hot still and motionless, the plums waiting to be picked.

Pounds and pounds of those super summer fruits we ate. From tree to tree we moved, selecting only the biggest and best.

'Crickey,' Sally Parker said, 'I couldn't eat another, not if you was to give me a pound note. I be that blowed out I could bust,' she cried sprawling herself out on the warm grass. We flung ourselves down beside her, shutting our eyes, listening to the soft buzz of the wasps and flies, we were as full up and contented as a sty full of newly fed pigs.

Suddenly I heard Mr Perrit's affected voice saying, 'I think there's someone in the orchard, dear, I'll just change my clothes and go down and see.'

Of course Mr Perrit tried to be what we called 'a bit on the posh side', and would not have dreamed of going down the orchard in his best suit, not if all hell was let loose, which was very fortunate for us, because as soon as he and his wife had disappeared into the house we crept out the back way and were paddling in the nearby Windrush when he finally walked down the orchard. He stared across at us, a bunch of squealing girls splashing about in the sunshine, then he shook his head and went back indoors.

A few days later, when we got home from school, Mrs Perrit and our Mother were chattering by the gate. Mrs Perrit was just saying, 'Are you sure it wasn't your Micky and Mollie? My hubby said they were down that way.'

'I'm sure it wasn't my children,' our Mother replied sternly. 'I kept them in most of the day because they'd tipped the boys out of the pram in the morning, so they spent the rest of Saturday ravelling. No. I'm sure you're mistaken, Mrs Perrit, and before you start accusing my children, you just get your facts right,' and she flounced off indoors her face red with temper.

'Now we're for it,' I whispered to Mick. 'She will ask us if we was down there and we shall have to tell the truth.'

A loud yell from the house sent us scurrying indoors—'Damn and set fire to it,' our Mother cried lifting a smoking saucepan off the fire. 'Drat the woman and her blummen plums, I hope somebody pinches the rest of 'um, she made me forget me pudding and the darn thing has boiled dry.' The pudding was quickly transferred to another water-filled saucepan.

'Go on, Mollie,' she said, handing me the burnt black pot, 'see if you can get that clean and hurry, I shall want it to cook the spuds in soon.' So I was dispatched to the back kitchen and scrubbed away with salt and elbow grease for what seemed ages before I could get the thing clean; by then our Mother had thankfully forgotten to ask us if we knew anything about Mrs Perrit's vanishing plums. What retribution would have followed had she found out that we were the guilty party did not bear thinking about at the time. But now, when I sample the delight of Victoria plums, I am magically transferred back to the tidy orchard in Ducklington, to the fat, ripe, forbidden fruit, the juice of long-forgotten summers, of hot fly-filled afternoons, and the cool evening peace of the Windrush.

Some of the jobs our Mother gave us to do were not always because we had been disobedient, but just to that we would learn to use our own initiative.

When we were quite small she would make us rag dolls, but as we got older we were encouraged to make our own. Giving Mick and I a pair of her old stockinet knickers, she said, 'Go on, see who can be first to make and dress a doll.' We slit the knickers in half, taking a leg each sewing it up and stuffing it with ravelling to resemble the body and head of a doll. Of course we did not use the whole piece of material. I suppose the finished doll was about sixteen inches long. While our Mother had always used a bit of black wool for doll's hair, we wanted something different, so we walked up to Witney and prowled about round the railway goods yard looking for thick string that had been thrown on the ground. When we had gathered enough we took it home, unplaited the coarse yellow string which made lovely blond, crinkly hair. Shoe buttons were used for eyes and nose and a bit of red wool embroidered the mouth. The clothes were also made of wool which we gleaned from around the seats in the Leys, a recreation park in Witney. It was to here on summer afternoons that the ladies from the town pushed their prams; while their babies were taking advantage of the fresh air and sunshine, their mothers chatted and knitted. Quite long pieces of wool, from casting off and on and unpicking mistakes were thrown down. Matchsticks were used as knitting needles, for small fingers matchstick knitting was ideal. The whole operation of making and dressing a doll took a matter of weeks, for much of our spare time was taken up with looking after the younger boys, doing errands and helping in the house.

But through the hidings and the jobs came something else. Our Mother was really preparing us for the future: she knew what she wanted for her children and went all out to see that everyone of us had a good chance of getting it. She certainly was not 'soft' with us as were many of the village mothers with their children. At the time we hated this strict attitude of hers, but it was for our own good in the long run.

Much to her disgust, our stepfather used to come home and tell us ditties or parodies that he had picked up at work. There was not really anything wrong in them, but it was just that our Mother did not encourage us in that sort of thing. Still, he used to argue with her and say that if he did not tell us them we should most likely pick them up from the other children.

'That,' she said to our stepfather, 'is taking the Lord's name in vain,' when he was singing a ditty to get young Ben to take a Beecham pill. These pills were not too bad if you swallowed them quickly, before the sweet powdery coating was sucked away, but after that they were quite bitter. And this pill that Ben had so far refused had lost all its sweet covering. Despite her grumbling our stepfather sang again:

> Hark the herald angels sing
> Beecham pills are a very good thing

> Easy to take and meek and mild,
> Two for a man and one for a child.

As young Ben opened his mouth to laugh, our stepfather popped the pill in, and it had gone down before Ben realized it.

One day I was in the back kitchen singing away as I washed up when, wham, I had a good cuff behind the ear.

'What was that for?' I asked our Mother, as I rubbed my stinging ear.

'That,' she said, 'was for singing that dirty song, and don't you ever let me hear you singing it again, or you'll get a clout the other side.' I was dumbfounded. All the kids were singing it, we had sung it at the top of our voices as we came home from school—

> There was a bonny Scotsman
> At the battle of Waterloo,
> The wind blew up his petticoat
> And showed his 'ow-du-do'.
> His 'ow-du-do' was dirty,
> He showed it to the Queen,
> And she gave him sixpence
> To keep it nice and clean.

Another time our stepfather was walking down from the garden unconsciously singing a parody to 'Sonny Boy'. Mother was in the wash-house and just as he passed he sang:

> I know what you're after
> That place above my garter.

'What did I hear you sing?' she yelled, rushing out of the wash-house and facing him. He did not answer, but she went on, 'I don't care what you sing at work, but don't bring your filth home. What if the children heard you?'

But she need not have worried, we had already heard it but were much too young and green to know what he was singing about.

Sometimes relations and friends would drop in unexpectedly to see us, often round about teatime, and most likely we would have nothing but a cup of tea to offer them. On these occasions, while they sipped tea and chattered to the rest of the family, our Mother would disappear into the back kitchen for a few minutes. Quick as a flash she would mix together flour, marg, sugar, a handful of mixed dried fruit, and an egg and spread it on to a sandwich tin and slip it in the oven of the valor oil stove which our stepfather bought her. Then she would come back into the room and ask sweetly if anyone wanted another cup of tea, and by the time the kettle had boiled again and the tea cups refilled, the visitors were thoroughly enjoying the hot, crumbly cake, which our Mother called 'rub up'.

Life was like that, you simply lived from one day to the next, for nobody could afford to keep much of a store cupboard. Even things like cake and jam were eaten almost as soon as they were made. But our parents fed us well, food came first and foremost in our house.

Almost every morning we had porridge for breakfast. Our Mother made it that thick you could have stood a flagpole up in it. But the skill came when she produced tasty stews and soups from next to nothing. Rabbits were always plentiful and we ate them often. The funny thing was, it seemed, that I was the one that nearly always got the head, which had very little meat on. If I protested about the lack of meat, the family would say, 'Go on—there's the brains, you eat 'um, you can do with them, they'll do you good.' So I would pick away at the head; there was a *tiny* bit of meat on the jaw-line, and of course the white soft brains, which, at the time, I really believed did me good.

One night we were all sat round the table, having just finished our meal, and Bunt remarked laughingly, 'The Lord be praised, the belly's raised!' and we all started tittering.

'What did I hear you say?' our Mother cried angrily.

And Bunt only about twelve at the time, repeated the rhyme, only to be rewarded with a good cuff behind the ear—for taking the Lord's name in vain. 'Where on earth did you hear that?' our Mother asked him, she was furious.

'One of the boys at school said it after he'd had his dinner,' Bunt explained.

'Well, don't you let me hear you say it again,' she cried. 'You know how quick these others pick things up. And less of that tittering,' she yelled to the rest of us, 'or you will get a good smack.'

At that moment I let out a loud cry, one of my baby teeth had come out. It had been loose for days, waggling about every time I had eaten anything. We scrambled down from the table, all eager to see the tooth burn.

'Burn, burn blue tooth, Please God send me a new tooth,' I said solemnly, flinging the tooth on to the fire, as I did so. Immediately a small blue flame sprang up from where I had thrown it.

'Ah,' our Mother remarked, 'it burnt quick and clear and bright, that means that your new tooth will come through soon and it will be firm and strong.'

This little ritual of throwing teeth on the fire was always carried out when any of us youngsters happened to lose one.

These were lots of funny little beliefs and sayings in those days—for instance, if you sneezed we used to say that it meant you would be kissed, cursed, cussed, or shake hands with a fool. When this happened in our house our Mother would immediately thrust out her hand, so that the sneezer might shake it. Not that she was anybody's fool, but it saved you being cussed or cursed, and at that time we were a bit too young for kissing to have any effect.

And if your nose itched, then you were going either to—

> Run a mile
> Jump a stile, or
> Eat a pancake in a field.

Itching or burning ears meant that someone was talking about you, and the saying was that it was

Right your mother
Left your lover.

And itching hands were significant too:

Scratch them on wood
Sure to come good

was one belief, another was if your right hand itched you would receive some money, but if your left itched then you would be paying some out.

But if the bottom of your feet itched, it meant that you were going to walk on strange ground. If your new boots or shoes squeaked when you first wore them, folks said that this was a sign that they had not been paid for, and children would tease each other unmercifully about this. I know I got a good hiding from our Mother one day, after I had suggested, quite seriously, to respectable Mr Hills, that he could not have paid for his, because his were squeaking like mad when I walked home with him from Witney.

And bad luck would surely befall you if you forgot to put a coin in the pocket of a coat or suit, when it was first new.

And there were peculiar country cures which people often practised. An old gypsy woman told our Mother once that the best thing to cure a baby's sore bottom or ease spreeze* on children's legs was ashes from elm wood. Simply burn some elm wood, let the ash get cold and then rub the affected parts with it. She also told her that bleeding could be stopped by laying a thick black cobweb across the wound, but I do not think she ever tried that one.

* Nasty rash caused through extremely cold weather.

13

Summer Days, Summer Ways

W E loved the hot sunny days of summer, the long hot, dusty days when we played almost all the time. Winter with its severe frost and snow was completely forgotten, and never it seemed had it ever rained, always it had been hot, sunny, and dusty.

Our stone-built cottage was cool enough, but outside the heat hit you like a frying pan. So we spent most of our time by the river. In the mornings our Mother would load us up with a big bag of bread and jam, and a bottle of lemonade made with a ha-porth of yellow sherbet powder to last us all day.

The shaded lane which led to Gooseham was waist high with nettles and purple vetch and grass, except for a narrow path that we had made where we constantly trailed along it. The lane led out to Wilsdon's field and to our beloved river Windrush. One summer the field was almost bare of grass, for the long, hot spell had lasted several weeks, and huge cracks had appeared in the ground and one of Wilsdon's cows had caught her hoof in one and as the poor animal had tried to free itself it had broken the trapped leg and the cow had to be destroyed, but at least the meat was good and it was later sold in one of the butcher's shops in the town.

The field was covered in cow-dung, cow clats as we called them, and they were sun-baked as hard as concrete and were thick with yellow horse-flies which stung us and fetched our skin up in big red weals. But even the cow clats had their uses, some of the villagers collected them up in this hard, solid state and put them on the copper fire where they burnt like wood, but let off a terrible smell as the smoke from the fire floated over the village in the still summer air.

And so the long hot summer wore on. Some of the wells in the village almost dried up, ours got very low, so low that, as we let the bucket down it scraped the bottom, disturbing the gravel and making the water cloudy. Mrs Wheeler's well was completely dry, even the ferns growing on the sides were parched brown. We leaned over gazing into its cavernous depths watching the newts darting and climbing about, desperate for dampness.

The drought meant hard work for villagers. All the housewives saved the water from the weekly wash for watering the gardens in an effort to save the withering crops, or to slosh down dirt paths to help lay the dust. 'When it do rain,' our Mother threatened, 'I shall rush out and stand in it with no clothes on, that's the only way I shall ever cool down,' but of course she never did.

Throughout the summer she was at constant battle with fleas, daily searching the hems of sheets and blankets for them, cracking them dead with her thumb nails when she did find one. It was not that we were flea-ridden like two or three of the families were, but when you played and fought or sat next to children who were, catching them was inevitable, one hop and jump and the little beggars would soon settle on a nice bit of fresh flesh. Our Mother only had to see a tell-tale bite on us and then nothing rested until she had tracked the offending flea down and firmly cracked and killed it.

Flies were a menace too. The only deterrent at that time was a tuppenny flypaper. This was quite an ingenious thing, a long, brown, sticky, treacly thing about two feet long. But when you bought it, it was cleverly rolled up inside a very small carton. You pulled the sticky strip out by a tiny loop whereby you hung the flypaper up, with the little carton that had held it still firmly stuck on the bottom end. Most people hung their flypapers up in the centre of the room, usually over the table where the flies seemed to congregate. They just flew on to the sticky strip, stuck to it and died. But I could never make out whether it was simply because they could not get away or whether there was, in fact, some poison on the flypaper. We were so plagued with flies in the summertime that a fresh paper only needed to be hung up for a short while before it was simply black with dying insects.

One day, bored with the long, hot, dusty day, we decided to play soldiers with our cousins and a newish boy to the village called George Wilkins. George was very popular with the children because he had a German helmet that his father had brought back from the war. We all fought George because he was the enemy, but we could not hurt him, at least not his head, because of the wonderful helmet. On this day George was shouting to us, 'Go on, you buggers, hit me, hit me', and we all set on to him thrashing him over the head with sticks. Suddenly George keeled over; he was as white as a sheet, his eyes were rolling, he was frothing at the mouth, and his arms and legs were making jerking movements. We were so frightened, we just looked at each other and then tore home as fast as our legs would carry us, daring anyone to breathe a word of what had happened. Later on we discovered that poor George was subject to fits, and our hitting him about the head had nothing to do with him passing out and foaming at the mouth. All the same he never asked us to play soldiers with him again, or whack him over the head.

Another morning during that summer our Mother announced that Mick and I were not to go out to play until we had each picked a cockerel. These were two that we were going to have for Sunday dinner. 'We might as well eat them as keep them for Christmas,' our Mother cried. 'They will eat me out of house and home, darned hungry things.' So she caught a couple of them and, holding them in her strong, brown hands, she stretched their necks and killed them, and handed one each to Mick and I to pick the feathers off. Then she left us to get on with it, the hot bodies, lifeless now, lay on our laps—they picked better warm our Mother reckoned. We pulled away at a few feathers, loath to work on this hot, sultry day. The little hen fleas began to creep up our arms annoying us, it was far too hot to do any more we decided.

'I know,' I said, 'let's hang um up in the hen run and let the other hens peck the feathers off for us.' Mick agreed that it was a good idea. So we tied the cockerels up by the legs and hung them up and sat back and waited for the fowls to do the work for us. It was hot and smelly sitting there in the muck-covered hen run but we did not mind, at least we were not doing anything. I fetched out a grubby piece of paper and a stub of pencil from my frock pocket and started to write my very first poem.

> Once I had a rabbit
> All of my very own
> And its little wooden hutch
> Was lodged upon a stone.

I decided there and then that I was going to write poetry and that when I left school I should not go to work but stay at home and write wonderful poetry. Goodness knows how long Mick and I sat there mumchancing* as the hot afternoon wore on.

Suddenly our Mother's face appeared round the side of the chicken run. 'I thought you was too darned quiet to be up to any good,' she hollered, her face red with annoyance. 'Get on and pick those birds, or I'll thrash you till you can't stand.' Of course we knew that she would not be as hard as that on us, but the threat of a hiding had us both picking feathers off those birds a darned sight quicker than we had ever done before. When we eventually crept out of the hen run our Mother was waiting for us; she just clipped our ears and sent us off down Gooseham to see if the boys, Ben and Denis, were all right.

We rushed off, thankfully escaping the threatened hiding. Down by the Windrush we paddled along with the rest of the village children. Mick and I swilled our faces, necks and arms to rid ourselves of the hen fleas. They do not live on humans, but they do irritate you while they are crawling about on you. Some of the bigger boys climbed up into the willow trees which stood like a row of drunken sailors along the river bank. Then the lads

* Thinking and dreaming.

leapt out of their perches into the river, splashing us all over so that we might as well have been swimming in our frocks we were that wet; but we soon dried in the warm sunshine.

Our strip of the river Windrush was mostly shallow and gravelly, a beautiful winding river. In some parts, the lovely green water weeds grew: they moved silently, floating and waving in that gentle stream, looking for all the world like the tresses of water maidens. Minnows darted around your feet and tickled your ankles if you stood still, but the crayfish kept well out of our noisy way only coming out at night when all was quiet and still.

Just a few yards downstream from where we swam, Wilsdon's cows would stand hock high in the Windrush, cooling themselves and drinking, their great pink tongues picking up the water, with the sun catching the droplets as they fell, turning them into rainbow colours so that they looked for all the world like jewels tumbling from a treasure chest.

There were a few deep pools along our stretch of the Windrush, like Parson's hole and Holland's hole where some of the grown-ups bathed. And running almost parallel with our river, but further away from Ducklington, was another stream called Cogg's brook, a much deeper and swifter flowing river. And it was in that river, somewhere between Ducklington and Witney, that a group of young men from the town bathed naked almost every Sunday during the summertime. Everybody knew that it went on, but it certainly did not bother us, nobody sneaked about to look or anything; anyhow we had seen boys bathing naked before and our young green minds did not know that grown-ups looked any different. But we knew that we were not supposed to go anywhere near and we did not. It was one of those things that were taken for granted. They were just a bunch of very respectable fellows, Oxford bagged and very with-it: shopkeepers' sons and bank clerks mostly, who enjoyed this perfectly innocent weekly jaunt and swim.

But one summer just before I left school I struck up a friendship, of which my Mother greatly disapproved, with a very pretty girl. Rosie Brown her name was and she was quite a bit older than I, about eighteen, I think she was. All the villagers said that she was fast and flighty, but I thought that she was marvellous and longed to grow up as pretty and popular with the boys as she was. Wherever we went the village lads used to follow, but Rosie would have no truck with them. 'Blummin' lot of hobble-de-hoys,' she said. 'I wouldn't go to the bottom of our stairs to meet any of um.'

Normally our Mother never interfered with our friendships, she left it to us to make our own judgement about people, but in this case she did try very hard to put me off going out with Rosie Brown, saying that she would lead me astray, but I could see no wrong in her. Then one day after a fierce argument about my friendship with Rosie, our Mother dared me ever to go out with her again.

I cried and sulked, but it did no good.

'If I so much as hear that you have spoken to her,' our Mother bellowed at me, 'I shall keep you in every weekend until you have learnt your lesson. You are not to have any more to do with her and that's that.'

But one hot summer Sunday afternoon I was mooning about over the meadows near our cottage when I met up with Rosie again and, forgetting my Mother's threat about keeping me in at the weekends, I readily agreed to show her a short cut over the fields to Cogg's brook, where she said she particularly wanted to go.

We trudged over the grassy meadows, it was hot and close and Rosie seemed to be in such a hurry.

Suddenly we rounded a bend in the river and she cried joyfully, 'Ah, there they are.'

And just a few yards away, frolicking about in the summer sunshine were several young men, laughing and splashing about in the river—then I realized who they were.

'We 'ent supposed to go anywhere near them,' I cried, 'our Mother ses if you do they'll chase you naked,' and I started to back away.

'Don't be such a silly,' Rosie said. 'They would be frit tu death tu come out of that water in front of us,' and she walked boldly along the bank and stood on the grass in front of the bathers scanning their faces. Seeing the one she was looking for she called out.

'Johnny, I've come to see you.'

'Go back,' the young man called in a very cultured voice, 'go back and I'll see you in the town tomorrow lunchtime.'

'I want to see you today, now,' she pleaded with him. 'I'll shut my eyes while you get out and dress if that's what's worrying you.' But the young man refused to move.

She came back to where I was standing.

'I'll get that bugger out you see if I don't,' she whispered to me. 'Just because he got his friends with him he don't want me, well, we'll see,' and she marched up to the neat piles of clothes, each topped with a clean folded towel, that the young men had placed on the grass.

One by one she picked up the heaps of clothes. 'Whose is this?' she called out and one by one the young men answered her and shouted to her to put them down. There was only one pile of clothes left. With a cunning look in her eye she gathered them up in her arms and began to walk very slowly across the field, away from me and the bewildered watchers in the river.

'You best get off home,' one of the men called to me. 'This is no place for you.' I stood where I was for a few minutes thinking Rosie might not like it if I went back without her.

Suddenly the young man who she had spoken to swam to the river's edge and rose out of the water. He looked like one of the Greek gods whose statues I had seen in a museum at Oxford.

Then he ran across the field after Rosie. She turned round and saw him coming, so she too started to run, then she tripped over a tussock of grass and went flying headlong into the field; at that moment the young man caught up with her and flung himself down beside her. I turned and ran for home.

A little while later I heard that the young man, a bank clerk, had married Rosie and that he had been transferred to another part of the county. And that I thought was that. But a couple of years later Rosie came home bringing a most beautiful child with her. The marriage had not worked out, the young man's parents thought that he had married beneath himself and never accepted Rosie and some time later they were divorced, a shocking thing in those days.

I became quite friendly with her again, she was not really as bad as folks made out. Her earlier behaviour was just a desperate attempt to get away from home. Then she told me what had happened to her before she and her father and stepmother came to live near our village.

'You see,' she told me, 'my mother died when I was ten and my father, desperate for someone to look after me, advertised for a housekeeper. Well, this person Eva came along and before you could wink they got married. They did not tell me until afterwards and I was that upset. You see I loved my mother; we three, my dad, her, and me was as happy as sandboys, and whereas my mother was very kind and loving, this Eva was as hard as nails and bossed us about something awful. I think that she was jealous of me and the fact that my Dad was fond of me. But she soon put a stop to that. They had a terrible row with my stepmother threatening to leave. After that there was no kind words or playful teasing from my Dad, only an indifference that I, as a child, could not understand. Oh, she fed me all right, but that was about all. Then, one day, coming up to my thirteenth birthday it was, quite suddenly she became nice and friendly towards me. She had a lovely silver watch, a round one about as big as half-a-crown it was. She wore it on a fine chain which hung round her neck. The watch had delicate engraving on the back of it and I thought that it was beautiful.

'Then she said, "Tell you what young Rosie, you shall have it for your birthday."

'Well—I was that excited I didn't know what to do and I couldn't understand why she should want to part with it, and I eagerly awaited my birthday, but just two days before she said that the watch was missing and she wanted me to swear that I had seen old Jake, a man who worked on the same farm as my father, and who sometimes popped in for a chatter, take the watch. She had walked into the town that afternoon and notified the police, and when they came I was to say that the old man had taken it. Of course I told my father as soon as I had the chance. There was a terrible row between him and my stepmother, then my father got on his bike and rode into the town and told the police that what she had said was a pack of lies. She thought that was the end of it but the next day the police came and gave her a good telling off. It appeared that she was a gambler and she used to bet on horses and had, in fact, pawned the watch. Apparently this was a put up job, her pretending she was going to give it to me and then say someone had pinched it. You see the bookie was worrying her for the money she owed him, so she had to find it from somewhere.

'Then a few weeks after that one of the fellows who worked on the farm attacked me as I was coming from school. Course I didn't really understand what he was doing, but I knew it was not right. He had a knife and I was frightened to death. Three times he "made love to me" as he called it before he let me go.

'"Don't you dare tell nobody," he said, "or I'll slit yer throat with this," he said waving his knife. I rushed home crying and hysterical, my clothes were all torn and I was covered in blood, I was in a terrible state.

'Then the police came and the doctor and then they took Jimmy away and locked him up and I think he died some years later still in the asylum where they put him. Well, the doctor said that he didn't think that I would be pregnant after such an attack, but my stepmother wasn't taking any chances, and for weeks after she had me jumping off five-bar gates, leaping from hayricks, and then she dosed me up with gin and vinegar and nutmeg, all these were old wives' tales of how to get rid of a baby. And all the while she kept saying that if I had a child nobody would employ me when I left school and that everybody would look down on me for the rest of my life. I can tell you that she made my life hell, and all this at thirteen years old. Still, thankfully, I didn't have a child.

'But from then on all I wanted to do was get away from home, I didn't care how it happened as long as I was not under the same roof as my stepmother. Anyhow you know the rest of the story.

'Then last year my stepmother went off with the postman, so I'm back home looking after me Dad and of course young John-boy.'

Then the war came along and I lost touch with Rosie, but I heard that in about 1944 she married a Canadian pilot and after the war went back to his home in Montreal.

I wonder if she ever thinks of those far-off days, of lush green meadows, flower-filled and speckled with butterflies, a river bank lined with drunken willows and the happy laughter of youth drifting over the cool clear water of Cogg's brook.

14

Winter

*W*HILE the summers of my youth seemed always to be hot and blazing, the winters in their turn were mostly very cold, at least so it always seemed.

'I reckon this cold weather comes from the Russian steppes,' old Mrs Adams remarked one day, her nose glowing multi-coloured in the frosty air.

And when someone asked Dan Dore if he was sweating, when the temperature was well below zero, his reply was, 'The only place I sweats is at the nose end.' And that was probably something that we all did, when it *was* cold.

We would set off for school wrapped up warm in almost everything that we had. 'Go on,' our Mother would say, 'run all the way and then you will be hot as toast when you gets there,' and we would all tear off at a rare pace, slapping our thighs and whinnying and snorting, shouting 'giddy up' to ourselves and rearing and galloping about like a lot of young colts, and our faces red and glowing when we arrived at school. On these occasions we stayed at school for dinner. We each had four thick slices of bread and dripping and a screw of newspaper containing a spoonful of cocoa and sugar. Miss Spencer, our headmistress, would put a kettle of water on the top of the huge tortoise stove, so that we could make a hot drink at dinner time—no milk, just cocoa, sugar and water. But to us, on those cold days, it was like nectar of the gods.

The classroom was as cold as charity, except for the immediate area by the fat, round stove, which was situated behind the teacher's table. My desk was very near to the door and when the wind was in one direction it used to whistle round my legs, causing me to have chilblains, at least that was what our Mother said caused them, for no other member of the family had red, swollen legs like mine. And every night, when the warmth from the fire made the chilblains itch I nearly scratched my legs raw. But, before I went to bed our Mother would cut a big, raw onion in half and give it to me to rub on my inflamed legs. Really all the onion juice seemed to do was cool them down, but at least it brought a bit of comfort for a while.

Mind you, one of the old wives' tales to cure chilblains was to immerse your feet in a full chamber-pot and bathe the chilblains. This I did—anything for relief—but again I think it only cooled my throbbing legs. Then there was the fact that I had to endure the indignity of bathing my legs in somebody else's pee. I must have stunk to high heaven during the wintertime, what with the smell of goose-grease and camphorated oil on my chest and onions and pee on my feet and legs.

That particular old wives' tale was also supposed to cure bald heads too, but I never heard of anyone trying it; if they did and it had not worked I do not suppose that they would have admitted defeat or the indignity. But the cold, hard spell of weather continued for several weeks.

Our stepfather met old Billy Tanner walking down the road one day muffled up in an old army coat and thick scarf.

'Cold enough for you, Billy?' our stepfather called.

'Ah that 'tis, Ben,' the old fellow replied. ''Tis that cold in my cottage I goes tu bed with all me clothes on and then I byent warm, and do you know?' he went on, 'you mightn't believe what I be going tu tell you, but that bin so cold in my bedroom this last few nights that have froze the piddle in the jerry-pot.' And he shuffled off his boots encased in a pair of old socks to stop him from slipping on the frozen ground.

Two years before this particular cold spell our two-holer vault lavatory had been replaced by a bucket lavatory, and while the old one only needed to be emptied twice a year, the bucket, with seven children and two grown-ups using it, had to be emptied daily. As soon as our stepfather came home from work he knew what his first job was. He would come into the yard, prop his bike up by the wash-house, go in and get his spade, and proceed down the garden collecting the full bucket on his way, and take the contents up to the end of the garden and bury it.

But during the extremely cold weather this became a bit of a problem. The ground was frozen solid. He tried digging a hole with a pick but it was impossible; so for a while the offending contents were strewn over the top end of the garden. By the time the weather got warmer some of the material had broken down but the paper was still there, blowing about in the garden, so we were sent to gather it up and make a bonfire of it.

Still, while the cold weather lasted we fed the birds and slid nightly on the frosty pond or on the flood-frozen meadows opposite our house.

At this time Bern, the eldest, had just left school and for about a year worked for a farmer Mr Parker of Barley Park Farm. One of his jobs during this particularly cold winter, was to help clear some woodland, so along with another young fellow, whose nickname was Skeecher, they hacked away with billhooks and hedge-slashers keeping themselves reasonably warm, and cutting and clearing away all the scrub, small trees and bushes. The big trees, of course, were left to the tree fellers to cut down. The lads had to work methodically, clearing up as they went along. First all the brushy sticks were set on one side, these had to be tied up in neat bundles of faggots. Later on these would be sold to local bakers, who used them to heat their ovens. Some cottagers bought them too, to chop up for fire lighting. Pea sticks and runner bean sticks would also be cut and tied up and these too would be sold in the village or in the nearby town. All the rubbishy stuff like black-berry bushes, twigs, and gorse had to be burnt, and all day long the lads would keep a huge bonfire going, always remembering of course to work with the wind in their faces and the bonfire behind them, so that they did not have the smoke blowing into their faces all day. With no other means of providing themselves with a hot drink, the lads would heat water from a nearby pond (sometimes ice) in an old tin that they found in the hedge, setting the tin in the red embers at the bottom of the bonfire. 'We 'as it just like tramps do,' Bern said, 'two spoonsful of tea and a bit of sugar, and we drinks it straight out of the tin and that goes down a treat.'

But that wood was a godsend to our parents—it saved them the expense of buying coal.

All her life our Mother was very friendly with a Mrs Bowles who lived further down the village. She was a widow woman, a Londoner with three daughters and a son. Betty was pally with the girls because they were round about her age, and they all used to go dancing together at the Corn Exchange in Witney on Saturday nights. And the Bowles family, like us, had a wind-up gramophone, so one Sunday night we would all walk down to their house and take a few of our records and the next week they would all come up to our house with a few of theirs.

They were lovely, unforgettable evenings, with lovely, unforgettable songs. We would all of us join in the singing, accompanying John McCormack as he sang in his rich, deep voice *Macushla, Macushla*, or Layton and Johnstone as they dreamily serenaded us with 'I'll bring a Love Song', 'My Blue Heaven', 'Have a Little Faith in Me', 'Shalimar', 'Souvenirs', and 'Goodnight Sweetheart', or the songs that a local man Moss Turner recorded, for a big record company—'With a Song in My Heart' and 'A Little Kiss Each Morning, a Little Kiss Each Night', lovely lilting melodies that still bring back memories of the happiness we found on those Sunday evenings. Of course with our one track minds we just had to spoil some of those songs, like 'The Sheik of Araby', which we insisted in adding 'without a shirt' after almost every line which made the song both funny and vulgar.

Most likely we would finish off the evening with nothing more than a welcome cup of cocoa, made with water and just topped up with milk, before we left for home. Then all the way back, and indeed all the next week we would be singing or whistling those songs.

One Sunday night we were walking back home having a good sing-song. As we rounded Collis's corner to the strains of 'Ramona', we met old Luke Atkins. He was wandering from one side of the road to the other. Luke was a beer-swigging, baccy-smelling old devil who was often the worse for drink.

'Lovely singing,' Luke called out in a slurred voice, 'but why don't you sing "Just Like the Ivy I'll Cling to You?"'

'Ah,' our stepfather replied laughingly, 'I reckons you'll want summut to cling to or else you will never get home in your state.' So we left old Luke there propped up against the wall while we made our way home on that clear, frosty night carolling 'Just Like the Ivy' especially for old Luke.

Then the temperature began to get a little warmer, and we woke up one morning to find the countryside covered in a deep heavy fall of snow. Every tree and branch and plant was covered in the powdery stuff as if a giant had come overnight and spilled caster sugar over the whole village. Snow was worse than frost as far as we and our boots were concerned. When it was frosty at least it was dry and so were our feet, but the wet, soft snow soon penetrated our boots, saturating our socks and stockings. We only possessed one pair at a time, so it was off with them as soon as we got indoors. Our Mother showed us how to stuff our boots with newspaper, which absorbed the damp and padded them out so they did not dry hard and wrinkled. So in the winter evenings the old fire hearth was filled with drying boots.

Wellingtons were coming into fashion, but we could not afford any. But I remember how excited we all were when Betty, who at the time was working at the laundry in the town, came home with a pair of Russian boots which were absolutely the height of fashion, leather they were and knee length.

When we were not sliding on the pond or visiting Bowles's we spent the rest of the evenings by the fireside. I remember once Mick passed away a whole winter by making a doll's cot from out of an old shoe box. She made a minute mattress and a pillow, sheets and blankets, then draped the lid so that it looked like a super baby's cot, only to realize at the end of the winter that she had grown out of dolls and doll's cots, and that she was almost old enough to go to work.

And sometimes, during the winter evenings, if he had not got a pair of our boots to patch up, or a puncture to mend, or his bike to repair, our stepfather would amuse us for ages by making shadow pictures on the wall with his hands. He was very clever at this, manœuvring his fingers so that the animals and things that he made became quite realistic, because in the flickering candle or firelight they looked as if they were moving. He also made the appropriate animal noises, and we were fascinated by his interpretations of foxes, rabbits, ducks, cats, and fighting cocks. To end with he always did a man chasing a ball across the living-room wall, the man had a long thin neck, and he made him disappear saying that he had gone to catch the animals up.

'That's it,' he would say, 'time you all went off to roost,' so we younger ones would go off to bed. The bedrooms seemed freezing cold, but we quickly got warm once we were in bed and cuddled up to each other. Our Mother would come up and throw a thick coat over our feet for extra warmth and we were soon fast asleep.

Some nights we children would pass the time away by swopping rhymes and jingles. Where they all originated from I do not know, but we seemed to pick them up a lot quicker than we did lessons, remembering and recalling them much easier than we did dates of famous battles and crowning of kings and queens—especially if they were a bit rude.

> One fine day in the middle of the night
> Two dead men got up to fight
> I went downstairs to let them in
> They knocked me on the head with a rolling pin
> The rolling pin was made of brass
> They turned me up and slapped my ass.

But another version went like this—

> Not last night but the night before
> Two tom cats came knocking at my door
> I went downstairs to let them in
> They hit me on the head with a rolling pin
> The rolling pin was made of brass
> They turned me up and slapped my—
> Ask no questions
> Hear no lies
> Here comes a blackyman
> Playing with his—
> Higher up the mountain
> Greener grows the grass
> I saw a nanny goat
> Sliding on his—
> Cock your leg over the rope lady
> I'm selling three balls for a penny
> Just as long as there's any
> Hit the monkey on the belly
> And you'll win a box of cigars

And so you could go on, linking each rhyme cunningly so that you really didn't say the rude words. Betty told us this one that she picked up in service, it was what a cheeky kitchen-maid actually said to her very bossy employer:

> Yes Ma'am, no Ma'am
> Ma'am if you please
> Shall I stuff the duck's ass
> With the shells or the peas?

And the girl was packed off at a minute's notice for saying that.

And with the coming of the motor car this little jingle was often recited:

> There was a little man
> And his name was Henry Ford
> He took a little bit of metal
> And a little piece of board

> He took a drop of petrol
> And an old tin can
> And put it all together
> And the darned thing ran.

Church singing was not left out either—we really had no respect for this harvest hymn:

> All is safely gathered in
> Docks and thistles tied with string
> Some was thick and some was thin
> But all was safely gathered in.

And instead of singing 'Safe in the arms of Jesus' we bawled out:

> Safe in the arms of a policeman
> Safe locked in Oxford jail
> Fourteen days hard labour
> For pulling a donkey's tail.

Conundrums we were very fond of and sometimes we had the whole family guessing on really the most simple ones:

> Stow on the Wold
> Where the wind blows cold
> And the cooks can't cook their dinner
> Take Stow from the Wold
> And Wold from the cold
> And spell me *that* in four letters.

Or this one that we would write in friends' autograph books:

> YYUR
> YYUB
> ICUR
> YY4 Me.

Then quite suddenly the cold weather was over and the rains of February came with the banks of the Windrush flooding our low-lying meadows. I came across these doggerel lines the other day, they were scribbled on the flyleaf of an old parish magazine. I think they must have been written by a local person, but I have never heard them before:

> The floods were out at Ducklington
> One cold November day
> And all the ducks of Ducklington
> Were lost or gone astray.

If these lines were penned in the days of my youth I doubt whether the ducks had gone far, probably on to the flood water in the fields over the road from the pond. Here they would most likely find a different diet from the one the pond provided, fresh, succulent worms, water snails, and beetles. But if the poem was written since the last war then the words are correct, the ducks have 'got lost or gone astray'.

For alas, there are no ducks now at Ducklington, and half the time there is no water in the pond either. I understand that some time ago it was cleared out, and cleaned so well that the Oxfordshire clay which lined it has all disappeared, and the only time there is water in it is when it has rained hard, and this soon soaks away. What a pity: that pond in our young days gave us so much pleasure, sliding in winter, playing mud pies in summer, and sometimes we were fortunate enough to find a duck's egg on the grassy bank. If we took it back to Mrs Collis she would reward us with a super piece of home-made fruit cake.

15

The Green Years

WHEN I look back to our growing-up years I realize that we were often very uncouth and cheeky. But it certainly was not for the want of trying, on our parents' part, to endeavour to make good citizens out of us. Both our Mother and stepfather worked hard and long, striving all the while to bring us up properly, so that when the time came for us to leave school and start work, we might stand a fair chance with the rest of the world.

And because of this, the memories of many things that happened during those green growing-up years come flooding back—how proud of us our Mother was when we excelled ourselves in the school concerts—when I, out of all the school, won the Bishop's prize, and when Bunt had a drawing of an angel pinned up in the classroom for all to see, a very unusual thing in those days. His class had been learning the poem *Abou Ben Adhem* by Leigh Hunt:

> Abou Ben Adhem (may his tribe increase)
> Awoke one night from a deep dream of peace,
> And saw within the moonlight of his room
> Making it rich, and like a lily in bloom
> An angel, writing in a book of gold

and Bunt had drawn and crayoned a most beautiful angel, complete with golden pen and golden book, although someone was quick to point out that the pen the angel was writing with was in his left hand. 'Anyhow,' our Mother said, consoling him, 'never mind, my boy, for all we knows half the angels in heaven might be left-handed.'

And almost always she encouraged us to take part in the yearly concerts. In fact, without bragging, I can safely say that the members of our family were nearly always picked to take the star parts in the school plays, with somebody or other finding a bit of bright cloth for our princely robes. Then one year, when I was about eleven, I was chosen to be one of a group of four fairies and we were expected to find our own clothes. White plimsols and white cotton frocks and pale stockings.

'No,' our Mother said firmly, 'you are not going to be a fairy and that's that.'

I cried, I sulked, and pleaded, but nothing would budge her from her decision.

On the night of the concert when parents were clapping and cheering the efforts of their children, I was perfectly miserable— worse too when the fairies came on the scene.

A few years ago I was shown some old photographs taken at these school concerts that we took part in. Amongst them was one of three fairies—the girls' faces were sweetly pretty, but the clothes, the black stockings, and one girl was wearing boots! I told our Mother about the photo.

'Yes,' she replied, 'perhaps now you can understand why I wouldn't let you be a fairy. I certainly did not want everybody in the village to know that I couldn't supply your clothes and shoes.'

But I did not see it like that. To me, it would have been no worse than me having to wear boots to school right up to the time I left at fourteen years old, especially as the other girls of my age were wearing shoes.

Is it just a middle-aged delusion, remembering the sun-drenched fields, when the long, hot summers timelessly slipped by, when grasshoppers leapt like kangaroos amongst the lush green grass and the yellow-hammers sang all day. Sometimes the mornings were unbelievably beautiful, with hazy mist hanging over the water meadows. Looking over the moors from our house you could see the herons leaping in the air from the stream, stretching their long wings in lazy flight, and the larks spiralling up out of the grass, flying almost out of sight, just a tiny speck in a blue summer sky, and yet we could still hear their sweet singing clearly on the ground below.

We spent so many happy hours playing by, and in, our lovely river Windrush. Our favourite bathing place was Gooseham. But further downstream, beyond the flour mill was a quiet place we called 'The Ham'. Here the river came through winding meadows, with the willow and hawthorn trees festooned with wild roses, almost dipping into the cool, rushy stream and the dappled sunlight shining on the water. No wonder we were as happy as bees in a buttercup, wandering along the river bank during those long, hot summer days.

We would often see the farm workers busy in the fields, hay carting and harvesting, dust covered, sunbronzed men they were with hairy chests like blackberry bushes, working tirelessly from sun up till sun down.

One day we came across Fred Franklin. He was lying under an 'azzie' bush dead drunk, an empty yellow stone jar lay on its side. I picked it up and sniffed—coo, elderberry I should think it was. We left him there sleeping as innocent as a new-born babe. But I'll bet there was ructions when the farmer realized that Fred had not been working all that afternoon. But Fred was also a good gardener and quite a character, and people would often seek his advice about gardening matters, like Mrs Truscot who was having trouble with her marrows one year. 'I can't get they flowers to set at no price,' she told Fred one day.

'Ah,' he replied, 'you wants to 'noculate um with a hen's feather, that'll do the trick, you mark my words.'

Another of his bits of advice was 'When the elm leaves be as big as a mouse's ear, thas the time to plant yer kidney beans.' Although our Mother said that Gloucester folk reckoned to plant theirs Stow Fair day which falls on or very near 12th May.

Old Fred had things to say about parsley too, when Mrs Salter complained to him that the seed she had planted had failed to come up.

'Ah,' Fred said, 'you got out of patience I expect and went and dug it up. That takes eight weeks fer parsley sid to germinate. You see,' he went on, 'that thur sid has to go down to the devil three times affor that 'ull ever start to grow, you just has tu give it time, that'll come through all right, but you go tu be patient. And another thing,' he said, 'don't you never transplant parsley neither. Thas one a the worst things you can do, it'll bring you nothing but bad luck and thas a fact.'

'Do you know,' Fred went on, 'we nevers reckons to buy no vegetables, I can grow all we wants. Mind you, in the wintertime my Missus 'er 'ull go awf and get some a they 'urricane beans, cos 'er likes 'um with a bit of oxtail stew, and I can't grow they.'

The hedge round Fred's cottage garden was always neat and tidy. But one year he was cutting it off almost to the ground. 'That's a bit drastic, isn't it, Fred?' our Mother called to him as he slashed away.

'Ah, missus,' he replied, 'come spring that hedge 'ull begin to stoul out, and he'll be as thick as thick by next summer.'

'Ah,' he went on, 'we don't half want some rain, don't we? I was telling the old parson the other day how dry it was, so he ses to me—

' "Well Mr Franklin, I had no idea it was that serious, I will offer up a prayer on Sunday, maybe that will do a bit of good."

'So I ses to him, "Well sir, begging your pardon, but as long as the wind's wur tis, you'll be wasting yer time".'

Fred gave our Mother a wonderful recipe for elderberry syrup. Excellent if you have a bad cold.

6 lb ripe elderberries
1½ lb sugar
Strip the berries from the stalks, put into a pan along with the sugar and simmer until the mixture is clear. Strain and bottle the contents. For a cold just put two tablespoons of the syrup in hot water and drink at bedtime.

To most of the villagers, our Mother must have seemed a bit unorthodox, to say the least. When other housewives were busy

257

with their weekly washing or ironing, she would be taking us off on some jaunt or another. It only needed the sun to shine for her to make up her mind that she would take us out. 'If that was to pour down with rain tomorrow, and I hadn't took you out today, it would be a day of sunshine that could never ever be brought back and we should have wasted it. I think the dear Lord sends the nice weather for us all to enjoy. Well,' she said laughingly, 'that's my story and I'm sticking to it.'

On our way down the village we would have to pass Mrs Topson's cottage and Mrs Bolton's. These ladies were both very houseproud, their one aim in life was to be a better housewife than the other. It was a proper fight on a Monday morning to see which of them got their washing out on the line first.

Giving our Mother a disapproving look, Mrs Topson remarked: 'Mornin' Missus, I'd a thought that you'd bin too busy a-doin' your ironing today, seein' as 'ow you managed to get your washing done yesday, to be traipsin' off with they children.'

But our Mother did not keep to the ritual of washing on a Monday, ironing on a Tuesday, bedrooms cleaning on a Wednesday, and so on through the week, as most of the village women did. She did hers when the spirit moved her. One of her favourite expressions she used when she went out and shut the door on the housework was that she had 'put a bit of salt on it, that'll keep it all right until tomorrow'.

Mrs Topson was busy hanging the clothes that she had ironed out on the washing line to air in the lovely sunshine.

'Ah,' our Mother said to her, knowing that it would rile the old lady, 'most of mine gets ass ironed—I just folds it up and smoothes it out, then I lays it on the chair seat and puts a cushion on the top and everybody that sits on it, helps to press it.'

'That wouldn't do for my Herbert,' Mrs Topson replied, folding her arms and pulling herself up in a shrugging position. 'Oh no, that wouldn't do for him at all,' she repeated, her mouth set in a thin, hard line.

'Ah well,' Mother replied sweetly, 'it's just as well I 'ent married to him then isn't it?' And she walked off with us towards the woods.

Mind you, there was some of our washing that did not even get ass ironed. In fact, when the weather was hot and sunny and the washing dried in no time at all, our Mother did not bother to fetch hers in before it got 'arched up', and really too dry for ironing. She would leave the sheets and pillow slips on the line until she was ready to make the beds—most likely late afternoon, then she would take them straight off the line and put them on the beds. If you have never slept in sheets that have been sun dried all day, *and not ironed*, then you have not lived. The delicious smell and the roughness of them is never-to-be-forgotten. The wonderment of drifting off to sleep at such a moment is heaven itself.

We called on elderly Mrs Carr, she had not been too well for a few weeks. 'Just popped in to say how are you, we can't stop,' our Mother called through the open door. Mrs Carr was a widow woman and quite poor, although she always kept two or three cats and made a drop of what she called (tonsil polish) home-made wine.

'Come in and set yerself down for a minute or two,' the old lady said to our Mother, she was glad to see someone to have a little chatter to. 'I wants you to try a drop of me last year's dandelion,' she went on, 'that ent a bad drop of tonsil polish, although I ses it meself.'

She had her very own way of producing the most excellent wines. She told us how she went about making her dandelion. 'I boils me flower heads up then when they be done I squeezes 'um between two saucepan lids, cos they be hot yu' see. Then I mixes the liquid with the sugar and a drop of lemon and orange juice, and when that's cooled down a bit I makes a slice of toast and spreads the yeast on it and just floats it on the top, and leaves it all to work for about a fortnight, affor I strains it off into bottles and corks it down. Course, if that haven't quite finished working they corks blows out, oh it's like being at the battle of Waterloo some nights, that it is.'

We children had a drink of water and then went outside in the yard to play with the cats while the women chatted. One cat was called Lionel, farty Lionel, because of his bad habits, and the other a piebald looking thing was called Albert, although both of them were females. Mrs Carr used to say that her two cats had produced more kittens than she had had suet puddings. 'As fast as they 'as 'um I drowns 'um,' she told us one day. 'I can't afford to keep no more than two or three cats at a time, so drowning 'ums the only way out. And they be useless as far as catching mice goes, I only keeps 'um for a bit of company.'

'I'll let you into a secret,' she announced one day, lifting up the red plush tassel-edged table cloth. 'Look, this is where I keeps me wine while it's a-working.' Standing on the floor underneath the table was her big red earthenware wine pan, it had a thick cloth over it. She lifted it up and showed us the contents. It was filled with fermenting mangold wine. 'Thas my own patent mouse trap too,' the old lady went on, 'I caught two more of they little beggars this morning. Ah they mice 'ull do that wine a power of good. You see they gets in to me wine pan arter that soggy toast and then they slips in and drowns, and that wine 'ull feed on 'um, that 'ull be a drop of good wine, you see if that ent.'

And although we children pulled faces at such a thing and pretended to heave at the old lady's tale, even we knew that wine fed on meat, because it was common knowledge that old farmer Kite, who made gallons and gallons of cider for his workmen, always reckoned to throw a sheep's innards into the brew, for it to work on. And his cider was not to be sneezed at either, 'twas some darned good stuff by all accounts.

And when our stepfather, who worked at a brewery, used to help the brewer, he used to tell us a similar story. This brewery used to brew the beer in huge round vats which held hundreds of gallons of boiling beer. Our stepfather used to have to skim the froth or barm off it before it cooled ready for bottling. And because there was always a lot of grain about the place, it was overrun with rats so they kept several cats to help keep the rats down. Now the rim of this huge vat was about a foot wide and the rats used to get on it to sample the barm. The cats then used to try and chase the rats off, running round and round on the rim until the rats more often than not made a dive into the beer and the cats went straight in after them.

Our stepfather would come home and say, 'Do you know I ent seen old Blackie,' one of the cats, 'for three or four days, but I reckons I knows where he is.' Then about a week later he would say, 'I've found what's left of old Blackie, his skin come up on the brew today. You mark my words,' he went on, 'when I see my old mates in the pub next week they'll say, "My word Ben, thas a drop of good beer this week" and I shall smile and agree with 'um, but I shan't tell 'um why.'

When I look back I marvel at the perseverance and energy coupled with a brightness of spirit which our Mother possessed. Even though, all through our growing-up years, she was dogged by acute hard-upness. Despite this, she seemed able to sail through life in a disordered, happy-go-lucky way.

She was always trying to make our cottage look bright and cheerful, and one day you might arrive home to find every curtain and cushion cover dyed rose pink, or even bright orange. She had great faith in Drummer dyes; with a couple of these she would transform the house whole, dyeing everything that she could lay her hands on.

And one year she bought an out-of-date paper pattern book from Margate's paint and paper shop in Witney. The book contained about a hundred patterns of wallpaper, all different of course, each measuring about two feet by one. Some of the paper was cheap and cheerful, while others were glossy and of much better quality, and she only paid sixpence for the book.

The very next day our stepfather came home with a lovely big stout wooden box, with a lid. It was so big that he had to walk home from work with the box perched precariously on the saddle of his bicycle.

Our Mother swooped on it like a bird after a worm. 'I can make a beautiful ottoman out of that,' she cried, ignoring whatever use he might have had for it.

The box, which had held glass was quite well made, and he said that he had given a man a shilling for it.

Choosing the prettiest floral patterns from the old wallpaper book, our Mother set about pasting them, first on the outside of the box. Blue and pink trellis and roses covered one side, with the true lovers' knots and forget-me-nots graced the other, with Chinese lanterns and willow pattern on the lid. The inside she papered with damask white ceiling paper. Then she got our stepfather to fix two hinges on the lid, on to which she tacked a big feather cushion. This provided us with an extra seat and also made a good storeplace for clothes.

We had it for ages. It stood in the recess under the window of the cottage. Of course through the years many different types of wallpaper graced its sides, but none of them seemed quite so beautiful as those odd pieces that our Mother first pasted on.

After the ottoman was completed she papered the larder with some of the odd paper. Normally this was simply whitewashed each spring, but the patchwork effect which we had that year was quite a change.

Even the lavatory got a new look. Instead of gazing at bare boards when you sat down there to do your 'bounden duty' we beheld bright blue kingfishers diving into green pools, surrounded by bunches of purple and green roses arranged in eastern vases.

One of our neighbours, Mrs Pye, did not approve of such things—'getting beyond yerself', she remarked when she learned that our Mother had papered the lavatory. Still, there were several things about our family Mrs Pye did not approve of.

One day our Mother was hanging out the washing, which ran parallel with Missus next door's washing line. While our Mother hung Betty's fashionable french knickers on our line, Mrs Pye was hanging what we called her 'free traders'. These were the old-fashioned, white calico knickers, two legs on a band, tight at the waist and knee, but with a rather peculiar slit all up the back and front.

'Oh,' Mrs Pye remarked with disgust, 'I don't know what the world's coming to, that I don't, it 'ent decent, that it 'ent,' she cried. 'I should have thought you'd a put your foot down and not allowed your Betty to wear such disgusting things as them' she said, pointing to the pale pink knickers. 'I wouldn't let our Flossie wear 'um,' she went on, 'cos I reckons that's tempting providence, that I do.'

'I've never seen anything more disgusting than those you wear,' our Mother replied angrily, 'these my daughter wears are not half as bad. At least there's a bit of material where it matters, in the crutch, and that's more than can be said of your "ever readies" because that's just what they are *ever ready*.' And she walked down the garden path, her head held high.

Mrs Pye's stays were a bit old-fashioned too. Each week she would wash a pair of them, stiff, foreboding, whale-boned, armour-plated things that were greyish white, with laces up the back.

'I must have two pairs on the go all the while,' she told our Mother one day, 'one pair on, and one on the line. I 'ent like you, you know,' she would remark, eyeing our Mother enviously, 'you can take your corselets off and wash up and go about without 'um 'til they be dry, not me, I should catch me death of cold, that I should.'

The thing was our Mother could not afford to have two pairs on the go, but at least she was not as badly off as old Mr Lines who lived down the village. His wife said that she used to wash his thick vest and long pants on a Sunday, and that he had to stay in bed until they were dry, so that he could wear them to work on the Monday.

Poor Mrs Pye, she was unfortunate really. She had, to use her own expression, 'a bladder no bigger than a walnut' and was for ever shooting off down to the bottom of the garden to the lavatory. I remember Mick and I got a good cuff round the ears when our Mother caught us, singing at the tops of our voices we were, as the old lady went by:

> Have you seen me daughter sir?
> She can't hold her water sir,
> Every time she laughs, sir, she pees.

'I really don't know where you kids picks up these things,' our Mother cried, 'I'm ashamed of you, I am.' And when she said that, we knew that she really was.

Only the day before she had heard young Ben singing a parody to a popular song, which at that time was considered to be quite rude:

> I passed by your window
> When you were undressed
> You took off your knickers
> And stood in your vest.

When she asked him who taught him it he replied, 'Our Mollie.' So bang—I had it again.

Mind you, some of the antics we got up to were enough to try the patience of Job, and I often wonder how in the world we got away with some of the outrageous things that we did.

One day about four or five of us village girls were playing in Rainer's backyard. We were having a high old time chasing and hiding in the many outhouses that they had. Lena, the daughter of the house, had a lovely plait of shiny hair, as thick as your arm it was, which hung down her back, whereas mine was chopped off short because I was always catching nits in it. I was chasing her up some old loft steps when I spied a huge pair of gloving shears, I took hold of them and Lena's hair, held her down and cut her lovely thick plait off at the top near her neck.

Needless to say, I was banned from playing in the Rainer's yard after that.

And once my brothers caught Alfred Knowles as he was coming home across the moors. They took his trousers off, tied his hands behind his back and tied a live grass snake round his neck and sent him on his way. His father was absolutely furious and came rushing up to our house to complain. Our stepfather, who looked upon the whole thing as a bit of tomfoolery, told him not to make such a namby pamby of the boy. This made Mr Knowles even more furious and he shouted at our stepfather saying, 'I'll pull your nose as long as a pound of sausages, that's what I'll do, your kids are like a lot of heathens, that's what they are,' he cried.

Another thing we got a hiding for was when we went down to Barratt's barn pinching locust beans and black treacle. The farmer used to buy these things to mix up with the cattle feed, and once the word got round that a farmer had got his locust beans and treacle in, then most of the children in the village made a bee-line for the barn at some time or other. Well, we made for the barn, creeping round the side so that the farmer did not see us. We stuffed our coat pockets with the sweet, hard beans and helped ourselves to the thick black treacle, drinking it from an old enamelled mug that we found in the barn. I think we must have had more than our share of the treacle, because we certainly did not need our weekly customary dose of Beecham Pills. We were up and down the garden to the old lavatory of ours for about twenty-four hours. 'Serves you right for pinching,' our Mother told us.

'I don't like the look of the weather,' our Mother remarked one super sunny morning. 'That's too bright to last.' I could not see a cloud in the china blue sky.

'I remember one of my Dad's expressions of very bright mornings,' she went on, 'he used to say that it was "too gay tu hold", and I reckon it's going to be like that today.'

'And look at that roof of our old wash-house,' she remarked, 'half an hour ago that was wet with dew, now it's as dry as a bone, that's another sure sign that it'll rain later on in the day, when the dew disappears quickly. Never mind,' she prattled on, 'I promised to take you all out today, so we'll go, but we shall have to look sharp and get out before the weather changes.'

It was only to be one of her wooding jaunts, but goodness knows what else we might come home with, maybe a lost dog, or an injured bird, or a handful of wild duck eggs, and always armfuls of wild flowers.

But just outside our gate we met Bertha Botherum. Botherum was not her proper surname, but a nickname that our stepfather had tacked on to her, because all she seemed to do was to 'bother' about other folks business. 'She's got too much of that the cat licks his backside with,' he remarked rudely one day, 'always going on about somebody she is.'

Bertha was very pale with a thin wisp of hair, and as skinny as a bean pole—too much running from one house to another gossiping is what makes her like that, the village people said. It was true too, she was never still, but for ever chasing about with snippets of gossip.

'Thought you'd like to know, missus,' she started. Our Mother tried hard not to listen to her outpourings.

'Oh Bertha,' she said, 'can't you find anything else to talk about except pregnant girls and dirty old men? Look,' she went on, 'look at that lovely sky, blue as blue, and you just come and take a peek at my wallflowers—you never see such colours and the smell nearly takes your breath away.'

So we all traipsed back into the yard.

'Yes, Kitty,' Bertha said, 'they be very nice and they smells nicer but did I tell you that Mr Miller been at it again?' Our Mother quickly shushed her, not wanting us to hear.

'It's no good, Bertha,' she went on, pushing us out of the yard, 'I can't stop jawing to you any longer, I've promised my children a walk and that's where we are going,' and we made off down the road at a fair pace leaving Bertha standing there open mouthed. 'Talks as her belly guides her,' our Mother remarked. 'Pity the poor soul's got nothing else to do.'

Then we met Mrs Ainsbury, she was puffing up to Witney on her bicycle, but jumped off quickly when she saw us. She was fat and round, and had what our stepfather termed as 'bikerider's buttocks'. It was true too—her rear end was as rounded as a cow's backside, but we liked her much better than Bertha.

'Where do you think you are all off to?' she asked.

'Well,' our Mother said, 'I promised I'd take um for a walk, I thought we could pick up a bit of fire-wood on our way back, but it won't be fine for long I'm afraid, just look at them aspen leaves. When they shows their petticoats like that, 'tis a sure sign that it'll rain before very long.' She was right too, a slight breeze had sprung up whipping up the leaves so that only the undersides were showing.

'I must just tell you about our tom cat,' Mrs Ainsbury said. 'You knows that lovely big cat of mine Joey. Well, I wanted him doctored you see, so my husband suggested that we should get long Harry from Cote to do it. Well he come last night and done it, but I shouldn't have let him if I'd have knowd. We was sitting in our living-room and in comes long Harry. "Wur is 'e then?" he asked, and there was my poor Joey a-sleeping on the couch so peaceful like. "Is this 'im?" he ses, catchin' hold of him. And before you could blink yer eye, he'd got his head stuffed in a sack, with the rest of his body sticking out. "Yer," he said to my husband, "ketch 'old of his neck tight, so he don't get out." Then he whips out his pocket knife, as sharp as a razor it was, turns the cat's backside towards him and before you could say Jack Robinson he'd cut out the necessary, and then, howling like a banshee that old cat streaked out of the house as if all the dogs in the kingdom was after him. Anyhow he seems all right this morning, long Harry said he would be, but I shouldn't have had it done if I'd have knowd.'

'Well, I won't hinder you no longer Kitty,' Mrs Ainsbury said, twisting her bicycle pedals round so that she could mount her machine easier, then she puffed off, hardly managing to squeeze herself between the saddle and the handlebars.

'What's a cat's necessary, Mum?' I enquired, as we made our way down the Curbridge Road.

'Never you mind,' she replied sharply. 'You and Bet hop over that gate and pick some flowers. And don't tread that grass down too much,' she called, 'old Albert will be cutting that any day now.'

We climbed over the rickety wooden gate and stood waist high in the field of moon daisies. I do not think I will ever forget that fleeting wonderful feeling; it was one of those never-to-be-forgotten tranquil moments. The slight breeze blew across the waving grass making it look like a beautiful green and white summer sea, cuckoos called from every direction and the hot morning sun bore down. We seemed to float about that green flecked sea, gathering moon daisies, ragged robins, buttercups, hens and chickens, babies rattles, clover and sorrel, disturbing bright butterflies and bumbling bees.

Our shoes and ankles were yellow with pollen from the buttercups, and our arms were full of those sweet summer flowers.

Then our Mother called us back on to the road again.

'Come on,' she cried, 'while you two have been mooning about picking them flowers, we have been busy finding all this wood,' she said, puffing slightly under her heavy load. Still wearing her big apron, she had gathered up the two bottom corners and filled it with chunky bits of wood. The rest of the family had a few sticks in their arms too.

'We had best make tracks for home straight away,' she cried, 'them rain clouds are coming up fast from the west, come on, best foot forward,' she shouted, and striking up with 'It's a long way to Tipperary' she led off down the road. We made our way behind her, straggling along, each carrying our treasures. We must have looked like a drawing of ancient Egyptians, bearing gifts to a Pharaoh.

It was a moment to be savoured, to be gently stowed away at the back of the mind, so that it could be brought out again, looked at and dusted, and stowed back again.

The next year Betty left school and went off to service, to work as a kitchen-maid in a big house miles away. For the rest of us the next few years were spent laughing and crying, playing and working, noisily and clumsily the days of our childhood sped by. Soon for us all those green growing-up years had gone for ever.

Another Kind
of Magic

�

To Mont
with grateful thanks

ჯჯჯჯჯჯჯჯჯჯჯჯჯჯჯჯჯჯჯჯჯჯჯჯჯჯ

I

A Cotswold Shepherd

IT was a fine Autumn morning—heavy with mist, an almost certain promise that the day later on would be hot and sunny. I cycled off to see my old shepherd friend Mark—a letter from him had read: 'Look out for a big flock of sheep, your side of Chippy*—you can't miss us, we be nine hundred odd.' Actually there's a thousand sheep in the flock, but like most shepherds he considers it unlucky to give an actual figure.

The swirling mist seemed to get thicker as I travelled higher, then quite suddenly only the valleys were shrouded, the rolling hilltops quite clear. A few fields away I could see the flock. I peddled off down into the valley again for a little way. Soon I felt the gradual climb but couldn't see much yet, but quite plainly could hear the sheep and one of the dogs—the old one I think it was. I got off my bike and walked, climbing higher. Suddenly, bursting out of the mist, there they were—nine hundred odd sheep and Mark looking like the Good Shepherd himself right in the middle of them. He wasn't carrying a lamb, but tending to an animal who seemed to have yards and yards of blackberry bramble twined round and round its body.

The wide grin, the twinkling blue eyes, the face ruddy with over sixty years of Cotswold air, greeted me.

'Dang me if I could see you a-comin', but I knawed as somebody was about, my old dog kept tryin' to tell I.'

The dog nuzzled up to him as if to say: 'See, I told you somebody was coming.'

* Slang word for Chipping Norton.

273

Mark took out his huge pocket watch. Automatically he rubbed its face with his thumb.

'You be just come right—'tis victual time.'

We made a bee line for the hut, the dogs following close at Shup's heels.

'They knaws 'tis victual time too,' he said, jerking his head in the dogs' direction. 'We 'en't 'ad narn a bite since six.'

The hut was clean and tidy and smelled of sweet summer hay, clover scented and warm. In one corner there were the medical supplies for the sheep—several tins of one thing and another for the prevention of many of the diseases that can attack the flock. On a large nail was a bundle of cut string, the coarse bag-tie sort for tying up wire and hurdles. Several old coats were draped over the hay-bales to dry—there were wellingtons, waterproof leggings, a spare cap, and a huge wooden block—it looked like a chopping block. This was Shup's seat. I noticed that he had neatly folded a couple of sacks and placed them on the top.

Catching my glance he said, 'Tha's in your honour—my backside's used to settin' on hard places.'

I took a seat while Mark sat down on a huge tin of sheep dip; the dogs waited outside the open door. He threw them a handful of biscuits.

It gives Shup the greatest pleasure to supply me with food when I visit him. He would have felt very hurt had I brought my own or refused his. Out of his bag he fetched the top of a cottage loaf, new and crusty. It was already cut through the middle. Another piece of paper revealed two lumps of cold bacon. Shup shared this between us. 'Yer be,' he said, 'that'll stick to yer ribs—wants a good bit of fat on yer entrails in this climate.'

Out came Mark's pocket knife. Holding his food in the left hand, he carefully cut a small wedge of bread and placed it under his left thumb—this was to keep the meat in place and to keep the food clean.

'Tha's what we calls a "thumb bit" in these parts,' he told me, the first time I saw him do it. Then with his sharp penknife he skilfully slivered off bread and meat in one swipe, putting it into his mouth with the right hand which still held the knife. I had visions of him poking his eye out with his knife blade, but realized he had been doing this too long to have an accident.

For a few minutes we munched away in silence. Then old Mark said, 'Tha's a thing as dun't taste like it used to, my wench—bacon. Never do this shop tackle taste like that as we used to cure ourselves. Why, when we was all young boy-chaps livin' at home my old dad allus kept a couple of pigs. We was brought up on taters and bacon. Thur was nine 'a we boys—all gret strappin' chaps we was too—ah—taters and bacon was our mainstay, and our mother cooked a bucket of spuds every day and thur was plenty of greens and swedes to fill us up. I don't think we ever went short of a bit of grub.

'You see, my wench,' Mark went on, throwing the thumb bit to the dogs, 'my father was head gardener up at the big house—my word he did grow some crops too—both for the squire and for we at home.'

I smiled and leant my back against the side of the hut. The sun's warmth had penetrated the wood. It was peaceful and quiet high up on these wide rolling hills. I could listen to Mark for hours. He had not lost his wonderful dialect and spoke a different tongue to most of the people in that lovely valley where the river Glyme wends its way toward the great lake at Blenheim.

Mark rambled on, 'It was like this you see, my wench, my father and the squire got on terrible well together, thought the world of him 'e did, treated him more like a friend than a worker.

'But at this particular time as I be tellin' you about, the squire was fair flummoxed—somebody was takin' his prize peaches, as fast as they ripened they disappeared.

'He'd already asked the local bobby, P.C. Jones, to 'ave a look in during the hours of darkness, but they couldn't seem to catch the culprit red-handed.

'So my father volunteered to sit up one night and keep watch—squire thought this was a very good idea, they never told a soul of what they planned to do in case it warned the thief away. That night the squire kept watch till half-past eleven, then my old dad took over.

'"You go off to bed, sir," he said, "I shall be all right sittin' in this yer greenhouse."

'But the time did drag so—sittin' still's hard work to an active man. Then about four o'clock in the mornin' my old dad sees somebody sculkin' around, 'twas still pretty dark and he soon lost sight of whoever it was.

'Out of his hidin' place comes me dad and up he went to the nearest peach tree, he picked a couple of 'um and was just stuffin' 'um into his pocket when a heavy hand dropped on his shoulder and the gruff voice of P.C. Jones said, "Ahh catched you this time, my man, ho ho, look who we've got here, this is the trusted head gardener who wouldn't pinch a pin is it, well, well, what's the squire going to say about this then?"

'P.C. Jones marched my old dad up to the front door of the big house and rang the bell, after a few minutes a sleepy housekeeper let them in.

'"Fetch the squire at once, Ma'am," he ordered, "we've got the culprit at last. Look what I found on him," he said, holding the two peaches in his hand.

'Course the squire couldn't believe his eyes when he saw me old dad held by the red-faced policeman.

'"Do you wish to make a charge, sir?" asked P.C. Jones. "Caught him red-handed I did."

'He didn't answer him but turned to my father and said, "You can go home now, Jacob, but I shall expect an explanation in the morning."

'"No time like the present, sir," broke in my dad quickly. Then he took a mighty sweep at P.C. Jones's helmet—it crashed to the floor and out of it rolled half a dozen of the squire's best peaches.

'Mind you, the squire didn't prosecute, but that finished P.C. Jones. He was sacked from the force and never spoke to my father again he didn't.'

I glanced at Mark. He was back in his youth again. His blue eyes had a far-away look—he was back in his hard, happy childhood of long ago. He caught my glance.

'Yer be I mumchancin' and no Friday pen up yet.'

Out came the huge watch, 'Time we was out in the field again. I likes to get a bit forrod with me pennin'—then by Friday afternoon I got me Sat'day and Sunday pen up. We can go on chattrin' while I works.'

Out with the flock again—we blinked in the brilliant sunshine. The sheep were grazing on cocksfoot grass. It had been cut in the early summer, but the wet season had produced a good crop, long and lush, so that the sheep had to be penned off on so much of it a day.

The speed at which Mark worked was amazing, and rolls of wire and hurdles were quickly fixed to the stakes which he whacked in the ground with his great crowbar (folding bar), while nimble fingers tied string to the posts.

The huge flock were a cross between Cheviot sheep and Border Leicesters, a much smaller variety than Mark had been used to shepherding.

'Are you getting more used to looking after this type of sheep,' I asked him, knowing full well that his heart was still with the old breed of Cotswold's.

''Tis a matter of havin' to get used to 'um, the ladies don't want a lot of fat meat these days, spoils thur figgers they all ses, but fer meself I allus did fancy both ship an' women with a good bit a fat on 'um.

'Do you knaw when you slapped a Cotswold ship on the rump, that was just like hittin' a quarten of dough, they was so fat.

'Still, even a shupperd has to move with the times, bless me soul, 'twassen't no good I a-sayin' as I couldn't look arter nothin' but Cotswolds, fer they be gone right out of fashion.

'They do say as there's only one flock left in the country, and they be kept on a farm 'tother side of Burford. 'Ent you ever sin 'um? Like young donkeys they looks when they be a-grazin'.

'Of course, 'twas quantity not quality that was produced years ago. Nowadays folks be more finicky about thur clothes—what man or woman wants to wear anything made out of that coarse wool what comes from they Cotswold ship, that all goes to the making of carpets and rugs. 'Tis wool from this sort of ship,' he went on, burying his great knarled hand in the lovely thick sheep's back, 'that you ladies likes for knittin'.

'But the fleeces from these yer cross-breds be only half the weight as they we used to have off the Cotswold ship. I've knawed the time when it only took two of 'um to weigh a Tod—thas roughly twenty-eight pounds.'

As Shup dismantled the pen that the sheep had finished with, I noticed, when he pulled a stake from the ground, that he quickly heeled in the hole.

'What do you do that for?' I asked him. I was fast learning more about sheep than ever before, but I didn't know why he did this.

'Well now, if I left holes like that all over the field I might have half the flock wi' broken legs, 'cos they'll graze this grass again when we've bin over it once. You see if I didn't heel the holes in they ship be just as likely to get thur foot stuck down 'um, and the dogs might do the same thing. And no shuppurd can risk that—nothin' upsets a man more than to have summut 'appen to his flock that could have bin avoided.

'But goin' back to Cotswold ship,' he went on, 'my old grand-father used to tell I that when they 'ad the ship fairs at Stow, thur 'ud be as many as twenty thousand ship thur and most of 'um Cotswolds, the rest was Welsh. A wonderful sight 'e said it was too—you see thur's five main roads that meets at Stow on the Wold—just picture it, thousands of ship pourin' into that town from all the countryside around—ah, must 'ave bin a wonderful sight an' no mistake.'

'Is that the reason you became a shepherd and not a gardener like your father?' I asked him.

'Ah, I suppose 'twas because I spent a lot of time wi' me grandparents, I was the oldest you see, and me parents was glad fer

I to go and stop with 'um sometimes—left a bit more room for they as was left at home. They do say as I be the spittin' image of me grandfather—my word he was a wonderful story-teller, he'd sit fer hours and tell I such wonderous things, I'll tell 'e about 'um sometime, when we got a bit more time.'

Not that Mark was still for a moment while he'd been chattering. His enormous hands were tying string to hurdles as neatly and quickly as a boy scout. He was a huge man—well over six feet tall—and he walked with a long springy stride, so that I had some difficulty in keeping up with him. He must cover miles a day—dismantling pens and putting up new ones, always keeping two days in advance with the pens. All day long he was bending—whacking—rolling up, tying up, and rolling out again, great bundles of fencing wire, as well as keeping a look out for any sick animals in the great flock. We gazed at the sheep—but to me every one looked the same; a sort of vacant look they all had which reminded me of a long-nosed white-faced maiden aunt of ours.

'No, they be all different,' Mark said when I remarked on the similarity. 'If any of these was put wi' another flock I could pick mine out in a minute, I knaws everyone of 'um.'

The Friday pen was now completed, and we stood on top of the hill drinking in the glorious scenery. The day was clear, warm and sparkling, the elms already tinged with Autumn gold.

'See that big clump of trees over there,' Mark said, pointing his long arm westerly, 'see, right on the skyline.' I followed the finger and found the clump.

'Yes—yes—I've got it, is it a special wood?' I asked.

'No—tha's just a covert of beech trees—beech grows well on these hills, but that big clump happens to be over thirty mile away on the old Stow–London road, the old drovers road we calls it.'

The arm swung round easterly. 'Ju knaw what that hill is then?' Two pairs of narrowed eyes were focused on the clear horizon miles and miles away. 'Tha's Cumnor Hill, Oxford, that is—mind you, that has to be clear affor that shows up like it do today.

'And behind these yer trees,' he went on, inclining his head, 'is the circus.'

I grinned. 'Go on, you're pulling my leg.'

'Tha's gospel,' he said; 'tha's what they calls thur winter quarters, but thurs somebody thur all the year round. They do say as thurs lions an' all sorts foreign animals penned up thur. Mind you, I takes perticler notice as I don't go by thur; I don't want to get 'et to death. I hopes to live long and die 'appy, and not end up wi' bein' fodder fer a lot of wild animals,' he chuckled.

'And back behind us, thurs nothin'—thurs nothin'ness between yer and Banbury.'

I turned and gazed at the expanse of rolling hills.

What Mark meant was, there was no landmark—nothing but miles and miles of green, gold and brown—lush, unspoilt Cotswold country, beautiful, and bountiful.

2

'Me Operation'

As a rule Mark only writes to me when he and the flock have moved a fair distance away, so I was surprised to see that I'd got a letter from him about a month after my last visit. It was rather a sad letter. He hadn't moved far but wrote to say that 'for the past week I've bin feeling so bad, I don't know how I gets through the day—I be in such pain—reckons I'll have to go and see the old quack, the rains getting I down too. I've had a wet shirt a few times lately, I've had nine top coats and macs all sobbled'd up and not one of them fit to put on, can't get them dry quick enough.'

I knew that he must be feeling pretty bad to write and tell me, for in all his year's he'd never had a day off for illness, so although the day was cold and missling with rain I set off to see him. The south-east wind cut across the Cotswold hills like a knife-blade, and the rain was so sharp and cold it felt as if it was making holes in my face; but the air was invigorating and I felt quite fresh and elated as I rode along.

Mark was sitting in the hut when I got there. He looked pinched and blue; his eyes that usually sparkle were dull, and he had a sort of hurt look about him. In the hut, jackets and coats hung wet, dismal, and dripping. The dogs came out from under the hut looking absolutely fed up with the bad weather and their unusually quiet master.

'You shouldn't a' come out yer on a day like this my wench, look at yu', you be all sobbled'd up wi' wet.'

'Never mind about me—a drop of rain won't hurt. Now what's this all about you feeling groggy,' I asked.

I could tell Mark was in pain. During these few minutes his hand had gone to his side more than once and he winced as he talked.

'Reckons it 'ave beat I this time gel. As soon as I've had a wash an' shave I shall go along to see the old quack tonight.'

I noticed that Mark didn't even want to smoke, so I knew he must be feeling pretty bad. He promised he'd let me know in the next few days how things were with him.

Four days after my trip to see Mark I got a letter from him, but it was postmarked Oxford. I ripped it open and was surprised to see not his usual home address but 'Radcliffe Infirmary' in spidery scrawl. The letter read:

This is a bit of a shock for you my wench. 'Twas for I too, but I've had it now and it's all over. When I got home that night after you'd been to see I, I'm damned if I could move, so our Fred goes off for the Doctor and he soon had I in that ambulance and I was in Oxford before you could say 'Jack Robinson'. . . . Could you come in and see I and I'll tell you all the news.

From where I stood in the corridor I could see Mark propped up in bed. A little nurse came out and opened the doors and said 'Visiting time' and we all trouped in to part off at the various beds in the ward. Mark caught sight of me and blushed like a youngster as I went up to him.

He was certainly in better shape than when I'd seen him last and chattered incessantly for the whole half-hour that I was there.

The man in the next bed didn't have anyone to see him and I was being sort of shared between them both. 'This is 'er as I tell'd 'e about Joe,' Mark said to his neighbour. Joe grinned—a quiet little man Joe seemed, anyhow he let Mark do most of the chattering. Only when visiting time was up did Joe have anything to say.

'A master fellow he is' he went on jerking his head in Mark's direction. 'I've never laughed so much in all my life as I have since he came round after his operation. Doctors and nurses all seem to like him and he says unbelievable things to them—he's making us all laugh all day. If he goes home before I do I shan't half miss him.'

I bade my two invalids goodbye with a promise to come again soon. Before I was out of the ward Mark was making the night nurse laugh. The sister remarked to me, 'He's a merry fellow that one—how pleasant life would be if all our patients were so happy' and she bustled off—stiff backed—rustling with starch.

One or two things cropped up within the next few days and before I had time to go to Oxford again there was another letter from Mark to say that 'I be off home on Wednesday, so if you don't come to see I before then I shall be at home.'

I waited a few days before setting out to see Shup again. Country folk love visitors of all kinds but there is a sort of reserve about them, I knew; for a little while Mark would like to get settled. I would let the family and near neighbours be the first to hear all the 'horrible details' of the trip to Oxford. Only when the excitement had died down a little would it be my place to visit him. So after he'd been home about a week I made my way over the hills once more and knocked at the door of his cottage. Getting no reply I went along to Shup's neighbour whose name I've never heard for he always refers to her as 'Missus next door'.

'I've come to see how Mark is' I explained to her after we'd said our good mornings. 'I've knocked at the door but couldn't make him hear. Perhaps he's still in bed?'

'In bed Missus, no that 'e en't—thur was no 'oldin' 'im once 'e got 'ome. Farmer 'ad to take 'im up to see the sheep as soon as 'e come out a 'ospital and 'e bin a goin' up thur every day since—not for all day, mind you, for 'e en't well yet, not be a long chalk 'e en't.'

She gave me the direction to the field where Old Shup would be—he certainly was a marvel to be out 'shupperin' as he called it, so soon after his operation.

As always, he was pleased to see me. I try to arrange to visit him during his dinner time, otherwise his boss might think I was encouraging Shup to waste time. Not that the old fellow would do that, for he belongs to the old school and has his own ideas about employees who don't give value for money.

Our dinner consisted of bread and cheese. I declined a huge raw onion that Mark offered, but the hot sweet cocoa that we swilled it down with was very welcome.

The conversation came round to operations and it wasn't long before I was rolling with laughter at some of the antics that he'd got up to in hospital.

'I reckons as 'ow they nusses used to get I goin' a purpose just to 'ear I a chatterin'. Course 'alf the time they couldn't understand me cackle, strikes me they en't never 'ad anybody from this part a the country affor—leastways tha's what I thinks.

'I wasn't feeling too bad when I fust got thur and I an' a few more had to wait in a little room fer a while, till they got the beds made I suppose.

'Well we be set thur a chatterin'—every one of us was worse that t'other be all accounts. Then a little nuss says "I shan't call Mr Adams again, I know he's one of you—now you just answer up." Then I thought to meself, tha's I—I en't never bin called Mr Adams fer this farty years—they all calls I "Old Shup" er "Old Mark". Then awf I goes tu see the one as they calls "sister". "Mr Adams," 'er says, so I stops 'er an' I ses, "Look 'ere Ma'am I en't bin called that fer this farty odd years, cyan't you call I old Shup er Old Mark like everybody else do?"

'You should a sin 'er face. I thinks 'er'd a liked to 'ave laughed but I s'pose it en't proper to 'ob nob wi' patients.

'"Well now" she said, very sternlike "really I can't call you any of those names." Then she thought for a minute and said "I tell you what we'll call you—Mr Mark—how will that do?" So I thanked 'er kindly and said 'tud do fine—so that was it. I was Mr Mark tu all on 'em.

'Ahh an' byent they nusses some grand little gels too, smashin' little figgers they got—thur yent no wench in ower village that got a figger like what they got, dang me if thur is.

'Fust day I was thur, one on 'um comes an' puts a screen round I. "Whatever you done that for" I ses to 'er? "You're going to be examined by the doctor" she said. "Well" I ses to 'er "I dun't see as 'ow that screen's necessary at all. I byent no different to anybody else as I knows on", an' 'er went awf a chucklin' an' laughin' to 'erself.

'After a few minutes the old doctor bloke comes along, an' we 'as a long chat. Talk about questions! He asked I all sorts a things, so I ses to 'im arter we got a bit friendly like "Well sir, when be you goin' tu 'ave a go at I?", an' 'e said "Tomorrow I think will be best Mr Mark." "Well then," I ses to 'im, "thee gyet that old knife sharpened up an' make a damned good clean cut on it—I dun't want none a this yer muckin' about." An' 'e laughed an' said "I'll do that—I'll see you tomorrow then Mr Mark."

'So next morning they brings I one a they white coat things an' some long white socks. "Go along to the bathroom and put these on," some pretty little nuss said. Well that white coat thing only come up tu me knees an' thur wasn't no fastenin' on 'im so I puts 'im on, with the openin' down the front and goes walking down the ward. You should 'ave 'eard that sister, proper fiery 'er was. "Get back in that bathroom you disgusting man an put that blessed thing on properly with the split up the back." Well 'ow was I to know—I'd never bin to Oxford affor in me life, let alone 'ospital. 'Course the other chaps in the beds all busted out laughin', proper uproar thur was fer a minute or two. Then I'd only got one a they white socks so out I goes agen "Sister" I ses "I thought I was goin' to 'ave me belly cut—not me foot" an' I 'olds me bare leg up to show 'er. That made 'er laugh. "Here's the other sock on your bed you silly man", her said to I.

'Well, awf I goes fer me operation an' affor I knows wur I be, I be back in bed wi' me belly that sore. One thing about 'ospitals they do let you 'ave a drop a beer. I 'ad 'alf a pint most nights, an' when I come round arter me operation that's the fust thing I asked for, and I got it.

'The old surgeon bloke comes to see I next day an' 'e ses "You're a remarkable man Mr Mark. I hear that you insisted on getting out of bed and making a trip to the lavatory an hour after you came round from your operation!"

'"Well, sir," I said, "'tis like this. You see I byent used to women tha's the thing an' as fer settin' up in bed on one a they chamber things—well, I couldn't."

'Well, come the day when the farmer's wife—'e as I works fer—'er said 'er'd come and fetch I out at 11 o'clock. Then a message comes to say as 'er couldn't get thur till three. I was settin' out in me dressin' gown when the old doctor comes along.

'"Hello Mr Mark," he said, "I thought you were gone home."

'So I ses to 'im, "I can't go wi'out me clobber can I?" "Without your what," he said.

'"Wi'out me clobber—me clothes" I told him, and he laughed and said, "I hope to see you again some time Mr Mark."

'And I ses to 'im, "I 'opes to see you agen too sir, but I shan't come if you be goin' to chop I about agen." And 'e went down that corridor laughin' fit to bust 'isself.

'But I feels champion now, the Doctor said that I should soon get well, because, 'e said I got a stummock as strong as a horse and I told 'im, no wonder, I 'as to work like one sometimes. Do you remember that awful winter we 'ad a few years back? That damned near killed I, and twas that what finished my old dog awf—he was goin' on fer fourteen you see and couldn't stand all the diggin' out we 'ad to do. That snowed fer days, the drifts was up to me shoulder—thas all we done my old dog and me was dig the ship out of snowdrifts—never lost one we didn't. I fell down twice, prit near done I was, but thur was nobody else to help, so I 'ad to pick meself up and get on with it. Tha's all we done they snowy days was feed the ship and dig 'um out of the drifts—ah some of 'um was eight and ten foot deep, I've never sin such snow all the time I bin shupperin'.

'But my wench, everything has its compensations—do you knaw the wool clip from ower ship the followin' summer was

1

more than two tons—much more than we usually has. Nature has its own way of lookin' arter things and they ship growd more wool to help protect um.

''Course its allus a top coat colder up yer than 'tis 'tother side of Woodstock.'

287

3

Amos and Rosie

CHRISTMAS had come and gone before I had a chance to visit Mark again. I'd had a long letter from him telling me where he had the sheep grazing, and a list of instructions on how to get to the outlandish place.

'When you get on the Chippy road, our side, look out for a signpost to Crowsford, turn right at Pee-wit corner and then left into White-way, turn right again at Will's grave, past a big field of brussel sprouts, a hundred yards past the sprouts there's a sharp turn left up a dark lane what we calls Hangman's Lane, we be up there.' These lovely country names were all right for the locals, but it was like double Dutch to me and I didn't see anyone to ask for miles and miles. It would be more by luck than judgement if I ever found Mark.

I was thinking of turning for home when I saw an old fellow out walking with his dog, but he was so deaf that I couldn't seem to make him understand what I wanted. I was just about to ride off again when he said 'You'd best come down and see the Missus, 'er 'ull tell you whatever it is you wants to know.'

Down the road and round a bend we went and, there in a clearing, stood a neat little cottage; propped up against an old outhouse were bundles of faggots and some slim straight bean sticks, and stacked near the front door a pile of freshly sawn logs.

I left my bike outside the gate and we went up the small front garden path. The old fellow opened the door which led straight into a bright warm room. 'Rosie,' he called, 'Rosie come yer, there's a young 'oman as wants to know summut.'

The name certainly suited her—she was pink and rounded, she reminded me of the old-fashioned moss rose that grows in our garden. She had a pleasant serene look about her as she came from the back kitchen, wiping her soap-suddy hands on her apron.

'Hullo, Miss, can I do anything for you? It 'ent no good asking my Amos, fer 'es as deaf as a post, 'e don't understand a word you ses to him. Come on inside,' she went on, 'its enough to strip yu out there today, set down for a few minutes and I'll find summut to warm you both.'

She disappeared into the kitchen but was soon back with a bottle of home-made wine; she moved across to the dresser for glasses.

'This is a drop of me special,' she said pouring out the rich red wine, 'this will warm the cockles of your heart. This here is Sloe, I makes all sorts of the stuff, we drinks a lot of wine, 'tis like medicine you know as well as being warmful.'

Amos stood his on the hob. 'He likes to stand his there,' Rosie rambled on, friendly like, 'ses it takes the chill off. I has to watch as 'e don't put it too near, else he would crack the glass an' that's happened before now.'

We drank the clear heady wine. I declined a second offering. 'I'm not used to it at this time of the day,' I told her, 'it would go to the weakest place and that's my head,' and we laughed.

'I'll tell 'im what you said later on—he'll chuckle over that I'll be bound,' Rose said.

I explained where I was making for and asked her if she would put me on the right road.

'You'll be looking for Mark I'll bet, he that shepherds for Master Haines. Well now, you 'ent no more than two miles away from where he got the sheep—you was on the right road all right.'

I said goodbye to Amos—he and the dog were still thawing out by the wood fire. 'Who shall I tell Mark I've been visiting,' I asked Rose as we walked down the path to the gate.

'He'll know if you ses carter Townsend and his missus, we've knowed Mark all his life, lived in the same village when we was younger and we've allus been friendly like.'

I set off again. The keen icy wind cut across from the east, but I was warmed with the good wine, a glowing fire and the welcome I had received from Amos and Rosie.

'I'll bet you had a job findin' we,' Mark said, 'I'd begun to give you up fer the day.'

I related my adventures to him. 'Ah-h course I knows 'um, I used to court Rosie at one time, and ower Fred used to be sweet on her sister what lives over at Campden. Funny thing,' he went on, 'none of we brothers married, though thurs plenty of time yet,' his eyes fairly danced, 'I might find one as suits I, if I looks hard enough,' he chuckled.

'I be just goin' to give the ship a bit extra grub—shouldn't be surprised if we don't get a fall of some sort, snow most likely, that winds got round eastways this afternoon,' Mark said as we trudged over the sodden ground to the building where the sweet smelling hay was piled high.

'See, you never knows on these hills,' Mark went on, cutting the string that held the tightly packed hay and releasing the smell of dried grass and summer flowers embalmed like tobacco flakes in the clumsy bales. 'You see my wench we mightn't be able to get yer for a day 'er so—not like the main roads; they clears quick with all the traffic on 'um. I've knowed the time when this very road 'ave bin blocked fer days. Course old Amos and his Missus be used to it, if you'd had a look in their larder you'd 'ave seen as they got thur supplies in ready, just in case we has some hard weather. They knows that they'll never get a baker's van er a milkman comin' along this yer narrow road just for a loaf of bread an' a pint of milk with the chance of gettin' stuck in a snowdrift, so they gets prepared like. And when we gets a lot of rain that cottage of their's floods summut dreadful—the water comes up through they stwon planks, sometimes they've come down in the mornin' and the chairs 'ave bin bobbin' about like corks. And did you notice they had got two or three of they home-made rag rugs on the floors, they sits a-makin' um most nights—well when that water rises a bit sudden like, they old rag rugs gets that sobbled up wi' water, old Rose got they hangin' out on 'e line fer weeks a-dryin'. But they don't want to move, 'ad the chance of a council house, but they won't go, they be got attached to that cottage they bin there that long. Course that's a tied cottage really, went with the cartering job, but old Amos's boss ses they can stop thur, you see none of the young farmworkers or thur wives want to live in an outlandish place like that with no conveniences er anything. So they lets um stay, the place would soon fall down if that was left empty fer long.'

Mark and I worked steadily along the field. I threw the hay bales from the back of the trailer while he drove at a snail's pace along the edge of the wire fence. We returned to the building for another load.

'I got a drop of tea left in me flask,' Mark said, diving into his dinner bag. And we sat down on the loaded trailer for a few minutes. Mark rolled himself a cigarette.

'I didn't tell you about the bad luck our gaffer had just affor Christmas did I? Well, you know 'e breeds a lot of turkeys—dang me if 'e didn't have about sixty of 'is stock birds pinched. Ah-h, three nights running somebody broke in. So old Fred Bailey, the farm foreman, suggested that two fellows ought to be on guard every night, well until after Christmas anyroad.

'And 'e said that 'e and 'is son would take the fust night's watch. And according to them this is what 'appened.

''Twas cold and frosty as Fred and his son Dick donned thur old army great-coats and wellingtons; they pulled thur caps well down over thur ears, laced thurselves with half-a-pint of ten-year old dandelion wine and set off for the field, guns under thur arms.

'As they walked through the village they 'eard singing, coming from the pub it was too.

'"I'll bet tha's old Walt Tovey, I can recognize his melodious voice a mile off," Dick said. You see 'e was givin' 'um his special "Lille Marlene", and that being a clear frosty night made it sound louder. "We'd best get inside and 'ave half a pint 'er two affor we settles down hadn't us bwoy?" old Fred said, and thur was a roar of welcome as they went in; I knows cos I was set in thur with old Ned.

'"Come on and have half a gaiger* with I," he called to 'um, "theet want summut in yer insides to keep you warm if you be going to spend the night out in that field."

'Arter they'd had three or four pints, all the foreman and his son did was brag about 'ow they was goin' to ketch the thieves red-handed. "We shall cop 'um tonight, you see if we don't, thur'll be no need for any of you others to keep watch, it'll all be over be mornin'," they said. "All we shall do is fire a few shots a bit low and scare the backside of 'um."

'They stuck in the pub till closing time, then made thur way off up to the field where the turkey arks was. It 'ad begun to snow— that nasty swirling blinding snow, the sort that gets you wet through in no time.

'"The best thing we can do" Fred said, "is to park ourselves somewur so as we can see 'um come in the gyet (gate)—they got to come that way, thur yent no other way to get in the field. We cyant stop out in this weather bwoy", Fred went on, "we shall get buried in the snow at this rate, let's see if we can fix up some shelter of some sort." Then Dick had a brainwave.

'"If we was tu get in this yer ark, we should 'ave a clear view if anybody come in the field and we should be in the warm too."

'So they snuggled down along with 'alf-a-dozen fat cock birds; 'twas warm and close in thur and they was soon fast asleep.

'Suddenly Fred woke up—for a few moments he couldn't make out where he was—then 'e nudged his son—"Hey wake up bwoy," he said, "we be on the move."

'They, turkey arks and all, had been pinched and was halfway to London on the back of a lorry.

'It was a few minutes before they realized what was going on. Then Fred said, "What be us tu do now then bwoy? Shall us lay

---

* Half a pint of beer or ale or even something stronger.

yer quiet till they stops somewur, then we can hold 'um at gunpoint, we still got the guns."

'"I got a better idea," Dick said, "If they two in the front was tu stop and go into a café, I could slip out and fetch a policeman smartish quick an' bring 'im back yer affor they makes awf agin."

'After a while the lorry drew up in a grimy back-street, in a big town by the look of the buildings they thought. Both of the men in the front jumped down and went into a house.

'"Go on bwoy, make a run for it", Fred whispered, "And dun't ferget tu find out the name of the strit we be in, else you wunt know were tu come back tu."

'Dick crept out of the ark and up the dimly lit strit. Twas about three o'clock in the mornin' and not many folk about. After walking up a couple of strits he saw a phone box, dialled 999 and asked for the police. The night duty copper listened at the wild tale that the fellow on the phone was telling him. Course he thought twas somebody having a joke.

'Then Dick said a bit urgent like, "If you dunt send somebody quick tu Fernstack Road thur'll be murder dun when they turkey thieves come up 'gainst my old man, I tell 'e you'll 'ave tu 'urry up else somebody's goin' tu get hurt."

'"You stay where you are young man," the policeman said, "and I'll send a patrol car round to pick you up and take you back to Fernstack Road, and don't do anything silly like shooting anybody."

'By the time the police got thur old Fred had got the thieves up agen the wall. He'd got 'is 12-bore gun held a bit close to 'um and was swearing summut terrible at the lorry driver and 'is mate.

'The police took charge of the thieves and asked Fred and Dick to go to the station too, and they'd see as they got back home all right.

'Then one of the turkey thieves turned to Fred and Dick and said, "how the devil you come to be so 'andy, to be here at the same time as we, did you follow us all the way up here?"

' "We followed you all right, only you brought us, we was in one a they turkey arks."

' "Well I'm b——" the other fellow said, "who'd a thought it, but now you comes to mention it, I thought that last b—— ark we put on the lorry was damned heavy."

'Ah, we've had many a laugh over that,' Mark said, shaking his head and chuckling.

All the time that he'd been telling me the turkey tale Mark had been busy feeding the sheep. The sky was already darkening and with a quick glance at the threatening clouds he said, 'See they little rough clouds there—they little uns, darker than the rest— they be messengers, and they be come to warn us that thur's bad weather a-comin', I'll bet we 'as snow by mornin'.'

'Then I'd better get off home, 'tis nearly dark now,' I said, pulling on my gloves.

'Ah-h an' do that coat of yours up at the neck, you'll be froze to the marrow affor you gets far. Now you hurry awf 'ome, and you mark my words, tu'll be all white when you wakes up tomorrow.'

The weather certainly had changed since I'd started out, and my fingers were soon numb with cold.

When I woke the next morning the outside world was strangely quiet—no sharp sounds, just muffled noises of early morning in the village, and I knew before I opened my eyes that Mark had been right in his prediction—the countryside was covered in deep snow.

Rose's Sloe Wine

Pick 1 gallon of ripe sloes (usually late September or early October). Roll these in a damp cloth to clean them.

Place them in a pan and pour a gallon of boiling water over them. Now put in five pounds of *preserving* sugar, cover with a thick cloth and leave in the pan for fourteen days, stirring often. Strain and put the liquor in a cask or earthenware jar. Fermentation will now proceed slowly and while it continues corks or bungs should be kept fairly loose.

When fermentation has ceased pour in a wine glass of brandy and ½ oz isinglass, then tighten up the bung or cork. Sloe wine takes a long time to mature so it is unwise to bottle it under a year. The longer you keep this wine the better it becomes.

4

Sorting Spuds

THE February winds blew cold and damp as I made my way to Furlong barn, where some hundreds of tons of potatoes were stored, and where I was due to help with the potato sorting.

The sorting had probably been going on since the turn of the year at Glory Hill Farm, but now some of the men were needed to help get the land ready for planting, so the 'casuals' had been called in.

As I rode along I could see tractors bobbing across the fields. The ploughshares were cutting deep into the rich brown earth, lapping it over in thick dark layers, and there was that lovely unmistakable smell of freshly turned soil. And following close behind the ploughs were hundreds of beautiful white gulls.

Some of the fields had been planted in the Autumn; in these the winter wheat was already thrusting its way through the earth like millions of tiny green spears. The elm trees were already 'thickening' and would soon be showing their minute pink flowers. Catkins and Pussy Willow were blooming in the otherwise bare hedgerows and here and there in the grass the first few flowers of the Coltsfoot showed up bright and yellow.

As children we were afraid to pick these flowers. Our nickname for them was 'Pee the beds'. If this happened we should have got a walloping, so they were left to bloom and grow, untouched by most country children.

I look forward to a few weeks potato sorting. I know that I shall be working with my old friend Nellie Walker. Nellie is in her late fifties; she is short and fat and very jolly. She lives in one of the farm cottages along with her husband Harry and their twelve children.

They are a happy united family, and Nellie is a fine mother who loves each and every one of her offspring with a strong maternal pride. And Harry obviously adores his wife and brood with equal pride.

Up until a few years ago the farmer that we are working for, like others in this area, stored his potatoes in huge outside clamps. Nellie and I used to get 'frezzed stiff' as she called it. We had to stand out in the fields for six hours a day handling cold 'taters'. The east winds used to whip round us, freezing us and numbing our hands and feet. When it snowed or rained, the work was at a standstill. But not any more. The walls in Furlong barn are a foot and a half thick. Its warm and dry in there and the work goes on all day and every day, uninterrupted by the weather.

Besides Nellie and myself there are three men in the sorting team. One man feeds the potatoes into the machine. He does this with a huge twelve tyned fork which is much wider than a garden fork. The prongs have small bulbous ends so that no damage is done to the crop, which quickly travels along two shaking trays. Here the potatoes lose any soil that might have been stuck on them, and at the same time the very small ones drop through to a separate container. The rest go up a fast moving elevator and it is here where our work starts. Nellie and I stand either side of the machine and we quickly snatch off any green or split potatoes which we drop into sacks that are hung by our sides. These potatoes are sold for pig-feed. Then the good clean ones travel on and drop into sacks which are fixed on to the end of the machine. The man working there has to move very quickly; he takes the full sacks off and clips empty ones back on. Another man is waiting to weigh off the hundredweight sacks and sew the tops up with the aid of a bagging needle and strong string. The third man stacks the full sacks in one ton lots.

We earn five shillings an hour—the same rate that we are paid for picking up the crop in the Autumn.

'Ah', Nellie told me one day, 'we was that hard up when we first got married that my Harry was glad to take any old job at the weekends. And one was to lift about three acres of taters fer another farmer. He had to dig 'um up with an ordinary garden fork *and* pick 'um up too. And what do you think he got paid fer doin' that?' she asked. 'A shillin' a sack full! Ah, 'e done that fer years, I used to help pick 'um up too. I'd take our Frankie and our Bobbie with me, that's me two eldest. They used to try and help, but they was more hindrance really, still the fresh air done 'um good.

'We was livin' about four miles from Painswick at the time, ever such a lonely place it was, just one farmhouse and two cottages fer the workers. But they was good folk to work for; ah I reckon we stopped thur fer about ten years.

'One day I thought I'd give the kids a bit of a treat and make 'um a nice treacle puddin'. It would be a change from the kitchen maids legs I'd bin giving 'um.'

Seeing my questioning glance she said, good humouredly, 'Ent you ever heard of puddin' called kitchen maids legs before? They be boiled puddin's with currants in, what you calls a spotted dog!

'Well, I sent our Frankie, who was about nine at the time, into the town to get this treacle. Just as 'e got outside the gate the lad next door said to him, "Wur bist goin' Frankie?" So 'e ses, "Down to Painswick to buy a tin of traycle and if you comes along wi' I, I'll let yu dip yer finger in." I ent never fergot that', Nellie told me laughingly, 'Can you imagine anybody walkin' all that way these days, just to dip thur finger in a treacle tin eh?

'Our next move was to Gaginwell, that ent far from here,' Nellie went on, 'Ah we stayed thur fer about four years I think. I remembers one old dear as lived next door to we said to I one day, "Missus ull you come into Chippy with I, I got a bit of shoppin' to do and I don't fancy goin' on me own, I'll pay yer fare if you'll come."

'Well, I wasent goin' to turn a chance like that down so off we goes. Her wanted to buy a new mattress her said, her was fed up with the old feather bed as her mother had given her.

'When we gets into Chippy her stalks straight into the co-op furnishing. Up comes a smart young fellow and asks her what 'er wants. "I wants a new bed," 'er said, crackin' her jaw a bit.* I thought you said as you wanted a mattress, I whispered to her. "Ah so I do," 'er said, "Young man tis only a mattress that I be hinterested in." So the young man ses to her, "Yes madam, what sort? Do you require a spring mattress?". "Oh lorks no," 'er replied, "I don't want one just fer spring, he got to last I all the year round!"

'Talk about laugh, that poor fellow didn't know wur to put his face.'

Nellie rambled on with her tales, she was in good form this afternoon.

'Ah, and one farmer as my Harry worked for allus wore leather breeches—he used to have 'um made special like. Well one year they had a college bloke working on the farm durin' the summer holidays, and what ever he was doing, this yer young man always wore leather gloves. So the farmer ses to him one day, "Why do you always wear leather gloves at work my boy?" "To keep my hands soft and white" he replied. "Well," the farmer said, "I've always worn leather breeches and you should see my backside, tis as brown as a berry!"'

The time passes very quickly as I listen to Nellie's endless chatter. She comes from a large family of eight boys and six girls. Her husband is also one of a family of ten, so there are many reminiscences and incidents to recall.

'We only had two bedrooms in our cottage, when we was young and all the family was at home,' she told me one day, 'so it was all the men and boys in one room and we girls and our mother in the other, twas the only way to be decent.

'And there was a fellow who lived next to us who's name was Harry Bell, but we used to call him "amorous Harry" cos he was a bit fast with the girls, sort of fancied his-self he did. Mine you he was good-looking and nearly all the girls used to chase after

---

* Putting her talk on.

him. And if any new ones come to the village I'll bet he was soon walkin' out with 'um. He got that he'd brag summut awful about his conquests. So the village lads thought they'd play a trick on him, and one of 'um offered to dress up as a girl to see if he could get off with "amorous Harry". Thur happened to be a penny hop in the schoolroom on this particular night. Course thur was no street lights in our village and twas as black as pitch outside. Off goes "amorous Harry" to the dance and as usual flirts with all the girls. Then my brother goes up to him and said "Thur's a smashing gal outside Harry, just up your strit, why don't you come outside and meet her?" So Harry, who was never backard at comin' forrod, was outside in a flash. He chatted this so-called "girl" up and then they went off down the lane with thur arms all round each other. And following close behind, unbeknown to Harry, was most of the lads. Well "amorous Harry" manœuvres the "girl" up against a stile and he soon begins his overtures. Suddenly he starts swearin' and shoutin' at the top of his voice, "you be a man you bitch! you be a man you bitch!" Then he took to his heels and run off home.

'Well that taught him a lesson, he never did seem quite so amorous after that. As a matter of fact soon afterwards he settled down with one of the local girls, they got married and he turned out to be ever such a good husband and father.'

Just then two of Nellie's children came into the barn. We were working a bit later than usual to get an extra big load of potatoes done.

'Can we go flowerin' Mum?' they asked.

'Yes,' she replied, 'but don't get your feet wet. I know what they're after', she went on, 'they always likes to bring me the first violets. I heard their Dad tell 'um this mornin' that he could smell 'um, when he was down Mill Lane yesterday.'

Nellie and I had been picking out some smallish potatoes. I wanted to make some wheat and potato wine, which is very much like whiskey if its made properly. Harry said that he could supply me with a pound of wheat, so on the whole it was going to be a very cheap gallon of wine. I promised to give them a bottle of it when it was fit. Nellie's didn't make wine, 'I ent got the time and I ent got the room,' she told me.

'Have you ever been down to the forest on Palm Sunday?' Nellie asked me one day.

'Forest,' I said, 'what forest?'

'Wychwood' she said, 'lots of people goes there on that day to visit the wells. Do you mean to stand there and say as you've never heard anything about it and you bin livin' in Oxfordshire all yer life!' Nellie cried.

'Well you see 'tis an old custom whats still kept up in the Wychwood forest and its called Spanish Sunday or Spanish Liquor day and it always falls on Palm Sunday. 'Tis the only day in the year that the public be allowed in the forest, unless you get a special permit fer bird watching and things like that. When we was kids we never missed goin', you see', she went on, 'we only lived three miles from thur and the night before we always got our bottles ready.'

'Bottles?' I asked.

'Yes, bottles,' she replied. 'That's the idea of going to the forest so that you can fill your bottle with the magic waters. Just before Spanish Sunday our mother would buy a piece of real black liquorice from an old lady in the village, she would chop it up and give us each a piece to put in our bottles, then along with that we'd put a spoonful of brown sugar and a black peppermint, and we'd hang our bottles up in the myrtle bush all Saturday night.'

'Why a myrtle bush?' I enquired.

'Well, that was to keep them safe from the witches,' she cried. 'The next morning we was up early and off we'd all go, gangs of us trailin' down to the forest. We had to walk about two miles before we got to the lakes or ponds, tha's what they calls the wells these days. And all along the grassy "rides" on the way to the wells there was little tiny springs, dozens of 'um all trickling down until they fell into the lakes. When we reached the biggest stretch of water, what the locals calls Lake Superior, we dipped our bottles in and filled them up. Then we'd shake the contents like billyho so as to mix it all up. Then we'd drink this concoction and it was supposed to cure anything that you had wrong with you. Mind you,' Nellie went on, 'an old fellow told I that hundreds of years ago somebody happened to find out that this water from the forest contained a lot of iron, and I suppose that was why folks started drinkin' it. And I reckons that the liquorice and sugar and sweets was added later, just to make it taste better, though the liquorice was a sort of medicine too. Mind you, that Spanish liquor always had the same effect on I as young rhubarb do. I don't think that many people bothers to take a bottle with 'um these days, they can get all the medicine they wants off the National Health. But I think its a good thing that folks still goes down to the forest on Spanish Liquor day, it'd be a pity if the custom was dropped after all these years.

'Do you remember I told you that the general public wasent allowed in the forest only on that day?' Nellie said. 'Well that ent exactly true. You see the people who lives in the villages that skirt Wychwood forest still have what's called "wooding rights" and they can go and pick up kindling wood on certain afternoons, but you can only bring out what you can carry in your arms because no wheeled vehicles be allowed in thur, except of course of men who works in the forest, you know, clearin' the old wood and that sort of thing.'

I was fascinated by Nellie's information about Spanish Liquor day and promised myself that I'd not let another Palm Sunday slip by before I made a journey to the wells at Wychwood.

We finished the potato sorting about the third week in March. Nellie and I probably wouldn't meet again until the next potato harvest, although there was talk that the farmer might purchase a machine to gather up the crop, in which case none of the potato picking gang would be employed.

We were experiencing typical March weather, high racy winds. Someone told me once thats what they were for—'to blow away the last year's leaves and make way for the young un's to grow'.

There certainly seemed to be a great spring cleaning of the land, the harrows were busy leaving the freshly planted fields flat and tidy. A wonderful month March, a forward looking month, with the wallflowers in bud and the crocus blooming bright and golden under the house wall. And although there may still be frosts and snow to come, Spring can't be far away.

A Good Wheat and Potato Wine Recipe

I LB OLD POTATOES
I LB WHEAT
I LB PRUNES
I GALLON WATER
3 LB DEMERARA SUGAR
I OZ YEAST

Bring the water to the boil, take off heat and pour into a large crock or pan. Add potatoes that have been scrubbed and cut up small. Add sugar, wheat and chopped prunes. Stir well until the sugar has dissolved. When cool add the yeast which has been spread on to a piece of toast.

Leave for three or four days. When working has finished strain and carefully pour into a cask, jar or bottles, cork lightly until all working has finished, as transferring the wine from the pan to bottles often causes the wine to begin to work again. Leave for six months. Strain again through wine filters. This wine improves with keeping.

5

Hoppy the Roadman

HOPPY the old roadman was one of the most fascinating characters in the village, and a conscientious hardworking man he was too. Keeping the roads tidy had not always been his job. For nearly forty-four years he had worked on one of the local farms; then one day, while they were threshing, he fell off a rick and that finished Hoppy's farmworking days.

After he got over breaking his hip he became the village roadman, and the place was richer for it. Almost anything the locals wanted to know, they asked Hoppy, and he nearly always had an answer for them.

He was a small, boney sort of man—'When I was a lad' he told me one day, 'I should have liked to have bin a jockey, but that would have meant going away to train, and our mother didn't want me to do that. So I started work when I was thirteen for farmer Harper and just stayed till I fell off the rick.'

He would often shout at me as I passed by on my bicycle—'I got a smashing little story for you my girl, come along at dinnertime and I'll tell you'. Hoppy knew I was collecting tales about country people, and he had a store of them packed away in his lively mind. Some of the stories that he related to me were uproariously wonderful, but unprintable; and Hoppy told them with such feeling too.

For the story-telling episodes we usually sat on the verge-side, wherever Hoppy happened to be working. With our backs against a Cotswold wall and the larks singing above he would almost relive incidents of the past.

304

There was the day when workmen had begun to demolish a row of derelict cottages in the village, and as we sat there lorries were passing by piled up with rubble and stone.

''Tis a shame knockin' they cottages down,' he said, 'I recons with a bit of money spent on 'um they'd a made good homes fer people. Course I can remember when they was proper smartish places, ah-h, you could rent one of 'um for three and six a week. I knows because we lived in one of 'um, when we was all at home; thirteen of us was brought up in that end cottage.

'And livin' next door to we was old Ben and Sarah Green, and they was allus quarrellin'. Nasty vicious quarrels they was too. If I'd a bin old Ben I should have left that old faggot Sarah years ago.

'I remembers one time when Ben had gone down to the Lion to 'ave a drink, and he hadn't bin down thur long when Sarah said as 'er was goin' down to drag 'im out.

'Well, down the village 'er stalks, and into the Lion. "Come on 'ome you wicked old beggar", 'er shouted to him, "wastin' yer time and money in yer." And to Sarah's surprise, instead of swearin' back at 'er old Ben said, "Righto me old wench, I be comin', I be just awf out the back—shan't be a couple of minutes."

'After waitin' for about a quarter of an hour Sarah ses to old Charlie, 'e as keeps the Lion, "You'd best go and see wur 'e's got to. He might 'ave 'ad an accident or summut, fell down your old lavartory I shouldn't wonder." But old Ben had gone out the back way and 'ad 'urried off 'ome—just to 'ave 'er one. And by the time Sarah 'ad got back, he'd gone to bed and he'd locked 'er out.

''Er banged on the door fer ages, but old Ben never took no notice. Then 'er got the clothes prop and tapped the bedroom window. After a bit Ben comes to the window, pokes 'is 'ead out an' ses, "What do you want now, you wicked old varmit?"

'"Don't ask such daft questions you silly old beggar" old Sarah shouted to him, "you come down an' let I in."

' "Oh no," Ben ses. "I don't encourage folks to be out all hours lolloping outside public houses. You go and sleep in the out-house, same as I've 'ad to affor now".

'Later on that same year old Ben was took bad, that bad as Sarah called in the doctor.

' "Well, what do you think of 'im?" 'er asked the doctor as he come down the stairs.

' "He's a very sick man Mrs Green. If he's got any relations you'd better send for them, he won't last long," the doctor told 'er.

'A couple of days arter this, old Ben took a turn for the worst, but old Sarah left 'im alone, 'er was busyin' herself about the house—there'd be 'er brother Tom a-comin' and that dragon of a sister of old Ben's, Clara, and 'er husband Sid, 'e as ate like a pig, and they'd want to stay overnight.

'Well, later on that afternoon Sarah 'eard Ben tappin' faintly on the floor with 'is walkin' stick, 'er went to the stairs door and shouted, "What do you want now then?"

'Old Ben called down in a weak voice, "Is that a bit of 'ome cured 'am you be cookin' Sarah?"

' "And what of it?" 'er ses to 'im, nasty like.

' "Well that do smell good, I fancies a bit 'a that fer me tea." Back come old Sarah's voice, as sharp as a knife, "Thee get on with thee dyin' you wicked old beggar, that 'ams fer thee funeral."

'And do you know,' Hoppy went on, ''er never shed a tear when old Ben died a couple a days later. Still 'er didn't enjoy 'er widowhood long. One night about a month arter, Sarah went out into the garden to draw up a bucket a water from the well, and folks recons that just as 'er bent over a gust of wind must 'ave lifted 'er off 'er feet and 'er went head fust down the well.

'When postman Townsend called with a letter in the mornin', he found the door open, but nobody about; 'e searched about a bit, then looked down the well and thur 'er was. Providence, tha's what our mother said it was.'

Hoppy took out his watch, 'we just got time fer another,' he said, 'I'll tell you one tha's a bit more cheerful, tis about one'a the cricket matches that we use to 'ave in the village years ago. My word, we had some humdingers then.

'Ah-h once every summer we played a damned good match with a team from Crowsbottom; you know the place, about six miles from yer, and the prize fer the winnin' side was a five gallon barrel of beer. And although 'twas a friendly match, each side allus done thur best to win—and the ones that did sort of felt as they was top dogs.

'Mind you,' Hoppy went on, 'the field was a bit on the rough side wur we played. The night affor this match as I be tellin' you of, old Jim Banks had got 'is herd a cows in thur and that old cricket pitch was fair smamsed up wi' cow muck. And some of the players finished up wi' more of it on thur clothes than thur was on the grass. But nobody minded, it all made a bit of fun with everybody takin' it in thur stride.

'Well, our fellows gets that Crowsbottom lot out fer sixty-eight, and they was certain that they could beat that score. But things didn't go too well, the fust seven of our chaps was out fer thirty. Then Bert Makepeace goes out to bat and 'e looked like stayin' fer ever. All we villagers was a cheerin' 'im on as 'e slashed away knockin' the ball for four, time and time agen. Ah-h and 'e made thirty-three affor 'e was caught out.

'That only left Hurdle Weaver, Smag Holly and Old Shackutts, and none of um 'ad ever scored no more than 'alf a dozen between um.

'Fust Hurdle goes out to bat—full of 'is self 'e was, but 'e was soon back agen, out fer a duck as usual. That left Smag and Shackutts to hold the fort. And our fellows begun to think as that barrel a beer was already gone to t'other side.

'Down comes the ball towards Shackutts like a bullet out of a gun and everybody 'eld thur breath a-waitin' fer the stumps to be knocked clean out of thur 'oles. But to the crowd's surprise old Shackutts hit that ball hard and sent it over the field—it bounced on the ground then shot straight up the spout of farmer Banks pump—you know one a they old lead pumps what folks used to pump thur water up from the wells with.

'That ball was stuck firm up the spout, one and another tried to get it down and all the time Shackutts and Smag was runnin' backwards and forwards, red-faced and sweatin' and the crowd a-cheerin' um on. Course they got thur six runs, long affor some-body got that old ball down.

'All our team ran out on the field, they picked up the barrel of beer then they set old Shackutts on the top of it and carried 'im off as if they was carrying the World Cup. My word didn't we all celebrate—I reckons as half the village was drunk that night. We drunk the pub dry and the landlord's wife finished up the night by givin' us gallons of 'er home-made wine.

'They carried old Shackutts 'ome at closin' time—drunk as a lord 'e was—hero of the day he'd bin, and the villagers never forgot it.'

Hoppy packed up his flask and paper into his dinner bag and hung it on his bike handles.

'I be goin' to do a bit a scythin' this arternoon,' he said, knowing I should want to stop and watch for a while.

He sharpened the huge curved blade with a grey-blue sharpening stone and then started to cut the verge-sides. It looked so easy, that slow steady sweep that he took, as he felled the swaying grasses, moon daisies and blue cranesbill.

I had tried my hand at scything once, but, as Hoppy said, 'It takes a bit of gettin' used to.'

Hoppy came to a patch of purple thistles, 'Dang nusaince, tha's all thistles be, I should 'ave cut 'um affor this' he said, taking a mighty sweep at the five-foot tall weeds. 'Do you know that little rhyme about these blessed things' he went on, wiping the sweat from his ruddy face.

Cut 'um in May they'll spoil yer hay,
Cut 'um in June 'tis a bit too soon,
Cut 'um in July, then 'um ull die.

'Course I suppose that saying's for farmers, not for roadmen; ah I should have cut 'um weeks ago,' Hoppy said.

I left him scything away, taking long, steady sweeps at the weeds with his newly sharpened blade. I had some shopping to do in the town but promised I'd stop and have another chat with him on my way back. I knew that he had a break for a cup of tea at about three o'clock.

The wonderful smell of fresh cut grass met me when I returned. I was amazed to see the amount of ground that Hoppy had covered. All along the verge-side layers of thistles and grasses lay wilting in the hot afternoon sun. I noticed that he had left some of the wild flowers growing—I stood watching him, skimming round a clump of blue cranesbill, he cut very close to them but not one fell under the sharp blade.

'I 'ent got the heart to cut 'um all down,' he said, looking at me, 'they be such a lovely colour, when they be full out.

'I found summut as I knows you'd like to see,' he went on, 'come and have a look at this little nest.' I followed him to a clump of blackberry bushes. There, suspended between two bramble sprays was the loveliest little nest, beautifully made of bits of dried grass and lined with horse-hair, in it snug and warm lay five green speckled eggs, awaiting the miracle of birth.

'I wonder how many journeys they little birds had to make before they had enough stuff to build that nest,' Hoppy said. 'Listen, can't you hear they birds a-scolding us because we be near their home.'

The pair were flitting about from bush to bush twittering and chattering trying to entice us away from the nest.

'Billy Whitethroats they be,' he went on, 'I allus knows summer's here when they arrives. Keeps me eye open for 'um I do, then suddenly one morning I sees 'um in the hedge, they seems to come back year after year to the very same place.'

As we walked away from the bramble bush the scolding died down and was soon lost in the hot afternoon air.

The scorching sun had dried the swathes of grass which Hoppy had cut earlier in the day into sweet smelling hay; he kicked at the layers with his foot. 'Ah, and thur it'll stay till it all disappears I suppose,' he said, 'and yets I minds the time when small farmers have bin glad to come along and gather all this verge-side hay up, and some of 'um used to let the cows graze the sides of the roads too, on thur way to and from milking.

'I'll tell 'e what my girl,' he went on, 'there don't seem many frogs about this year. As a rule when I be scything they little beggars be hopping about like mad things in the grass. No, I can't say as I've seen more than half a dozen this summer. 'Tis all that spray tackle whats killing 'um off, it 'ent natural fer animals to be destroyed like it—they 'ull be having a go at we next,' he said laughingly.

'Ah, I suppose that old Cuckoo 'ull be going back any day now—I ent heard him calling for a day or so now. 'Tis funny, all winter we longs to hear him and before you knows where you be, they be all gone back to Africa.

'Thurs a good bush of Elderflowers over in that field,' Hoppy said, inclining his head. 'You don't want to pick 'um from the side of the road if you can help it, they got too much dust on 'um.'

I promised to come and gather some the next day, when I hadn't any shopping to carry. You must gather Elderflowers just at the right time for wine making—not with any of the flowers still in bud, for that will make the wine taste bitter, and not with any of the tiny flowerets falling or that will make the wine taste like Elderflowers smell, which is not very pleasant. I make both Elderflower wine and Champagne, the latter can be drunk two weeks after making and is the loveliest most refreshing drink imaginable, and a great favourite of ours.

During the night we had a heavy thunderstorm so I waited a couple of days before setting out to gather the Elderflowers. You must also pick them when they are dry and with the sun shining on them if possible.

Hoppy had moved a couple of miles further down the road. 'To another part of me *length*' as he calls the four or five miles of roadway that he has to keep clean and tidy. As usual he was pleased to see me.

'You knows the right time to come don't you my gel,' he said jokingly, 'I was thinking twas time I stopped fer me afternoon drink. I reckoned as how you'd be coming today, so I left enough fer us both to have a mouthful.

'We'd best set on the wall today,' Hoppy went on, 'that grass still strikes up a bit damp. My word, that didn't stop to rain did it? All I've done since is clean out they little gullies—you know the little channels what I digs in the verge-sides so that the water will drain off the road. They was all blocked up with hay and rubbish. It's funny', he said, 'that I should be ending me days as a roadman, for my old father done the same job for the last seven years of his working life. Mind you, conditions be a lot better than they was in his time, at least we got fairly good road surfaces these days. I've heard him say that 'twas nothing but dirt and stones then. And one of his most useful tools was a mud scraper—ah a bit wider than a garden rake it was. Course with all the horses and carts a-coming off the fields and they dirt roads, you can imagine how clapered up they'd get after a storm. Well he used to scrape this yer mud off the roads and pile it up on the grass. And after a bit, that dried and powdered down very fine. And during his dinnertime he used to sift this dirt and sell it to the local builders for 1s. 6d. a cart-load. I suppose they used it to mix along with summut else for building purposes. And another way he earned a bit extra was by selling beech leaves, fer compost. You see thur was quite a big beech wood along the road where he'd got his "length". Well one of the farmer's wives from the next village was a very keen gardener, and every week in the autumn-time her 'ud bring two or three sacks and drop 'um off on her way to market. And my dad would get 'um filled up ready for her to collect on her way home. Ah, he used to get 3d. a bag fer they. Threepence don't seem much these days, but I'll bet that was as good as a five shilling piece to my father.'

Just at that moment a dog fox slipped quickly and quietly over the wall about two hundred yards up the road from where we were sitting. He crossed the road and was over the field before we could get our breath.

'Crikey,' Hoppy cried, getting up to start work again, 'he's damned hungry, or his family is, fer him to be out at this time of day. I'll bet he's got his lair in that old quarry over at Westfields. Have you ever seen fox-cubs at play? Lovely they be to watch, pity they has to grow up to be so destructive. I remembers once when I worked on a farm, my gaffer had got a broody hen sitting on some ducks' eggs, her 'ad been set thur about a couple of weeks and one morning he went to feed 'er and thur 'er was set thur with no yead, a fox 'ad et it off, and that wasn't all, 'e ad bit the yeads off six of his pullets too. 'Twas his own fault really, 'twas too much trouble to go and shut 'um up at nights. Course he took perticler notice to shut 'um up arter that.'

Hoppy kicked over a freshly made mole-hill on the verge-side, 'Busy little beggars ent they,' he said, 'when I was a youngster I used to set traps to catch 'um. I used to get 6*d.* a skin for 'um, but nobody seems to bother to catch 'um these days. Ah, and talking about traps, have you ever sin one a they awful man-traps? Poachers' Penalty they was nicknamed. Terrible things they was, break a man's leg if he happened to get caught in one. Course they never bin used in my time, but I knows where there is one—still in the wood wur he was set all they years ago, and do you know my gel, he's all tangled up in the branches of a big beech tree, it just grew through the iron work I suppose. I expect when they used it, that there beech tree was just a sapling.

'Not that you can compare a mole trap with a man-trap or a gin trap fer that matter,' Hoppy said, 'but seeing that mole-hill reminded I to tell you about it.'

'I remember seeing a man-trap hung up in the yard of the Bull Hotel at Burford,' I said to him. And as I rode home I thought of another poaching tale that one of my old pals had told me, but that will have to wait for another day. Now my one thought was the Elderflowers that needed picking over, ready to make wine and Champagne.

Sarah Cook's Elderflower Champagne

2 HEADS OF ELDERFLOWERS
1½ LB WHITE SUGAR
1 GALLON OF WATER
2 TABLESPOONS OF WHITE-WINE VINEGAR
1 LEMON

Pick the heads when in full bloom. Take off any green stems however small. Put the blossoms into a bowl, sprinkle over the juice from the lemon, grate the rind and add this along with the sugar and vinegar. Add the cold water and leave for twenty-four hours. Strain into bottles and cork firmly and lay the bottles on their sides. Do not disturb for two weeks when the champagne should be sparkling and ready to drink. Do not try and keep this drink, as you would wine.

6

Missus-Next-Door

MIDSUMMER DAY had come and gone before I had the chance to visit Mark again. It was one of those perfect June days—the grass verges were waist high with (Kek) Cow parsley, Moon Daisies and Hemlock, and in the fields huge red balers thumped out hay bales at an alarming rate, and following in their wake sunburned men who loaded them on to trailers. Cattle stood under the trees idly flicking flies from their warm, pink bodies, and there wasn't a cloud in the china blue sky.

I made for the hamlet where Mark lived; he was having a few days holiday after almost three hectic weeks of sheep shearing. His first words to me were:

'You'll never guess wass goin' to 'appen to we—we be movin'.'

For a moment I hardly believed it, then he went on, 'You needn't look so surprised, my wench—I byen't going far—only up to the top end of the village.'

'But why?' I protested, 'I thought you loved your little old cottage. And what about the garden?', I added, knowing that his tidy plot was his pride and joy.

'Well you see 'tis like this, you can blame it all on to that operation I had. You knaw that little district Nuss that used to come in an' 'ave a look at I—arter I'd 'ad me stitches out? Well, 'er must 'ave reported what conditions we lived under—used to go on summut dreadful about ower cottage—and last sprintime Missus-next-door 'ad a fall, an' that same Nuss used to come an' see 'er—an' 'er told Missus-next-door as 'er'd complain to the Council about fetchin' water from the garden and trapesin' all down that garden path to they lavatories—and that rain

314

comin' in, you 'as to set in thur with a umberala up when thas rainin'.

'We only heard about it yes'day. Good job Gaffer got they two cottages empty up the top end—they used to be used fer the cowman and fer one a the tractor drivers, but they both got such gret families they bin moved up to the Council 'ouses. Mind you they cottages bin done up—they recons they be nice, cosy little places now.'

We were sitting outside Mark's cottage, the garden was ablaze with colour and summer glory, there were masses of flowers everywhere. Over the walls trailed honeysuckle and roses, and cushions of pinks and pansies spilled over the flagstoned path.

Poor old Mark—having to leave this—he and his brother had lived here for nearly thirty years. I had seen the cottages 'up the top end'. They had been vacant for almost a year and the gardens were waist high in nettles and docks.

'Ah-h but 'tis only temp'rey, just while they be doing ower cottage up', old Mark said, almost as if he was reading my thoughts. 'We shall be back yer in about six months—well, tha's what they ses—but you knaws what they builder chaps be, keeps knockin' awf fer tea they do, like as not tu'll be a twelvemonth affor we be back. Course, we knawed as 'ow they was condemned years ago, and Missus-next-door 'er was born in 'er cottage—and 'er's goin' on fer sixty-five and thur en't bin a darn thing done to um since 'er bin married and tha's farty years ago.

'We 'ave got the 'lectric mind you, but Missus-next-door 'er got none, a paraffin stove 'er cooks by in summer, and that old fire oven in winter, and 'er still got the old oil lamps what 'er lights of a night; course they uses candles in the bedrooms.

'And 'er roof—you can see from yer, 'es in a terrible state, that rains in summut dreadful in the bedrooms, and thurs pots and buckuts all over the place when tha's rainin', to catch the spots—ah-h and sometimes before they gets into bed, 'er and old Charlie—tha's Missus-next-door's husband, they has tu move the bed round if that rain starts comin' in in a new place, leastways tha's what they tells we.'

'Why ever hasn't she complained about the conditions, surely people aren't expected to put up with that sort of thing these days?'

'You 'aven't 'eard nothin' yet,' Mark said. 'We still 'as to fetch all our water from this tap in the garden—mind you we allus used the well water, then one day one a they sanitation men come pokin' round and said we wasn't to use the well water no more. And they put us this tap in and now we 'as the water from the main—leastways tha's what they thinks, but ower Fred and me we often 'as a drop of water from this yer well—thur's nothin' sweeter nor clearer than well water, though mind you in summer we do get newts in thur. But they little beggars don't 'urt—we chucks 'um back in again. I recon's everythings sent fer a purpose—p'rhaps they newts etts summat in that water as might do we some harm.

'Course tha's another thing the sanitation man said 'e 'ud get done, that lavatory of owern, but I recons they fergot all about it. Tha's the place—that little old stwon buildin' at the bottom of the garden.' From where I was sitting I could see the tumbledown 'little house'.

Mark went on, 'Now if I thinks a minute I shall remember just what that sanitation man said about it.' And he pushed his cap on to the back of his head and scratched his thick white hair.

'Ah-h, now I remembers—'e said 'twas a dreadful little 'ole—'e wants to pay we a call when I be emptin' 'im sometimes, 'e 'ud think as twas a dreadful little 'ole all right. All 'e done was just poke 'is yed round the door—and that was enough fer 'im. I suppose 'e was one of they town chaps what be used to they water closets. But we dun't take no notice, we be used to 'um.

'But we be lucky really, we 'ave got an old sink in ower 'ouse—mind you thur yent no 'ole fer the water tu run away, we brings it outside an' chucks it down the drain. But Missus-next-door 'ent got a sink to stand a bowl in—'er's a lot worse off than we really.

'And every time you 'as a bath you 'as tu fetch that old tin bath in—'e 'as 'angs up thur on the wall—then you lights a fire in the old wash-house copper, and when that water is nice and hot—thur you 'as tu sit—a stack a' coal on one side and a great bundle of faggots on 'tother—an' in winter the wind whistles under that old door—that east wind just sets in thur. I tells 'e, I don't 'ave no more baths than I be obliged to, that 'ud give I the pnemonia quicker than anything I recons.

'Course, it'll be all so different when they've done these cottages up, they be goin' to take all the stwon flags up in the kitchen, an' put a decent floor down. And when they've put a new roof on, Missus-next-door won't know what to do with all 'er pots and buckuts what 'er got up in the bedroom.'

'Is she looking forward to an easily run home', I asked, 'or would she rather jog along as she's going now?'

'Well, 'er recons that 'er won't knaw what to do with 'erself all day—you see thur won't be any stwon floors to scrub—no oil lamps tu clean and fill—no runnin' in and out with bowls and buckuts of water—and no more standin' in that freezin' cold wash-house to do 'er washin'.

'Old Charly 'ave offered to buy 'er one a they washin' machines, but I thinks 'ers too old in the yead to start using one a they contraptions.'

Just then Mark's neighbour, Missus-next-door came out. She had laid a tray with pretty rose-covered china—her best I should think, and several chunks of home-made cake—seedy, raisin and fruit.

'I thought you'd like a drop of tay, 'tis a thursty sort of day. Well if you bent thursty,' she said, looking at me, 'I knaws 'e is, for 'e chatters that much as 'e can't 'ave got a bit of spittle left in 'is mouth. Did 'e tell 'e as we got to move—fancy havin' to shift at my time of life—like rootin' up one a they old elm trees. Come and see I affor you goes', she called to me over her shoulder, 'I got one or two little orniments as I think you'll like; 'e says you be fond of little curios.'

I thanked her then—and again when she gave me two blue 'vawses' as she called them, lovely delicate china they were.

'You really shouldn't give me these—they might be quite valuable,' I said.

'Never mind about that, I might break 'um when we moves— I'd much rather think you had got 'um safe in your house. I knows as you'll look after 'um fer 'e ses you got quite a little collection. Perhaps movin' out of this yer hollow might do I a bit of good', she went on, 'fer I've 'ad the yeadache fer that long I fergets what its like not to have one.'

'What does the doctor say, or haven't you been to see him?' I enquired.

'Oh bless me soul I've bin to see him many a time, he have put it down to all sorts of things; now 'e ses that its me tith whats causin' me yead to ache so. 'E ses to I one day—Mrs Hawkins 'e ses, if you was to 'ave your tith out you'd 'ave no more yeadaches. So I ses to 'im, Doctor, if you think thats what 'tis I'll 'ave 'um all out—though what in the name of wonderment me yeads got to do with me tith I don't know.

'Well, I 'ad 'um all out, proper goormless I looked too, and I with me mouth as empty as a new born babe.

'Then come the time fer I to go and 'ave me pressure took. All that chap kept doin' was to keep puttin' a gret lump of 'ot putty in me mouth, made I as sick as a dog it did. So I ses to 'im after 'e 'ad bin muckin' about with me poor mouth fer about half an hour, "Look yer young man, if its all the same to you I won't 'ave no artificials—never thought 'twas all thus fuss and bother. I've 'ad the yeadache fer forty years and I recons I can put up with it fer a bit longer."

'Then the doctor said that it might be me stummuck. So I ses to 'im, 'old 'ard doctor, if you thinks I be goin' to 'ave me stummuck out you got another think. I byent 'alf the woman I was before I 'ad me tith out. Lord knows what I should look like with me stummuck out as well.

'Oh 'e did laugh, but 'e still thinks as I ought to persevere and 'ave some artificials, although they do say 'tis like walking about with a mouthful of gravestwons.'

I bade her goodbye and hoped that both she and Mark would be settled in the cottages up the top end of the village by the next time I came to visit.

Doris Bracknell's
Elderflower Wine

3 PINTS OF ELDERFLOWERS
(measure them in a pint cup, jug or basin)
3 LB SUGAR
2 LEMONS
2 ORANGES
1 GALLON WATER
½ OZ YEAST

Pick all green stalks from Elderflowers, place in a saucepan and cover with water, bring to the boil and simmer for fifteen minutes. Add the sugar and the rind from the lemons and oranges, bring to the boil again and simmer again for a further fifteen minutes. Strain into a pan and add the juice of lemons and oranges. Mix the yeast with a drop of warm wine, place on a piece of toast and slip this on to the top of the wine. Leave until all fermentation has ceased, then bottle and leave at least six months. Now strain through paper wine filters—this will clear any sediment.

7

Cotswold Friends

THE first two weeks in July had been dull and wet, but at last the weather had changed for the better. The sun shone on the ripening corn, turning the landscape to the colour of a lion. This is 'between time'—the hay harvest and silage cutting is over—the corn, not quite ripe, stands waiting motionless, the bustling days of harvest are yet to come.

I was off to visit my old friends Ethel and Fred Atkins. I'd had a card from them days ago reminding me of a long promised visit, couple with the fact that Ethel had written 'we be just got into a nice bit of pigmeat'.

I pushed my bike up a steep hill; there was wild thyme growing by the dusty roadside and here and there the verges were blue with drifts of meadow cranesbill, and fat brown bumble bees flew drunkenly about in the sleepy summer haze.

I zoomed down into the valley and passed over a humped-back bridge, underneath which a gentle stream trickled and sang. At the water's edge large patches of purple loosestrife stood straight and soldierly. And by the old stone bridge a little group of wide-eyed, pink-faced children dawdled, their arms filled with jam-jars and fishing nets. In some of the cottage gardens lace curtains had been draped over ripening currants and raspberries, in a vain attempt to keep the yellow billed blackbirds at bay.

Ethel and Fred were waiting for me; I was given such a royal welcome. Going into their house was like entering a miniature jungle, plants chambered up, hung down, wandered and sprawled over window sills and ledges. Licking tongues of cacti caught your sleeve, drawing you into the steamy jungle. Pots of geraniums were packed closely on side tables and shelves, and amongst it all Ethel and Fred sat like a pair of bright-eyed, red-faced gnomes.

'We be glad you be come,' Ethel said, ''E bin talkin' of nothin' else fer days, and we be got into the nicest bit of pigmeat as you ever taisted. And Fred was up that early this mornin',' she burbled on, 'you see my dear, we be goin' to have our own new taters today, first of the season, and he've picked some a they green winsors, 'e ses they be just fit, we knows as you loves a few broad beans boiled in the bacon water; thur yent nothin' nicer nowhere than that. Lorks 'ow I do go on,' she cried, 'yer be I a-chatterin' and I ent even put the kettle on.' She scuttled out to the back scullery still chattering.

'We be goin' to have you all to ourselves for the rest of the day,' she said excitedly. 'My Fred said to I this mornin', "Missus" 'e said, "by eight o'clock tonight that old tongue of yourn 'ull be fit to drop out, dang me if 'e wont."'

We wandered out into the beautiful garden. 'You be just come right,' Fred said, as he proudly showed me round. 'That won't never look no better than it do now.'

Every flower that ever grew in a summer garden was blooming there; the long border was a blaze of colour and there wasn't a weed in sight. Beyond the rustic fence, where Clematis, Honeysuckle, and Roses tumbled, was a splendid vegetable garden.

'Plenty of pig muck, thas what makes the tackle grow,' Fred told me when I complimented him on his wonderful crops. 'Come and have a look at our youngsters,' he went on, and we made our way to the top of the garden where two young pink pigs grunted happily.

'They byent very old but they be doin' nicely,' he said, scratching the backs of the animals. 'You got to make a fuss of 'um, pigs loves a bit of fuss—they thrives on it!'

Arms folded we leaned on the top rail of the pig run. It was built just the right height for this pleasant pastime—no words were necessary—we just leaned and gazed—gazed and leaned, while the pigs greedily ate the cabbage leaves that Fred had thrown to them.

'Well mother,' he said turning to his wife, 'its about time that dinner was done, I be fair famished.'

'By the time we gets down home it'll all be just ready to "strain up",' she answered happily.

We entered the cool kitchen. Ethel had laid the table with her best linen. She had placed a bowl of gloriously coloured sweet peas in the centre and their delicate smell filled the room.

The meal was first class; the bacon was done to a turn and the young potatoes and broad beans simply melted in our mouths. Raspberries, freshly gathered that morning and made into a delicious tart, swilled down with Ethel's Elderflower champagne, completed a wonderful meal. We moved out into the garden.

Here was all the peace and quiet that anyone ever wished for. Ethel and Fred had lived here for over forty years, they were happy and contented and loved every stick and stone. The words of Amos Alcott came into my mind: 'Who loves a garden, still his Eden keeps'.

The unmistakable smell of jam-making floated over the privet hedge. 'That's my neighbour,' Ethel explained, 'her said her was a-goin' jam-makin' this afternoon. I've made quite a lot meself: raspberry, blackcurrant, and his favourite gooseberry', she nodded in the direction of Fred's sleeping form. 'I don't really make jam with me raspberries,' she went on, 'its called "preserve", and you don't have to boil it, and it tastes just like the fresh fruit. And its a lovely colour too. I'll give 'e the recipe, if you'd like it. Once you've made it this way you'll never make ordinary jam again. Then I makes home-made wine with all the tail-end fruits, thas what I calls me mixed-fruit wine—thas nice and sweet, and course its a lovely colour too. Fred's favourite that is,' Ethel said proudly.

'I remembers that was my father's favourite too. He was head keeper at Catsford Park. Did I ever tell you about the time 'e got shot?' she went on, not waiting for my answer. 'I was about eleven at the time and our Mother was expecting a baby and because she was near her time I was allowed to stay up to keep her company while my father went out to try and catch some poachers. You see he had been losing a lot of pheasants, and fer the past week 'e'd bin going back to the spinneys at night-time to see if he could catch the thieves. Well about two o'clock in the morning he comes staggering in—he'd bin shot in the arm and another bullet had grazed his leg. And when he took his hat off, there was a bullet hole right through the top. If that had bin two inches lower he'd never bin alive to tell the tale. You see, keepers used to wear brown hard hats something like a bowler only higher in the crown. Well, as soon as it was daylight I was sent off with a note for the doctor. Mind you our Dad only had about four days off from work. And he never did find out who took a pot shot at him that night.

'Anyhow, about thirty years after the shooting a very peculiar thing happened. By then my father had died—nothing to do with the shooting mind you, no, I thinks 'twas pneumonia what took him off in the end. Well, my mother was still living in the same cottage, and we girls had married and left home. One day there was a knock at the door, and a big smartly dressed middle-aged man stood there, brown as a berry he was. Then he ses to our mother "Mrs Hackett isent it?" sort of talking down his nose.

'Yes, I'm Mrs Hackett' her said.

'Then this man blurted out, "Mrs Hackett I've come home to confess". Our mother sort of thought that her ought to know who it was, so her asks him indoors. Then he blurts out again, "I've come back to confess, all these years and I've never forgot that night when I killed your husband."

'Then our mother realized who it was. Twas Jack Arnott who used to live over at Little Cowpens. And this was the man who had shot my father. At the time they thought that he might have been the poacher, but nobody could find out where he'd gone. Some said as he might have joined the army, but nobody was sure. He was never heard of again until the day he knocked at our mother's door.

'Talk about relieved when he learned that my father didn't die on that night over thirty years ago.

'Course then our mother had to hear the full story. How this 'ere Jack Arnott took aim and he knew that he'd hit my father, cos he went down like a log, and when he didn't get up and chase him well he was proper scared. So Jack took to his heels and run and run—all through the night. He slept in hayricks and sheds, only moving after it was dark until he got to Cardiff, wur he joined a ship and in time he got to Australia. He'd got on ever so well, a respectable married man he was. But he just had to come back and make his peace. All they years of worrying, and all fer nothing. Still,' Ethel went on, 'you couldn't help but admire the fellow fer coming back as soon as he could afford it. Anyhow he went back home a very happy man. After that he always kept in touch with our mother—and each Christmas he sent her a big parcel, filled with tinned foods of every sort.'

Fred began snoring loudly. 'Hark at him,' Ethel said, 'he bin that busy getting it all to look nice fer your visit, now I suppose he thinks as how he can relax a bit. A cup of tea, that'll wake him I'll be bound,' she cried, and she scuttled indoors to put the kettle on.

The scents from the flowers—pinks, stocks, and roses—wafted across to where we were sitting, and the peaceful afternoon wore on.

'I'll tell you about another man who lived in our village,' Ethel said after we'd settled down again. Sid Thomas his name was, and he was the local sweep. Ah, he'd sweep my mother's chimney fer the top of a cottage loaf.'

'For the top of a loaf?' I queried.

'Ah, like as not her hadn't got no money in the house. Folks was so hard up in them days. I can remember when the village cobbler would sole yer boots fer a whole loaf and he'd do it while you waited. And women used to go out and get blackberries and walk into Oxford and sell em for 2*d* a lb to the jam factories.

'Still I was a-telling you about the sweep fust go awf. He was such a kind man, all we kids loved old Sid, nobody called him Mr, not even we children. He'd got a lovely donkey that pulled a little trap, and after he'd finished his chimney sweepin' he'd take a few of us children for a ride round the village. Mind you we had to take something to give the donkey to eat, sort of payment for the ride. We would cadge carrots or apples, or perhaps a bit of bran from our mother. And once,' she went on, 'he took us all round Faketon Hall park, that was about three miles out of the village. It must have been about 1909, and some sort of royal event, coronation or something special, anyhow he gave us little Union Jacks to wave as we jogged along in his trap.

'Ah, an' once he went to prison—for assaultin' a policeman. Mind you he used to get terrible drunk. He was the night he was arrested. But he was such a well-loved man that a lady, and I mean a real educated lady, paid for the hay for his donkey all the time he was in prison. And another time when thur was a general election on, he painted his door-step and his donkey and trap bright blue, just to let the people know who he was a-voting for. He tore round and round the village shoutin' and hollerin' politics at the top of his voice; course he was drunk as usual. The police tried to catch him, but he just managed to stumble indoors so they couldn't arrest him. He used to tell everybody that when he died he didn't want anybody to grieve and that he wanted a band to play at his funeral, and they was to play cheerful music. The day he was laid to rest a brass band come over from the next village and they played all old Sid's favourite songs, what he used to sing in the pubs. The folks was a-cryin' and singin' at the same time. We kids even had a day off from school. And Sid's wife and two sons followed in his trap with his faithful old donkey in the shafts. Ah, 'e certainly was a nice fellow, I don't think thur was anybody who'd say a bad word against him, except the police.

'Mind you, the village was a rough old place at that time. One old man used to tell us that just fer a bit of excitement on a Saturday night, he and some of the other young fellows would take off their jackets and dangle 'um in front of the pub windows. This was a challenge to anybody inside to come out and have a fight with 'um. Dreadful place it was fer fightin', it was. Still I suppose they had to liven up the village a bit and that was the only way they knew.

'Ah, an' long before my time thur used to be a witch in our village—well so my old granny used to tell I. Mind you, over the years I expect the story have got exaggerated a bit, but I do recall her a-tellin' about this perticler one.

'Saleena they used to call her; mind you her was quite clever really, 'er could cure all sorts of things. But 'er could be very nasty if folks upset her. Well, there was this big bully who used to tease 'er and say as 'er hadn't got no magic. Once or twice 'er threatened him and said as 'ow 'er would cast a spell on him if he kept on. Well one day in the street he started on 'er again, so 'er ses to him "George James, I've warned you affor, and now I means it, I be goin' to put a curse on you that'll last till you die or I die. You shall dance along the rooftops every time thurs a full moon and nothin' on earth 'ull stop you."

'Well 'e goes swaggerin' off down the street sayin' as twas a lot of poppycock, but sure enough come the next full moon thur 'e was up thur a-dancin' along the thatched roofs of all the cottages. So when the next full moon was due 'e got some of the menfolk to tie him down with big strong ropes, so as he shouldn't go runnin' around again. But long before midnight thur 'e was a-dancin' about on the roofs again. This went on fer quite a long time and poor old George got that thin and bad, with worry. So some of the village men planned to catch old Saleena and try to kill 'er. But 'twas easier said than done. Witches be funny things to try and kill. Well they caught her and eight of 'um held her down in the pond to try and drown 'er, that took 'um four hours before 'er was really dead. Then they had to find somewhere to bury 'er; you see you can't bury a witch on consecrated ground. So they takes her out of the village to what was called Highwayman's Corner; 'twas a little three-cornered piece of grass at the crossroads. They digs a grave and buried her there and soon old George James was his old self again, no more runnin' about on the roofs at full moon. But yers the funny bit, and I knows its true cost I've seen it. That three-cornered piece of grass wur they buried old Saleena is still thur, and right in the middle of it thurs a strip what measures two feet wide by five feet long whats never had no grass on!'

''Tis true,' Fred said, seeing my unbelieving glance, 'I've seen it meself, but don't you ask neither of us wur 'tis 'cos we shan't tell you, 'cos that would bring us bad luck. But now you knows the story you just keep your eyes open for it and perhaps one day you'll come across it, like we did. I expect you've passed the spot dozens of times, but didn't think anything about it.'

The sun had left the garden, and for a moment I felt a shiver run down my back. Ethel noticed it. 'Come on my dear,' she said, 'don't take too much notice of what we tells you.' But the story intrigued me and I vowed to look for the bare patch two feet wide by five feet long on a green triangle—somewhere in the county.

There was a bag of 'they winsors', a root of young potatoes, and a little joint of bacon all ready for me when I left for home. 'That,' Ethel said, 'is a treat for "himself",' the name she has conferred on my better half.

I had spent a wonderful memorable day with my two old friends, one that I should remember for many years to come.

Ethel's Mixed Fruit Wine

Pick all tail-end fruits—raspberries, strawberries, gooseberries, black and red currants—place in an earthenware crock and add a gallon of boiling water to every 4 lb of fruit.

Leave for four days stirring daily. Strain through a jelly bag. Add 3 lb sugar to every gallon of liquid. Heat very gently until sugar has dissolved (stirring all the time). Pour back into crock. Leave to ferment for another four days. Bottle off, corking lightly until all working has ceased.

Ethel's Raspberry Preserve

4 LB RASPBERRIES
5 LB GRANULATED SUGAR
½ OZ BUTTER (TO GREASE THE SAUCEPAN)

Put the raspberries onto a large meat dish and put into a warm oven. Place the sugar on another large dish and put that also in the oven. When they are hot tip both fruit and sugar into a large saucepan over a very low flame and continue to beat the fruit and sugar together until the sugar is completely dissolved. Pour into jars and tie down. This will keep for years.

8

'Tempory Move'

I⊤ was early Autumn before Mark and his brother moved 'up the top end cottage'. Missus-next-door followed the week after, and these two neighbours, who for so many years had lived side by side in the old cottages, were neighbours again in more modern surroundings. At least they would be spending the winter there, for as I rode past the old cottages I noticed that 'they builder chaps' hadn't started work on them. Already every window pane had been broken and Missus-next-door's roof looked as if it would cave in at any moment.

Mark had got the sheep grazing nice and handy; it is'nt often that they are penned so near his cottage that he can pop off home at midday and get a fresh cup of tea.

Mark was eager for me to see all over his 'tempory home' as he called it; it certainly was an improvement on the old place. He chattered excitedly as we walked round the comfortable little house.

'The best thing we done fer years was come up yer to live,' he went on, 'when we comes home at night thas just like a bakehouse oven in this livin' room, arter that bin shut up all day. See this "Aggur" cookin' thing, thas what keeps the house warm, and thurs always plenty of 'ot water. And if I 'angs my old jackuts up affor we goes to bed they be nice and dry by mornin', and we can 'ave a bath just when we likes.

'When we come up yer fust go awf, Missus-next-door said that 'er 'ad a bath every day fer a week—didn't like to waste the water 'er said—strikes me 'er had more baths in that week than 'ers had in a twelvemonth down at t'other place. Course, when you 'ave 'ad to carry all yer water in and out fer so many years, you gets careful like, and all these luxuries what we got up yer took a bit of gettin' used to.

'Ah'n flush lavatories we got too, just outside the back door; none of that traipsin' up the garden no more. And what do you think of ower garden now then? Some difference to what that was when we fust come up yer.'

Mark must have worked like a Trojan to get the garden as ship-shape as it was. Only a few months ago it had looked like a wilderness. 'Course 'twas the wrong time of the year to plant much,' Mark said, as he proudly showed me a good bed of spring cabbage plants. 'Just got they in on time,' he went on, 'you should always get yer spring cabbage in by Michaelmas, then they got a good start affor the ground gets cold; an' I got me a few Gilly flowers and Sweet Williams planted too.'

What a wonderful gardener he was, I thought, to have turned a wilderness into such a tidy plot. Still, I supposed it was some-thing that he had inherited from his father.

'I can't understand fellows these days,' Mark said, as we wan-dered back down the long garden path, 'they be fer ever buyin' a bag of this and a bag of that to try and make the tackle in thur gardens grow; this is what they wants,' he went on, prodding his stick into a great pile of farmyard manure, 'you can't beat it, nobody never used anything else years ago.

'Ah-h, and when we was young we 'ad to go out with a bucket and shovel and collect hoss-muck; plenty about thur was, fer hosses was used fer most everything. Nowadays if you goes out to gather some 'arter they've 'ad one a they Jimmykana things, folks looks at you as if you be daft. A powerful lot of good hoss-muck does. Ah'h brings the colour out in the roses that do.

'I've told you before that my old father was a gardener, up at the big house, and 'e swore by animal manure, and they growed some good crops in they days.

'He used to tell we all sorts of tales of a winter's night when we was all at home. Course I can't remember 'um all. but thur's one or two as I shall never forget.

'Thur was this man he knew whose daughter was gettin' married—mind you the old fellow 'ad begun to think as 'er was never goin' to get wed fer 'er was goin' on fer fifty before any chap looked at 'er. Anyhow this old fellow was goin' to give his daughter away, and the gel wantin' the weddin' to be all posh-like said to 'er father—"Dad, you'll have to get a new hat. I byent goin' to church with you with that old 'un, you've had him this twenty years as I knows on".

'So come Saturday the old fellow walks into the nearest town, four miles away, to buy himself a new trilby.

'He gets back 'ome about five hours later without a new hat. "And why didn't you get a hat", the daughter said, her was in a rare old temper 'cos the weddin' was the next week and the old man wouldn't be able to go shoppin' again before the great day.

'"Well", the old chap replied, "they 'addent got one me size. I went into every shop and the biggest any of 'um 'ad was size 7⅜ and you knows that I takes a 15½ collar and my head's bigger than my neck 'ent it now."

'Darned old fool, wasn't he!' Mark said, and we laughed while he poured out another cup of tea and he went on story telling.

'And another tale that 'e used to tell we was about the village postman. You see my gel, it wasent only letters that they 'ad to deliver years ago, oh no, 'twas a recognized thing fer the postman to pick up the medicine from the Doctor's surgery and deliver it at the same time as he delivered the post, specially to people as lived in out-lying places. Course, in they days medicine 'ad to be paid for, and thur was an extra charge on the bottles, so it was very precious stuff specially to the working class.

'Well, one winter's morning Postman White was cycling off on his rounds, there'd been a frost overnight and the roads was like glass. Suddenly he skidded—he went one way and his bike the other and the contents of his bag scattered all over the road.

'The letters was all right, but a bottle of medicine that he was carrying for old Mrs Ward was smashed. Now the postman noticed that on a piece of broken glass the label was still intact, so 'e put that carefully in his pocket. When 'e got to Mrs Ward's he told the old lady that her medicine wasent ready, but that he'd be sure and bring it the next day.

'When he got home that night, the first thing he done was to ask his wife if 'er'd got some Epsom salts in the house, lucky fer him 'er had. So 'e dissolved some in some hot water, and when twas cooled down a bit 'e fills up another medicine bottle with the mixture, then 'e steamed the label off that bit of broken glass and stuck it on the one containing the Epsoms and delivered it to Mrs Ward the next morning without battin' an eyelid.

'About a couple of weeks arter 'e called on the old lady again, this time with a letter.

'"Ah'h Postman," she said, "I've been wanting to see you," and the first thing Postman White thought was that 'ed bin caught out. Then Mrs Ward said, "Could you call at the Doctor's and ask him if he would please send I another bottle of medicine—the same sort as he sent last time. That have done I a power of good, I ent felt so well fer years."

'Mind you I dun't know how 'e got out of that 'un I'm sure, still I'll bet he had many a chuckle about they salts, I knows I have,' Mark said as he looked at his watch. "Well, this won't do my wench, we've had a good chatter and now 'tis time to get back to the sheep, be you comin' to 'ave a look at um?"

'No, not today,' I told him, and as I turned my bike towards home Mark whistled for the dogs and went swinging down the lane.

⅊⅊⅊⅊⅊⅊⅊⅊⅊⅊⅊⅊⅊⅊⅊⅊⅊⅊⅊⅊⅊⅊⅊⅊⅊

9

'Tatering Tales'

THE beautiful autumn weather that we were having certainly suited the gang of potato pickers. Picking up spuds is hard work, but if the sun shines this irksome task is made much easier.

We'd had a few slight frosts, for this was mid-October. Already some of the leaves on the elms and oaks were golden, and dew-wet cobwebs hung like miniature cartwheels on every twig and bough. There were blackberries in the hedge—gleaming black and shiny—but we country people don't pick them after October the 10th because after that date they say 'the devil's piddled on them'. But I think the proper explanation is that by mid-October we've usually had a few frosts and this, along with the misty mornings, makes the fruit go mouldy and it would upset the stomach if eaten.

It is pleasant working out in the afternoon sun. A few of us have stripped off our warm jumpers. Some of the women have brought their young children with them and the youngsters play contentedly, building castles in the rich brown earth. The field that we are working in is bounded by water; I am fortunate enough to be working at the river edge, and in the quiet moments I've caught sight of some beautiful pink speckled trout, and the water rats swimming into their holes in the river bank. One of the tractor drivers pointed out a badger's set to us, but of course there was no sign of Brock.

One day we caught a glimpse of a Kingfisher, but only for a fleeting moment did we see the flash of its brilliant blue wings. A few late scabious bloom on the verge-sides and in the hedge the sloes are almost ripe. As soon as we've finished spudding I shall be back to gather some for wine making.

It is rather sad that this season will see the end of the 'potato picking gangs' at least in this area. Because, one by one, the farmers are buying huge potato-picking machines which only need three or four men to operate. But this year, and for more years than some of the old 'uns want to remember, gangs of housewives have earned pin-money this way each autumn. So too have a few local retired men, who usually load up the trailers with full sacks of spuds or help to store them in the sheds and barns.

Only a few years back most of the farmers round here stored their potato crops in great long clamps outside in the fields, where they were covered first with straw and then with soil to keep out the frost. But the indoor method that they are using now is much easier and there is no risk of frost.

One man who has helped with the potato harvest for years is Jack Brookes, an upright seventy-five-year-old. He comes from one of the other villages and rides to work on his wife's bike— 'Cyant cock me leg over me own these days,' he told me. 'I be that ett up with the rhumatics.'

For nearly fifty years he had been a gardener, but retired when he was sixty-five. Now, like us, he joins in with the potato harvest. 'Provides I with a bit of baccy money and keeps I out of the wife's way fer a bit,' he said laughingly one day.

Sometimes I help with the heavy lifting jobs, and work along-side Jack, and we chatter away as we carefully store the hundreds of tons of potatoes in the huge old stone barns.

'Ah, I started work when I was thirteen at that old mill in your village, fer a shilling a week,' he told me. 'I used to have to walk four miles over the fields to get thur. Three or four lads from our village worked thur too and we used to sing and laugh on our way to work, and we used to pinch turnips from Farmer Bank's fields too. I allus was fond of turnips, I reckons they does you a power of good, ah, and walkin' do too,' he went on, 'I shouldn't be as fit as I be today if I hadn't walked the hundreds of miles that I have.

'I was only earnin' four and six a week when I was seventeen, then one day our mother heard that Lord Parks wanted a garden boy—they kept eight gardeners and six garden boys—and they was good people to work for too. So I smartens meself up and went along to see if I could get the job, but there was twelve other young boy-chaps there after it. And I thought how disappointed our mother would be if I didn't get it. "Be polite and honest" she said to me before I left home that mornin'. Well, I got the job and I stopped there till I retired, ah, and I was head gardener for the last fifteen years.'

He has been married twice and refers to the ladies in his life as 'my wife as is', and 'my wife as was' when he's talking about them. We were chatting about cooking one day and he said, 'Thur was one fer cookin' my wife as was, 'er could make a meal fer seven of us out of nothin' but a few bones and vegetables out of me garden—and the gret big currant duffs 'er used to make, full of lumps of suet they was, "butchers plums" we used to call they pieces of suet. My wife as is, 'ers a good cook, but her'll never come up to my wife as was, not fer cookin' 'er won't, 'ers all fer this new-fangled way of doing it, a packet of this and a tin of that and thurs yer dinner; wholesome enough I suppose, but I sometimes wishes as how I could set down to one a they smashing dinners my wife as was used to turn out.

'Still, its no good thinking about that now is it?' he went on, 'thur 'ent many people as makes suet puddin's these days, spoils thur figgers they reckons, ah, and I should think all this liftin' 'ull do your figger a bit of good won't it?' he said to me as we emptied the sacks of potatoes piled high on the waiting trailers. The tractor drivers were certainly coming into the barn with their huge loads at a rare pace, the weather had been good for days and the ground was dry and firm, and everyone was in a good mood. Each day we were all allowed to take a few spuds home. I usually picked out some big ones, 'jackty Taters' as we call them, for field potatoes always seem so much bigger than those we grow ourselves. The crop this farmer grows are *Majestic*, which suit the soil very well in these parts. Later on some of us will be asked to come and help sort this crop, but that won't be until January or February. At last the cry goes up 'dinner time' and Jack and I carry a bale of straw outside and sit in the sun to have our meal. We are certainly ready for the break, for we've been hard at it since nine o'clock.

'I never did tell you about old Charlie Douser did I?' Jack said after we'd finished eating. 'He lived in the same village as I did when I was a youngster. Do you know I never heard him called anything else but Charlie *Douser*, but he must have had another name. Like as not he was the first fireman that we ever had in our village, and you never saw him without a long pole, with a piece of flannel nailed on the end in one hand, and an old bucket with water in, in the other.

'You see most of the cottages and some of the barns was straw-thatched, and a spark from a bonfire or one from the blacksmith's forge could have easily set the village on fire, if it hadn't been for old Charlie and his bit of flannel on the end of his pole. Course, the only water we had was in the wells—there was a lot about the village, at the backs of the cottages. And although Douser always carried water with him, he could soon get more if a fire got out of hand—not that one ever did, but there was one or two near goes as I remember.

'When a fire did break out, the warnin' was given just by a good loud "holler" of "fire! fire!". All the houses was clustered close together and within minutes old Douser would come runnin' up the street, his long legs coverin' the ground at a rare old pace. He was one of the tallest men I've ever seen, about six foot eight he was, with gret long arms, so with these and his pole he could easily reach the roof of any of the low thatched cottages. He'd work like a trojan and have that fire out in no time at all.

'Of course winter was Douser's busiest time, with all the cottage fires lit for cooking, and firework time kept him busy too. Though thur wasent much money for fireworks in them days, but we used to have a bonfire and gather sacks of conkers and chuck 'em on thur, and they'd bang and explode better than any fireworks.

'But thur's one bonfire night as I shall never ferget. We boys was havin' a merry old time, goin' round the village from one kid's bonfire to another, when suddenly there was an urgent shout to "get the kids out of the way! quick, get 'em off the road!" And we was shoved into a walled garden. We peered over the top and saw this flamin' torch like a gret ball of fire tearin' down the hill towards the centre of the village. The women shrieked, kids cried, dogs barked, and old mother Broadbent flung 'er apron over 'er head and shouted that the end of the world was drawin' near. But old Douser had done some quick thinkin', he guessed what the fire ball was, he'd seen the lads of the village go swaggerin' off up the hill laughin' and chatterin', thur eyes full of mischief. Douser noticed too that workmen had been mendin' the top road and they'd left barrels of tar by the roadside. The boys had set one of these tar barrels alight and had started it on its journey down the hill. From the garden wall we watched absolutely terrified as that flamin' barrel got nearer and nearer. "Quick, give us a hand!" Douser shouted and he lifted farmer Dore's big iron gate from its hinges. Six or seven men rushed to help him and as the barrel reached the houses they held the great big gate right in the pathway of the fast movin' barrel, to divert it away from the cottages at the bottom of the hill. It was travellin' at such a rate that it nearly knocked that strong body of men off thur feet. Then it smashed against the opposite wall—paused—then went careerin' down the road past the church and into the village pond. Them boys come down the hill a bit shame-faced I can tell you, they didn't realize what a lot of damage they could have done. Anyhow the boys' fathers dealt with them, awf come thur leather belts and every lad had the biggest thrashin' of thur lives, in front of the whole village too.

'Mind you,' old Jack went on, 'nobody ever done anything like that ever again; which was just as well really, because the next year a "widder" woman from the Midlands come to our village fer a holiday and, do you know, 'er swept old Douser off his feet, married him and took him off to spend the rest of his life in a crowded city. But we often used to talk about him and the day he saved our village.'

A tractor roared into the yard, the women rose stiffly from where they'd rested their weary bones and walked slowly down the potato rows, ready to start again. Old Jack and I reluctantly got to our feet, ready to start another three hours hard work. I should have to wait till the next dinnertime before I heard more stories from him.

'Talkin' about blacksmiths,' he said to me a few days later, 'did you know old Gossop Taylor, he only retired last year? He was a darned good smithy too, I used to walk down to see him most mornin's. Nobody took his job on when he give up; pity, thas a nice little place. Course, three or four of we retired men used to go in thur fer a chatter every day, that was nice and warm in thur too, but talk about a dark little hole, couldn't see to tell the truth I used to say. I did laugh one mornin',' he went on, 'it happened to be one a they very dull winter days and old Perce Hill walks in and he said to Gossop "I can't understand you workin' in the dark like this, why dun't you 'ave a skylight fixed in this yer roof?"

'"Ah well" Gossop said, "If I done that, the kids 'ud chuck stwons up an' break the glass, wouldn't 'um?"

'"Well" old Perce said, "You could allus throw a sack over it so as they couldn't see it, couldn't you?"

'Folks do say some comical things sometimes don't 'um my gel', he went on, 'we had a fellow livin' next door to we durin' the war, 'e come from up north somewhere and damn me if I could understand him fer ages. He hadn't bin livin' next to we very long when he knocks at our door. I goes and he ses in a foreign sort of language, "can I have a loan of yer tomboy?"

'"Me what?" I ses.

'"Yer tomboy," he ses.

'Well I looked at him and he looked at I, neither of us knew what to say—for I didn't know what he wanted—he knew but couldn't tell me, well not in my way of talkin' anyway.

'So I ses to him, "I got no tomboy here, all our gels be married and lives away." Then he burst out laughin' and said, "I don't want to borrow your daughter, I wants to mend the missus's shoes and I wants to borrow your tomboy to do it with." I still didn't cotton on as to what he meant so I ses to him, "you come and have a look in the shed, perhaps you can show me what 'tis you wants", and do you know what he was on about my gel, he wanted to borrow me iron foot. Course we had a darn good laugh after that.

'Ah, and another funny little bit I heard the other day made I laugh, though really it was quite a serious thing. I happened to overhear the village grave digger tellin' a stranger about his work, and this was just the words he used: "Ah, I be grave digger in this yer village an' I takes a pride in me work. I digs 'um good and deep, then when they've laid the coffin in, I don't just chuck the earth straight in, oh no, I packs moss and pebbles round and makes it good and firm, ah, and when I've finished with 'um they be thur fer life."

'You see my gel, our little cottage is just agen the churchyard and thats how I overheard him a talkin'. And before I fergets, my wife as is said to be sure and ask you to come and have a cup of tea with us, as soon as the spuddin's over.'

But the spuddin' hung on longer than we thought. We had a few wet days that held us up and then when we did start again the going was pretty hard, with tractors and loads of potatoes getting stuck in the mud. The gang of women got smaller too, for the ones with the little children stayed at home. A muddy wet cold tater field is no place for a small child. And what had started out as a nice open-air job in the sun ended with mud up to our eyebrows and we were all thankful when the last load was carefully stored away.

However, a few days later we had some more nice warm days, 'St Luke's little summer' we call those last few bright days of Autumn. So I went along to gather some sloes that I had seen growing in the hedge of one of the potato fields. I make both Sloe Wine and Sloe Gin—the gin being much more expensive and much more potent than the wine; both are very nice. The trouble is we only seem to get one good year in about four with sloes, so I make an extra amount when they are plentiful to make up for the poor seasons.

After I'd gathered as many as I thought I needed, and prickled myself on the sharp thorns, I made my way to the village where Old Jack and 'my wife as is' lived. They were so pleased to see me, and I was shown round the tidy garden before going indoors for a cup of tea.

'Come and have a look at the rest of the cottage' Jack's wife said, 'though 'tis very small, just two up and two down, still 'tis big enough for we—tin bath, and lavatory down the bottom of the garden—we've never been used to anything else so it don't come amiss to us,' she told me happily. Old Jack followed behind close at our heels. 'I wants you to see the lovely view we got from the bedroom window,' he said. The cottage overlooked the churchyard.

'See,' he went on, 'the ground drops down sharp just beyond the church and then it rises again, see that wood, thas about four miles away, "Pinnocks" we calls it, thurs nothing nicer than to lay a-bed on a summer mornin' just when thats gettin' light and watch the daylight float over the wood and the fields, and the birdsong regler wakes you up but we don't mind. I brought the vicar up yer when he first took over this parish, and he was lookin' out of the window and he said "what a wonderful panorama Mr Brookes, you are lucky to live in such a delightful spot." So I ses "Yes sir I am, and do you know that you and I can see beyond the grave." He turns round and gives me such a funny look and said seriously "I have no claim for that, if you have." Then I grinned and said, "just take a look at your churchyard sir, and the graves, and the fields beyond—that's what I meant, we can see beyond the graves." Course he had a chuckle about it after, he's got used to I and my little jokes now.

'I thinks we be in for a hard winter,' Jack said as we settled ourselves down for more tea. 'I was sayin' to my wife the other day, the onions have got a good thick skin on um, thas a sure sign of a cold winter.'

'Haven't you heard that little rhyme about onions?' she asked me:

> Onion skin very thin,
> Mild winter coming in;
> Onion skin thick and tough
> Coming winter cold and rough.

'And the moles,' Jack cut in, 'they be going down already, thas another sure sign. You see they goes down deep 'cos the worms and insects what they lives on goes down, and the reason for that is so that they will be frost free. I wonder what warns 'um that ther's a hard winter a-head.'

'Ah,' he went on, changing the subject, 'I'll tell you about the time I made ten shillings in about two minutes, easiest money I ever earned in me life. 'Twas like this, I was walkin' home from me allotment one day and Squire Mayson comes up to I.

' "Oh Brooks, you are just the man I want to see," he said, "I wonder if you would come and have a look at my orchard, its been laid down with new fruit trees this two years and there's no sign of growth yet." Course I knew what 'e was on about, I'd noticed they trees meself and I knew they wasent doing very well, and I knew the reason. Mind you I didn't let on to him as I'd noticed 'um.

'Well we reaches the orchard gate and the squire goes to open it. Beggin' your pardon sir, thurs no need to go in, I ses, I can see what's wrong with 'um from here. You see, you had the orchard carefully ridged and furrowed, thats all right, the mistakes in the plantin'. Your men set the tree roots in the furrows, 'tis too damp, how would you like your feet in water all the time sir? All you wants to do is to get the trees replanted on the ridges, they roots will go down if they wants a drink. Then the squire puts his hand in his pocket and gives me a ten shilling note, that seemed like a fortune because at that time I wasent earning no more than three pounds a week.

'Mind you, a gardener has to be a very knowledgeable man and a tidy man too. You see, me gel, a gardener's like a housemaid, 'e makes the beds and emps the pots, no offence mind you, but you must admit 'tis right.

'We shall get quite a sharp frost tonight I reckon,' he said as he saw me to the gate, 'see how clear and red that sun's going down, good job you got your sloes today, they can stand a few mild frosts, but if that's a bit sharp they goes all soft like and no good at all.'

'Don't wait till next taterin' season before you comes again,' his wife said, ''e do so love somebody to chatter to.'

I didn't remind her that we had, in fact, just witnessed the end of potato picking by hand, the end of a way of life that had lasted since potatoes were first grown in this country many years ago. The machines would be a much easier way of harvesting them, and more economical; but not half as much fun, and I for one was going to miss it.

Mark's Sloe Gin

1 LB SLOES
3 OZ CASTOR SUGAR
1½ PINTS GIN

Wipe the sloes clean and prick each one several times with a large needle, throw into a Kilner type jar, now add the sugar and screw down the lid. Leave until all the sugar has dissolved. Now add the gin and remember to shake the jar slightly about every other day for three months. Strain and bottle, cork tightly and store for a year (if possible).

10

Ship Dags

*T*HE cold hard weather of the past winter had given way to a lovely early spring. Already the snow-white blackthorn blossoms showed up like patches of mist against the still bare branches in the hedgerows.

The birds were taking advantage of the mild days, blackbirds especially were chack chacking away, announcing to the world that they had staked a claim in the nearby hedge. All around the fields had been planted with corn, carefully harrowed, then left clean, tidy and bare to await the sun and rain of April. In the giant elm trees which skirted the hamlet where Mark lived, dozens of squawking jet black rooks were busily tidying up their last year's nest.

Mark was in the garden. He already had a visitor, a smartly dressed pale-faced young man; they were gazing into a trench which the shepherd had dug, a long deep trench which reached from where they were standing to the wall.

'You waants tu dig one like this fer yer kidney beans,' he was telling the young man, 'I allus do, I leaves it open like this for weeks to let the sun and air get into it before I fills it up with me dags, the finest thing in the world fer kidney beans is ship dags.'

The young man looked puzzled, 'What the devil are you talking about' he said laughingly to Mark.

'Well, you knaws what ship dags be surely, 'tis all that claggum tackle what we cuts awf 'um', Mark went on. 'You see about a month before the ship be sheared they 'as tu be tidied up, cos you can't send mucky fleeces away, an' when they ship eats too much young grass, arter being fed on swedes an' hay all winter, they gets

343

what we calls the gripes an' instead of the muck leavin' 'um it gets all matted round the wool. Ent you ever sin a ship runnin' about with gret lumps of wool an' muck round its backside? Well, this all 'as tu be cut awf, then when shearin' time comes round they be all nice and clean. What you waants tu do is to get 'old of some a this an' fill yer kidney bean trench up with it. You see, my boy, the wool 'elps tu 'old the moisture an' the muck 'elps tu feed the beans, an' if you does just what I tells yu, you'll 'ave kidney beans as long as yer arm. I'll tell you what' Mark said, 'if you likes tu come along sometime early in May, I'll give you a sack of daggin's, I shall be starting to clean the ship up then -ah-h, about the fust week in May.'

'And talkin' about ship daggin', one Spring I was a doin' me daggin', I'd got some of the ship penned up, sortin' out the ones with the dirty backsides then cuttin' awf all the muck with a pair of hand shears. I noticed that a car 'ad pulled up, and two men and two women—thur wives I suppose, was 'aving a look round the countryside. Then the men gets out of the car an' walks over tu see what I be doin', and fer a few minutes watches I workin' away. Then the ladies joined 'um. I'd just got 'old of a ship what was fair clapered up with muck round 'is backside an' one a these women takes one look at what I be doin' an' said, "How disgusting" tossin' her head in the air as 'er spoke.

'I looks up at 'er an' ses "What do you mean disgusting Maam, if your Mother 'adnt done the same thing fer you, you'd a bin in a fine pickle by now I'll bet." Her just stood thur for a minute lookin' at I with 'er mouth open, then they all cleared off.

'I often wonders if I shall ever run against her again', Mark said, as we laughed over his tale.

'He's one a they town fellas,' Mark told me, inclining his head towards the departing figure of the young man as he walked off down the lane, 'come to settle in these parts and don't know the next thing about gardenin', so I be goin' to give him some of my valuable advice fer what its worth.

344

'And talking about kidney beans, don't you ferget my wench, get 'um planted by Stow fair day May 12ths, we allus keeps to that date round these parts.'

'My next door neighbour said a funny thing to I the other day,' Mark went on, as we strolled up the garden path, ''e was tellin' I about a mole what had bin makin' a mess of his gardenin'. He said, "that old mole went zig-zag right across my seed bed—ah-h like a shot out of a gun 'e went." Damned old fool, how could summut go zigzag *and* like a shot out of a gun!

'I brought you a couple of mangolds home,' he went on, 'we opened the bury yesterday, just to give the cattle a bit of a change of grub, so I collared two of the biggest I could see, I knowed as you likes to make a drop of mangold wine about this time of the year.'

The mangolds lay on the path, they glowed bright orange and yellow in the pale afternoon sun.

'What's the news about your cottage? I've come over specially to find out when you're going back,' I asked him.

'Well the truth is my wench, we bent goin' back, we'd rather stay wur we be, you never see such a difference they've made to our old place—not the sort of home fer workin' chaps like we.'

'Whatever has happened? I thought you were longing to get back, and you've kept the garden planted too,' I cried.

'Well fust go awf they've put we a potty little front-room grate in—thas no good to we. I likes a fireplace wur you can set a pot with a bit of bacon on to boil—you got summut to watch then. Now if we went back thur, and we'd got a bit of bacon cookin' on the 'lectric stove, I should have to keep goin' in and out, from wur I was settin' by the fire, out to the kitchen to see if 'twas done—an' look at all the 'lectric I should use. And another thing, 'ow be I goin' to get my jackuts dry—sometimes I got six or more all soakin' wet arter that bin peltin' down with rain all day. And they've put the lavartory upstairs—now do you call that good plannin' for a couple of farm workers to live in—an' we a-comin' 'ome from work all clapered up with mud? No, I told Gaffer as it 'ouldn't suit we at all, and if its all the same to 'im we'll stop wur we be.'

'What about Missus-next-door? Is she going to stay too?'

'No, thas the funny part, 'er likes 'um 'er ses, and 'ers goin' back as soon as 'ers is finished, but we shall stay wur we be.'

I could see that nothing that I or anyone said would budge Mark and his brother from the warm comfortable cottage, so I just let him ramble on.

'Ah-h we got a very good system ower Fred and me, we does most of our work on a Sunday, 'e farms out the house while I does the cookin'—I recons to make a couple of big fruit cakes and a pie affor I puts the Sunday joint in. Then once a week me sister comes and does the bedrooms out and does the washin'—thas 'ow we manages.

'But thas enough about our troubles,' Mark said, 'I bin a-thinkin' of one er two tales to tell you, I promised I'd try and think of some my old Dad told I. I never did tell you the one about Silas Moore did I? He was the village carter round these parts, journeying between Oxford and all the villages that lay along the way, and he'd fetch and carry most anythin' folk wanted. Used to go shoppin' fer the ladies too, 'eed buy combs and corsets, flannelette nightgowns and calico knickers, he didn't mind what it was, 'e took it all in his stride.

'But 'e 'ad one fault, he used to get dead drunk. Regular on a Wednesday when 'e come home from Oxford Market he'd call at all the pubs along the way, and affor 'e got home 'e was as tight as a tic.

'But 'e knowed when 'ed had enough and every Wednesday arternoon he'd pull up at a quiet spot called Bell Bridge and sleep it off.

'Well, one day some of the local farm labourers who was workin' in a nearby field thought they'd play a trick on the old carrier, and as soon as he dropped off to sleep they un-hitched his horses and turned 'um out into a field. Then one of the men sat under the cart and waited for old Silas to wake up.

'About five o'clock that arternoon Silas woke. He set bolt upright in the cart, then looked round fuddled-like, a-scratchin' 'is head, wonderin' where 'e was. Then 'e said to 'isself "Silas Moore, I recons you be dead, well if its I, that is, but if it ent I, who be I?"

'Then 'e noticed that his horses was gone and said "Well, if it is I, I've lost two hosses, but if it ent I, I've found a cart!"

'Mind you, my old Dad said that arter that episode Silas went a bit steady on the beer fer a while—but it didn't last long, he was soon sleepin' it awf again on Wednesday afternoons.

'Ah-h another tale I remembers was one 'e used to tell about the days when the corn was all cut with scythes and thur 'ud be six or seven men at a time scything away in a field at harvest time, and in they days 'twas right and proper fer the farmer who employed 'um to supply a certain amount of beer or cider for the men. And every now and then the gang of hot thirsty workers 'ould stop and each 'ould take a swig from the big stone jar—you knows the sort, with a handle near the narrow neck. The fellows 'ad a knack of restin' the jar on thur shoulder and the beer or cider was drunk straight out of it.

'Course the jar was always kept in the hedge to keep the drink cool-like.

'Well, a pal of my old dad's was called Sid Parker, and 'e used to work in one of these yer gangs and 'e told 'im about the way they cured one of the chaps who was a bit greedy like. Jimmy 'is name was, they reconed that 'e 'ad twice as much drink as 'tothers. So they played a trick on 'im. One day when they was workin' in the field old Sid come across a nest of new-born mice and he and the other fellows dropped um into the beer jar, they knew 'twas prit-near empty. When they got round to wur the jar was kept, Jimmy made a bee-line for it—allus first 'e was.

'He took a good long swig and finished the lot—then 'e coughed a bit and wiped 'is mouth with the back of 'is 'and and said, "that beer's got a bit thick. I recon farmer's got to the bottom of the barrel; that last drop had hops in, I know."

'Course the rest of the gang busted out laughin' and holdin' thur sides and the tears a-runnin' down thur cheeks.

'Then they told Jimmy what they'd done and 'e was as sick as a dog. But that larned 'im, 'e never reconed to take first swig of the jar after that.'

While Mark had been story-telling the sun had moved round to the West and had begun to set red and rosy, lighting up the fluffy clouds till they looked like candy floss.

'Ah-h, looks like another fine day tomorrow my gel, "red sky at night—shepherds' delight". Course you know what they ses when 'tis red sky in the mornin' don't you, red sky in the mornin'—shepherds' warnin', ploughboy take yer coat.'

I had to admit that I hadn't heard the last little bit about the coat, but then I was always learning new things from Mark. He was such a knowledgeable man—this man of the hills—he knew about the habits of birds and beasts, wind and weather, a man who during his long life had never been away for a holiday—never been away from the wide hills that he loved so much. Yet he was content—content and happy—a man that anyone would be glad to call his friend.

Jessie Pratley's Mangold Wine

½ OZ YEAST

5 LB MANGOLDS	2 LEMONS
1 GALLON WATER	2 ORANGES
3 LB SUGAR (either demerara or lump dem makes a darker wine)	

Scrub the mangolds but do not peel. Cut into smallish pieces and place in a saucepan with the water. Boil until tender. Strain, add sugar and rinds of oranges and lemons to the strained liquid and boil for a further twenty minutes. Allow to cool. Add juice of lemons and oranges. Mix the yeast with a little castor sugar and place on top of the liquid. Leave to work for seven days. Strain and bottle lightly. (During the seven days while the wine is working keep the pan covered with a clean dry cloth.)

II

Bill Brown and his Missus

ONE thing about doing casual work for more than one farmer, is that you do meet a variety of people. And on one of the farms I made the acquaintance of Bill Brown. We had a lot in common, a genuine love of the soil and simple things of the countryside. So I always jumped at the chance to work alongside him for a few days. We found plenty to chatter about as we slashed away at weeds or singled out sugar beet.

This particular year Bill and I had been asked to help with the hoeing on the farm where at one time Bill had been fully employed, and although there was no need for him to work he loved to be asked. He would shake his old head and say to me, 'Ah, they can't do wi'out we old uns, we has to come and give 'um a hand every now and then.' Whether Old Bill included me when he said 'we old uns', I don't know. Bill, by the way, was in his seventies and I in my forties.

On this lovely May day we had been hoeing all morning, the sun hot on our backs as we worked. But despite the heat old Bill still wore his 'weskit', and thick cord trousers yorked up just below the knee, a striped working shirt, a large straw hat and heavy boots.

'I'll bet I be cooler than you', he said, eyeing my red sweating face and bare arms; he was too, yet I was clad in the minimum of clothes.

At dinnertime we sat in the cool of a giant elm tree, to have our 'vittalls'. Bill never called food anything else but 'vittalls'. It was either 'me mornin' vittalls, me nuncheon vittalls or me night vittalls'.

Some days we would sit and eat in complete silence, depending on now Bill felt. Other days he would tell me vivid stories of his youth; they might have been harder, but he reckoned that they were much happier times than the present ones. He used to say 'I be glad I was born in a cottage wur thur was allus piles of stew and mountains of dumplings.'

A young fellow who worked on the same farm went careering down the road on a great smelly tractor; this set old Bill going. 'Look at that damned young fool', he said, 'break his neck if 'e 'ent careful. The trouble is these days, if it 'ent got a seat on it, they don't want it. These young uns don't know nothin' about walking; our old gaffer always liked us to walk with our hosses—nowadays thas all they wants to do, set on they soulless things. But give I hosses anytime, they be near human, you can talk to 'um and they knows what you ses to 'um, too, and they got souls all right—that I be sure of. Course when I got retired from this estate me poor hosses got retired too; broke my heart to see they go off to the knackers yard, thur was years of good work in they hosses, same as thur was in I, and I be good fer another ten years and I be gone seventy. Course, when the old squire retired, and his son took over—'e as we be working for now—'twas very different. "Clear out all the old stuff" he said, I heard him, "men and machinery, and the horses will have to go", 'e said—a liability tha's what 'e called us old uns. Fair knocked I over fust go off, but they was very good to we really.

'Ah, the young master come to I just before I retired and said, "You and your wife can stay in your cottage as long as you like, you shall have it in writing." And he said they would give I a small pension, so they couldn't be fairer than that.

'Course I've worked yer all me life, boy and man—come to help in the stables when I was twelve and stayed yer regler till I was sixty-five.

'Mind you, this young gaffer got the right ideas—got to move with the times, but with all thur new-fangled methods, they won't produce no better crops 'er cattle than we did. His father was always winnin' prizes at cattle shows, and 'e'd let his men go in fer ploughin' and thatchin' contests, and I'll bet you nine times out of ten 'twas ower chaps what won.'

We had a slight pause while old Bill finished off his bread and cheese. Then he went on. 'Lot of alterations goin' on up at the big house. Young master 'ent goin' to live thur—well so 'um ses. I've heard tell that they've sold it for an agricultural research place, he's goin' to have the bailiff's house done up fer 'e and his young wife; plenty big enough fer them 'e ses.

'Then all they outbuildings and stables be goin' to be made into up-to-date flats and houses fer the farm workers and thur wives, thas why they didn't want the cottages as we old uns lives in.

'Mind you, I shouldn't want to move, not at my time of life; we've lived in ower cottage all 'er married life, and my missus 'ave lived thur since her was about seven or eight.

'When I retired they let I have all me old horse brasses. Carter 'e ses to I, you have these, I don't see as how anybody else is entitled to them but you. So we've got 'um all hung up, and me old drover's whip. The missus keeps they brasses shone up a treat. I should like as many pounds as times I've polished 'um, when I was working—lovely they brasses allus looked.

' 'Twas a nice sound they made too, a-jinglin' and janglin', and them hosses that proud, a-tossin' thur 'eads up when folks admired 'um—ah-h hosses be near human, I tell 'e what, the last two I had was called Beauty and Rastus, and I recons as they knowed every word I said to 'um.'

Here we had another pause in this fascinating tale of Bill's, while he swilled down his food with a bottle of cold tea. 'Nothin' like cold tea for a thirst quencher,' Bill was always telling me, 'and never drink between meals, 'specially when you're doing field work. 'Tis fatal, the more you drinks the more you wants to.'

'Funny thing', Bill went on, 'My missus ses to I the other day, "you might think this queer" 'er said, but I been thinkin' of old Beauty and Rastus such a lot today—keeps wondering if they goes to heaven along a we'. So I ses to 'er, "whatever made you think about them, they bin dead this past ten or eleven years, you gets such daft idea's in that old 'ead of yours."

'"Never mind," 'er said, "I just can't get 'um out of me mind, keeps wondering if tha's what they green pastures be for, what they sings about." Fancy my old missus a-talkin' like that. I told her the older 'er gets the sillier 'er gets.'

But I could see that what Bill's missus had said had moved the old fellow and he turned his head away and blew his nose very hard.

Time to go back to the hoeing—the sun beat down, and the sultry afternoon wore on.

'Get some thunder affor long I shouldn't wonder,' Bill said, when we stopped for a breather at the end of one of the rows, 'thur's a lot of they wapsy flies about, proper spitful they be too.'

We were both very thankful when five o'clock came. Bill looked tired and suddenly very old. He ought to give up this casual work, but I suppose he'd worked hard all his life and to use his own expression, 'he just couldn't abide to set still'.

The next day Bill didn't turn up for work, and as I moved steadily up and down the endless rows I couldn't help feeling just a bit worried. The farm foreman had been to say that Bill had had a bad turn in the night and wouldn't be at work today, but he added, 'if I know anything of old Bill he'll turn up tomorrow, you see'.

But old Bill didn't turn up again—he died the following day.

I called to see Mrs Bill a little while after; I'd heard that she was giving up her cottage and going to live with her youngest sister in a nearby village. 'I can't stay here be meself,' she told me, ''tis no good, I be for ever seeing my old Bill everywhere. Its best fer I to go and live with our Dolly, 'ers a widdow woman too. We always did get on well together, and I don't see why we still can't,' and she busied about, carefully wrapping her crockery in newspaper.

We began to talk about Bill, for he and I had worked together so often, and I knew just when 'my missus made her jams and wines' and when old Bill put his early 'taters in.

I told her that Bill had mentioned about the horses Beauty and Rastus and of her thinking of them so. 'Ah-h that was a most peculiar thing,' she went on, 'do you know, I'd had them horses on my mind for days. Then that night as he died, all he wanted was they horse brasses, and 'e kept asking for 'um, so I gets up on a chair and fetched 'um down off the wall. Then he said to I, "we shall want these soon missus" and he stroked 'um and went off to sleep. I tried to take them away from him—thought that he'd lie on them and make himself uncomfortable like, but he'd got hold of them that tight. So I left them there.

'Then about four o'clock—just as 'twas getting light and the birds was a-singing thur little hearts out—he wakes up, and seemed bright and well, he did. So I ses to him, what about a nice cup of tea Bill? He looked up at me and said, "I got no time to set yer drinkin' tea missus, I be awf to fetch Beauty and Rastus, and we be a-goin' out into the fields agen, out into the green pastures". And that was it, he just smiled and died, still caught hold of his brasses he was too.'

A few days later I saw a tractor and trailer carrying Bill's Missus's bit of furniture over to her sister's, and a pathetic little lot it was too. Mrs Bill had told me that she was going on ahead. 'I don't want to see the old stuff going out of the cottage,' she said, 'I wants to remember the place when 'twas full of life, not empty and quiet.'

About a twelvemonth after old Bill died, I was back on the same farm again. The first thing I did was to ask if anyone was living in Bill's old cottage. One of the young tractor drivers answered and said: 'A couple of months arter Mrs Bill left, the gaffer had it pulled down—'twas falling down anyroad—no good for nothing. We used the stones and rubble to fill up the ruts in the gateways.'

That evening something compelled me to go to the spot where the cottage had been. A stranger would have never known that there had ever been anything there, other than a field. For now, where the old place had been, corn was just coming through—the little cottage had stood in the corner of the field, and now it was just a field, with a lighter patch of earth that the mortar and stone dust had left. This was the only visible sign that anything had ever been there.

I walked about the patch of light soil—little bits of broken crockery that Bill's missus had used had been brought to the surface with the ploughing. I felt sad and quite depressed that this happy little home was no more—Bill had gone and his Missus I heard was ill.

The sun was low in the sky as I turned to go home. Suddenly I saw something glinting on the top soil; I picked it up, and knew at once what it was. It seemed as if old Bill was by my side telling me: 'When we got married I was only earning sixteen bob a week, and my old dad said to me, "I got nothin' else to give you but this—always keep it and you'll never be hard up." 'Twas a golden sovereign. So I had it put on me watch chain; 'twas safe thur, fer I should have had to have it cut off to have spent it. Anyhow it always looked nice, and as me old Dad said, while I'd got that I couldn't be hard up—mind you, thur was hundreds of times that we could have done with that to spend, but somehow we always managed.

'But a few years ago I lost it while I was a-digging me garden; we searched every bit of soil over but we never found it. You see it had bin on that chain so long, it had worn right through. In time we give up looking for it, give it up as a bad job, but I should have liked my eldest to have had it.' Poor old Bill, I thought, never mind, I'll ride over to the village and give it to his Missus; it might cheer her up a bit.

About three days after my find I cycled over to see Missus Bill—it was about six miles to the village where she lived. It was a lovely fresh spring day, and the air was like champagne. Everywhere was the lush green growth of a Cotswold springtime. Cattle, sheep, and lambs were enjoying the fresh young grass, larks sang high above in the warm sunshine. It was one of those rare, May days that you never forget.

When I reached the edge of the village I began to look out for someone to ask where Mrs Bill lived. I knew the house was called Kingfisher Cottage, but had no idea where it was.

A woman busy gardening told me the way. 'Ah' she said, 'you means her what come over from Tansworth to live with her sister, their cottage is about the tenth from here. But', she added, 'you're a bit late arn't you?'

I thanked her and moved off quickly, wondering whatever she meant. As I neared Kingfisher Cottage I could see a little knot of people by the gate; they were mostly middle-aged and elderly, and dressed in black. They stood quiet and still while men lifted a coffin on to a hearse. I knew at once why the woman had said 'you are a bit late arn't you?'

12

Cotswold Spring

It was nearing the end of May. I had heard from Mark that he had started to shear the sheep.

'We are in the old barn at Little Brackton', he wrote. Little Brackton is a very small village, one tiny church built in 1612, a manor house, five or six farmworkers' cottages and some old cotswold barns.

Mark had told me once that Little Brackton had been 'a smartish place' centuries ago. This could easily have been so, for there were several overgrown old orchards and many hillocks and mounds as if quite a number of buildings had once been dotted about. Now the manor house was the home of the farm foreman and the little church was only used occasionally.

Yet it was situated in a delightful valley, sheltered on three sides by wide high hills—green and lush, lush and green, that's how it looked on this lovely May day. Many of the fields in this quiet spot were carpeted with green and gold—gold from the millions of buttercups and dandelions which spattered the green grass. Giant Whitsuntide candles (horse chestnut blossom) graced the old knarled trees, and hedges of creamy-white May garlanded some of the fields.

'All in a rush with richness', is what Gerard Manley Hopkins wrote of the month of May, and how right he was.

In the little copsies and woods, carpets of bluebells glowed almost purple in the trees' shade. On the verge-sides sweet-smelling cowslips nodded their key-like bunches of flowers. When I was a youngster we children used to sometimes call them 'Freckled Faces' because of the orange markings on the flowers,

another country name for them is 'fairy flower'. A few late primroses, 'pimiroses' my gramp used to call them, bloomed on the
bank. And the air was scented with the delicate perfume from the
pink and white crab-apple blossom.

I crossed the field towards the barn where the shearing was in
progress. Dotted about were dozens of sheep already white and
shorn. It must be wonderful for the animals to be free of all their
thick winter wool, especially as the weather was uncommonly hot
for May.

The great tithe barn where Mark and another man were hard at
work was over three hundred years old. The huge door was open
on one side, and the sweating men were in their shirt-sleeves. It
was fascinating to watch them, how gently they handled the sheep
and how skilfully they sheared them. Now-a-days they use electri-
cally operated shears, but for many years Mark had sheared by
hand. A third man was kept busy folding and rolling the fleeces
and piling them on the floor.

When Mark saw me he stopped for 'blowings', a few minutes
to get his breath back. Carefully he rolled a cigarette.

'Look at um my wench', he said, holding out his enormous
hands to me. 'Soft as a baby's bum they be. 'Tis the lanolin what
does that', he went on. ''Thas wur yer lanolin comes from my gel,
out of ship's wool. You pays dear fer that when you buys sham-
poos and hand cream; come and do a bit of shearin' and you can
have any God's amount fer nothin'. Do you know before we
started shearin' my hands was as rough as a nutmeg grater? And
look at me clothes, they be all clapered up with the tackle, me
trousers be that stiff with all this greasy lanolin, they stands
upright when I takes 'um off at night time.

'Still, about another week and we shall be done I reckon,' he
said, pushing his cap back off his sweating head and giving it a
good scratch. 'Ah, thas goin' well this year, we've 'ad it dry you
see, and that makes a lot of difference. You get they ship all
clagged up wi' rain and you got to wait till they be dryish-like
uffor you can get goin'.'

'Where do the fleeces go, now that the wool staplers at Charlbury have closed down?' I asked him.

'Ah, they comes all the way from Thame to fetch these, thas the nearest place now, and I think the next one's as far away as Devon, since that un at Charlbury finished.

'I'll tel 'e what my gel, we shall be stoppin' fer tea soon. You see we works till eight o'clock, but at four we has a good half-hour break. We can have a bit of a chatter then, cos I got one or two little stories as you might like to hear. Why don't you go and ask the foreman's wife if you can have the key of the church? You'd be interested to have a look in thur I'll bet.'

'We don't get many asking for this,' she said as she handed me the great iron key.

I walked through the overgrown churchyard, and spent a little while in the peace and quiet of the remote little church. Then made my way once more over the springy turf towards the barn.

Mark and his workmates were already digging into their dinnerbags, fetching out great hunks of home-made cake.

'My blessed,' Mark said, 'you don' half want some grub at this game, you see we leaves home affor seven in the mornin' and that'll be knockin' on fer nine affor we gets back. I don't know about these chaps' he went on, inclining his head towards his mates, 'but all I wants to do when I gets home is have a damned good wash and go off up the wooden hill to bedfordshire.'

He finished his food and came outside. ' 'Tis better out yer', he said, 'the smell regler gets down yu in thur.'

We climbed the steep grassy hill. I was puffing, but not Mark; he strode up the high banks like an Olympic champion.

'Wonderful view from up yer,' he said when we reached the top. 'Ah, as near to heaven as I shall ever get I recons.'

It certainly was peaceful and lovely up there on that pleasant May afternoon. The world all around was fresh and new and the greenest green. Cuckoos were calling and larks singing and the air was clear and sparkling like wine. Half-way up the hill we had stopped to look at the source of a tiny spring, magically trickling out of the grassy bank.

'The purest clearest water in the world,' Mark said, cupping his hands to catch some. We both savoured the ice cold water. Mark splashed some over his hot face, the sun caught the falling drops, lighting them up like tiny jewels.

'I've planted a few roots of watercress, in this same spring a bit further down in the valley,' Mark said. 'I be hopin' fer a good supply of it in a year er so, you wouldn't get no frogs nor frogspawn in that, thas runnin' too fast.

'Ah, an talkin' about water reminds I of a young lad who worked on the same farm as I did at one time. He was allus called Grubby, Grubby Taylor, damned if I ever knew his right christian name. They called him that fust go off when 'e was at school. Proper dirtly little 'erbert he was too. 'Tis funny how a nickname 'ull stick. Yet when 'e growed up he was as smart and clean as any of us, but thas it, till his dyin' day, he'll allus be called Grubby Taylor by we village folks. Course thur was a big family of 'um and thur was no tap water in they days and none of yer bathrooms neither. The only way water was hotted was by the old washin' copper but I don't recon as they had their copper on a lot.

'Well, as I said, he worked on the same farm as I, and that dirty little beggar used to come to work wi' a fortnight's dirt on him. Then one day some of the older chaps thought they'd teach him a lesson, 'twas on a Thursday and Gaffer had gone off to market. Arter dinner they ketches Grubby and strips all his clothes off and chucks him into the old hoss trough out in the rickyard. Then they got an old brush what Carter Hicks used to brush his hosses down with and they fairly scrubbed him all over.

'The dirt was proper grammard in round his neck, you could'av planted onion seed in thur. It took four of 'um to hold him down, and 'e looked a different boy arter. That scrubbin's seemed to bring him to his senses for 'e never did seem to look quite so dirty again.

'Well, when the war broke out, off 'e goes and joins the army. And do you know my gel, he met and married a gel who's father worked in a soap factory, and arter the war Grubby joined him and the last I heard he had worked hisself up and is one of the firm's directors. I often wonders if 'e ever thinks of the day when 'e was stripped and scrubbed in the rickyard.

'Mind you,' Mark went on, 'his Gramp was a rough old fellow. I never did know how 'e earned a livin', for all 'e seemed to do was a bit of hedgin' and ditchin' and odd jobs. Yet 'e brought up a big family and he had a donkey and cart.

'But one day I see him do a very cunnin' thing.

'I was supposed to be hoein', but we'd had a sudden storm and I was shelterin' behind a hayrick. When up the road and past were I was standin' goes one of the mill wagons piled up wi' sacks of cow cake. The driver was set up front with his shoulders hunched up, he'd got a sack over his back and head cos of the pourin' rain. Well, up behind the wagon comes Grubby's Gramp, Faggot Taylor, and one of his sons. They was pushin' old Faggot's donkey cart and just as they got right up close to the mill wagon, Faggot suddenly jumps up onto the back of it. Then 'e lifted up the sheet that was coverin' the load, whips out his pocket knife and slits a great gash in one of the sacks, and into the cart falls some cow cake. Then 'e cuts open another and then another till his donkey cart was nearly full. Then 'e jumped down off the back of the mill wagon, flung the sheet back over the sacks and 'e and his son just dawdled along home with their load. 'Twas all over in less time than it have took to tell you. I wouldn't mind bettin' as that wagon driver never did find out who slit they sacks.

'Now this next story as I be goin' to tell 'e happened in our village. Mind you, 'twas affor we was put on the sewer; still, that was only three years ago.

'Well, one of our neighbours, Jim Potter and his missus, 'ad got Jim's Auntie Laura stayin' with 'um fer Easter. This Auntie come from London and 'twas the fust time as 'er had visited 'um. Course the time come when 'er had to pay a visit to their "little house" at the bottom of the garden. Well, back 'er comes a bit worried like, "Jim", 'er said, "the door of the lavatory won't shut properly, why don't you do something about it, get a key my boy and lock it up." Old Jim looked a bit puzzled like, then he said, "Auntie Laura, we've bin livin' yer fer the past twenty years and we've never 'ad a bucket of muck pinched yet, so why should I lock it up now?"'

Mark and I had a good laugh as we strolled back down the grassy bank. It was nearly time for him to start work again, and time I set out over the hills again too. When we got to where my bicycle stood, Mark said, 'Hello, you got a flat tyre my wench, that comes of leavin' yer bike in the sun. Ah, that reminds I of an old fellow who used to come round these parts sellin' sausages years ago. One day he had a puncture and he' got nothin' to mend it with and he was miles away from home, so 'e stuffed the front tube with sausages and got back that way. But you got no sausages, so we shall have to have a go at pumpin' 'im up.'

Mark blew up the tyre, which thankfully kept hard.

'Try and come over again, affor we finishes the shearin',' Mark called as I rode away.

The next few days were taken up with gathering dandelions and making them into wine. Of all the sorts I make, this seems to be the most popular. My neighbour goes to the trouble of picking out all the yellow petals to make his, but having made and savoured both sorts I think the one using the whole flower is best, and of course not half so much trouble.

We were now into June, and the weather had turned quite cool. Only a week had passed since I had last made my way over the hills to see Mark, yet there was a great upsurge of growth everywhere. The grass fields which had not yet been cut waved and rippled like huge green seas. Gone already were the Whitsuntide Candles from the horse-chestnut trees, and a few early dog-roses trailed over the hedgerows.

'Good job you didn't put off your visit any longer,' Mark said, ''Cos we shan't be yer arter tomorrow.'

The three weeks hard work of shearing was almost at an end. The men were working against time, anxious to see the finish of it. Only a few sheep waited patiently and quiet in the pen. I watched as the last half-dozen were sheared; the last animal ran out into the field, the men straightened their backs and it was all over for another year.

'Ah, we shall be glad to see the backside of this lot,' Mark said, nodding in the direction of the great piles of fleeces stacked almost to the rafters at one end of the barn.

'They be comin' for 'um tomorrow; we shall help load 'um up and then we hopes to have a few days off. 'Tis a bit easier on the farm once the shearin's done. This is when the farmer "sits and takes his ease" fer about a couple of weeks, though thur yent much easetakin' at this lark,' he went on, 'fer gaffer have already started cuttin' fer silage. I don't think he's goin' in fer much hay this time.

'This yer,' Mark said turning towards the men who had been working with him, 'is Jacko and Thumper, old Thumper was sayin' that he'd got a little tale to tell you but he's a bit on the shy side. Come on Thumper, come and set down yer fer ten minutes, we ent got nothin' to do till the foreman comes to take we home.'

Thumper, a short stocky red faced fellow, came over and sat down.

'Well,' he said, 'I don't rightly know where to begin.'

'At the beginnin', you gret lappen,' Mark said grinning.

'I suppose its alright to tell you this,' Thumper said nervously. 'I mean, seeing as how you might put it in that little book of yourn. But a fellow come to see we the other night and he told it to us and we did have a laugh my missus and me.' I assured him that I had no first claim on any of my 'little stories', because someone or other had told me them. He seemed to buck up a bit when I said that and started speaking in his lovely broad dialect.

'Well, some years ago, a country bumpkin went to Burford fair. Course they didn't have many outin's in they days and this was a real treat fer him. Well, fust go off he trys his luck on the hoopla stall and after two or three goes he wins. So the man on the stall gives him a tortoise fer a prize and this yer fellow goes awf with his winnin's as proud as punch. Well, he strolls round the fair fer a bit and comes back to the hoopla again and has another go and he wins again. This time the stall-holder asked him what prize he wanted. "Ah, summut different this time", he said, "the meat in that pie I won was alright, but the crust was a bit hard, I had to throw that away".'

Just then the farm foreman came to collect the weary men. I thanked Thumper for his contribution and hoped that some day he would think of another tale to tell me.

'Next time you comes, my gel', Mark called, 'I shall be down home, tha's if you comes along within the next ten days.'

I promised to do that. We should have more time to chatter then.

My favourite recipe for Dandelion Wine

3 QUARTS FLOWERS
3 LB SUGAR
1 GALLON WATER
1 LB RAISINS
2 LEMONS
1 ORANGE
1 OZ YEAST

The flowers must be freshly picked. (Nip off the smallest pieces of stalk as any left on will make the wine taste bitter.) Put the flower heads into a large bowl. Bring the water to the boil and pour over the dandelions. Leave for three days, stirring once each day. Strain. Now add the sugar and the rinds only of the lemons and orange. Turn into a saucepan and boil gently for an hour. Put back into the bowl and add the juice of the lemons and orange. Leave until cool (not cold) place the yeast onto a piece of toast and place on top of the wine. Leave for three days when it should be ready to strain and put into bottles (do not quite fill bottles). Divide the raisins and slip into the bottles. Do not cork tightly until the wine has finished working. Then strain once more through paper wine filters. Made in June this is ready for drinking at Christmas.

PS. Always keep the wine covered with a cloth during the making period.

❧❧❧❧❧❧❧❧❧❧❧❧❧❧❧❧❧❧❧❧❧❧❧❧❧❧❧

13

All on a Summer Day

NEARLY a year had passed since Mark and Missus-next-door had first left their tumble-down old cottages to live in the temporary ones 'up the top end of the village', and while Mark and his brother had decided to stay, because of the convenience—Missus-next-door had settled back in her original cottage and she had sent a message to say that she would like me to call and see her and the renovations.

So one sweltering August day I set off to see her. It was hot, and very tiring with dozens of midge-flies—thunder flies some people call them—sticking to my sweating face. It was certainly very sultry and would probably end in a thunderstorm.

With half my journey behind me I thought I'd rest a while. A tall beech tree offered both shade and comfort and I soon settled down with my back against its smooth trunk. As I sat there cooling off I remembered another weary traveller. He was an old fellow known in these parts as 'The Witney Man', and the expression, 'I've got the Witney Man' is still used round here, especially by the older people when they are feeling tired and weary, for some of them remember the man who was given this nickname and why.

Many years ago the only method of cooking was either by fire or paraffin oil. And one progressive firm in Witney used to deliver paraffin oil, lamps, stoves, and wicks to many of the housewives living in the outlying villages. One of the men who worked for this firm was called Frank Pratley, and his delivery area was round Stonesfield, Coombe, Fawler, and Finstock. It was quite an event for the villagers when once a week he came driving through the village in his horse and cart. 'Yer comes the Witney man' they would call to one another, and they would pick up their tin cans and jars and crowd round his cart to be served.

He was a kind man and if any of them had trouble in fixing a lamp wick, or their stove smoked, he would always put it right for them.

Well, after one hot trying day Frank Pratley turned towards home. He got as far as Norlie (Northleigh) common, which looked cool and inviting. He tethered his horse to a tree so that he could get a good feed of grass, then stretched himself out in the sweet-smelling bracken and went off to sleep. Back in Witney the owner of the paraffin shop had begun to get a bit worried. It was 7.30 p.m. and Pratley not back from his journey. So he asked two of the other men to take a horse and cart and go and look for him. Anything could have happened to man, horse and cart, for it wasn't like Pratley to be late.

Well, they found him curled up on Norlie common sleeping as peaceful as a baby. Of course he never lived it down, they were always teasing him about it. And after that episode, anyone who felt tired and listless had the complaint known as 'The Witney Man'. And I had definitely got that complaint on this scorching hot day.

I wasn't going to curl up and go to sleep, but it was peaceful sitting there under the big tree, along the quiet road which would eventually lead to the hamlet where Missus-next-door lived. In the field opposite to where I was resting, men were busy harvesting. A giant scarlet combine charged up and down the field at a fair pace, stopping every now and then to discharge its load of golden grain into a waiting trailer. It all seemed so easy, this way of harvesting—at least much easier than in the old days.

I thought as I sat there what knowledgeable men farmers and farm workers have to be. They have to understand drainage, medicine, mechanics as well as soil and seeds, beasts, and weather. It certainly was a lovely day. Such beauty there was all around, with every field and fold throwing up a different hue. It was like gazing at a giant patchwork, of lovely muted greens and golds and rich brown earth, and the stone walls which part the fields running like a lace thread across the wold.

There were wild flowers on the verge-sides—gay mauve scabious, candy-striped mallow, purple vetch, and yellow bedstraw. It was one of those days when every sound is 'sharp set' as we call it. I could hear a dog barking way off in some lonely farmyard, and rooks cawing, but I couldn't see them. A church clock down in the valley chimed the hour of three, it was time I set off over the hills again.

A lovely smell of freshly baked cakes met me as I walked into Missus-next-door's spick and span cottage. I sniffed. 'Yes', she said, 'I've made yer favourite, seedy en't it? I remembered you said you liked seedy, and I've made a bit of what I calls me special gingerbread too.'

I was glad of the hot sweet tea, and her cakes were delicious. 'Ah, I'll give 'e the receipt affor you goes if you'd like it,' she said, after I'd complimented her.

The improvements made to Missus-next-door's cottage were marvellous, and she was very pleased to show me round. 'Mind you', she rambled on, 'that electric stove took a bit of getting used to, arter cooking with nothing but paraffin and that old fire-oven fer years; but I manages.'

'I can't really understand why old Mark and his brother don't want to come back', she prattled on, 'what could you want better than this? Course I suppose when you comes to think of it, it ent so convenient as the one they be in, what with 'e havin' to dry his jackuts and things.'

'They're getting on well with the harvest round here', I said to her, after we'd settled down to another cup of tea.

'Ah', she said, 'I was a-watchin' 'um out in that thur field only yes'day and I thought how different it was to what 'twas a few years ago, before the combines, when a good farmer had got six or seven great ricks in his rickyard. Course they don't have nothin' like that now-a-days, I used to enjoy a bit of threshin' work, we reckoned on that round yer to buy a bit of warm clothes fer winter. When that old threshing machine drawed into farmer Baines' yard we women knowed as we was all right fer two or three weeks work, cos every farmer in the village would have his threshin' done once the threshin' tackle and the men got yer. We used to start work just after seven in the mornin' and keep on till half past four in the afternoon, with an hour break at midday. My word, that fust days threshin' nearly killed we, tossin' they sheaves all day. 'Twasn't so bad when you was right on top of the rick, pitchin' 'um down, but when you got three parts down the rick and you had to toss they sheaves up on to the threshin' drum, that was when it made yer muscles ache. I didn't mind when we was doing wheat ricks, but when we got on to barley that was awful, full of dust, and they barley hales* used to stick to yer clothes, nearly sent you mad a-scratchin'. When you got home the best thing to do was to strip awf and pick 'um out yer vest and knickers. Mind you', she went on, 'we used to have a damned good laugh—ah, and talking about strippin', I remembers the time when George Franklin took all his clothes awf when we was threshin' up at High Barn Farm once, bitter cold day it was too.

'Course when they ricks had been stood in that rickyard fer months, they used to get that full of rats and when we got towards the bottom you had to watch out. The farmer and any kids what was about used to stand thur waitin' with great sticks and try and kill 'um as they rushed out; the dogs used to catch 'um too.

'Well, on this day as I be tellin' you about, we'd got right down to the last few sheaves and nobody thought thur was any more rats left. Suddenly old George tosses up a sheaf and then 'e lets out such a yell, "E's gone up me trousers", 'e shouts, and 'e starts dancin' about in the yard tryin' to shake the animal down, but we could see that the rat was up near his backside. Thur was such a yellin' and a-shoutin', then the farmer hollers "take 'um awf, take

---

* Barley hales are the little whiskers on the end of the seed.

'um awf or 'e'll eat you alive", and old George was fair goin' mad screamin' and dancin' about.

' "That's it", Bert Abbot shouts, "take 'um awf affor 'e eats yer doings." That done it, 'e does no more than strips awf, naked as the day 'e was born, and awf runs the rat across the yard with the dogs followin' after it. Ah, old George was lucky not to be bit, but I should think with all the noise we was makin' the poor animal was frit to death.

'After that we took particular notice to tie the bottoms of our trousers with a piece of bagtie string. Well they was our husbands' trousers really, thur was not such things as women's trousers in they days. Well if thur was, we couldn't afford 'um just fer a few weeks threshin'.'

Missus-next-door refilled our cups. And the beautiful summer afternoon wore on; it was as cool as a church in the stone cottage.

'I'll tell 'e another little tale' she said, 'thas if you got time to listen.'

I assured her I'd got all the time in the world. I've learned over the years that if country folk want to talk the best thing to do is to let them, for you're sure to hear something worth while.

'You might think that this is a bit far fetched', she went on, 'but its gospel truth; happened to my eldest brother it did when 'e was about seventeen. You see 'e worked for a pig killing man and sometimes his gaffer would give 'im a bit of meat or offal to bring home to our mother. We was a big family and her was very glad of it. Well, one night just as 'e was leaving work his boss ses to 'im, "yer be Ted take these chitlins home". He'd got no bag or basket to put 'um in so 'e slips 'um into his trouser pocket, not realisin' thur was a hole in it. Now on his way home 'e catches up with a young girl from our village, walkin' home from work her was, and our Ted being a bit sweet on her gets awf his bike and walks alongside her, trying to get off with her like. They hadn't bin walkin' very long when the girl suddenly shrieks out "what's that", pointin' to a piece of chitlin that was danglin' below our Ted's trouser leg. Quick as a flash he whips out his pen-knife, cuts awf the piece that was showin' and chucks it over the hedge, and the poor girl fell down in a dead faint, and, do you know, 'er never spoke to our Ted again after that.'

Missus-next-door and I roared with laughter over her tales. 'Have you got time just fer a short un?' she asked, 'then I shall have to start cookin' fer my old man, 'e gets in just after five and 'e likes his meal on the table when 'e comes in.

'Well now, this happened at one of our Women's Institute meetings a few years back. I shan't tell you the woman's name although her bin dead this ten year; but on the night I felt that embarrassed for the poor woman, though I don't think 'er ever knew what 'er said. But I thinks some of 'um in the audience did, the way they laughed.

'"Twas like this you see, this yer woman was the one chosen as the deligate to go to the Annual general meeting what they holds in London every year, and the person that goes has to give a report about it to her own W.I. So 'er starts talkin' about the trip and the meetin' and her said "We was all settled in the Albert Hall and then the meetin' started with the hymn Jerusalem and we all sang out with lust." Well, I ask you my dear, we don't do that sort of thing at W.I. meetings now, do we?'

'Not at ours anyhow,' I assured her.

'Now about this yer cake receipt you wanted, I'll just write it out for you', and she scribbled away quietly for a few minutes.

We'd had a wonderful afternoon and I promised that I would come and see her again one day. But that day never came. Three weeks later dear Missus-next-door was walking home in the dimpsy light, well on the side of the road too, when a car driven recklessly by a young fellow knocked her down and she died three days later without regaining consciousness.

I often think of her, and the wonderful stories she told me. She loved what she called 'a bit of company', a bit of company that we often shared. And I still have the two nice blue 'vawses' that she gave me. I thought it would be a fitting tribute to her to finish this chapter with her 'receipt' for what she called 'me special ginger-bread'.

Missus-Next-Door's
Special Gingerbread

Sift together 8 oz of S.R. flour, half a tablespoon of ground ginger and half a teaspoon of mixed spice. Into a heavy pan put 4 oz margarine, 4 oz soft brown sugar, 4 oz golden syrup and 4 oz of black treacle. Heat gently until sugar dissolves. Cool a little. Beat together one egg and a gill of milk. Add this and the melted ingredients to the flour and mix well. Pour into a well-lined meat tin and bake in the middle of the oven for 1¼ hours until firm to touch. Gas No. 3 or electricity 333. Allow to cool before removing from tin.

14

World Without End

FOR a number of years my old friend Mark had threatened to give up his job. He'd stayed on long past retiring age, because his boss kept saying that he couldn't find anyone to replace him. The truth was that if Mark did retire, his boss knew that he would have to employ two men to do the 'shuppering'.

But a couple of bad winters, coupled with the fact that he had developed acute arthritis in his right hand, which Mark attributed to years of whacking in posts with his heavy folding bar, helped him to make up his mind. So I was not surprised when he told me 'I've jacked it all up and so have gaffer.'

'What! Your boss given up farming,' I cried.

'No, just the ship,' he said, 'he couldn't get a shuppard nowhere. 'Tis a seven day a week job you see, my wench, you got to go and have a look at 'um even on a Sunday, and the young uns wun't have it not at any price. So 'e sent 'um all off to Bicester market and finished with 'um altogether.'

'Course,' Mark went on, 'I shall have to do a bit of summut, if its only to get some beer and baccy money. Any road, I couldn't abide not doin' nothin'. But I byent rushin' into anything. Thurs bin two or three arter I already, to go gyardnin' for 'um, but I byent goin' to have much of that this wet weather. I shall be like they old hedgehogs, I shall hibernate and come out fresh and eager in the spring.'

We were now well into November and the weather had turned cold and wet. Almost silently the yellowing leaves were falling from the great elms, fluttering lifelessly to the ground to lay dejectedly at our feet. It was the end of their life, those patchy yellow leaves that had gladdened our hearts in the Spring with their delicate greenery. Some people get sad over Autumn, but I like to think that its really just the beginning of another year's growth. There were still golden leaves clinging to the beech branches; soon they too would fall, only to be scooped up again by eager gardeners. The only other colours in the hedgerows were a few scarlet hips and a glint of gold here and there where gorse bushes had established themselves.

'You knaws what they ses about gorse don't you', Mark said, after I had remarked on the lovely blooms for the time of year.

'Kissing's out of fashion when the gorse is not in bloom. But 'tis always in bloom, at least you can allus find a flower 'er two bloomin', no matter what time of the year it is; and you knaws kissin's never out of fashion,' he said good-humouredly.

'And talkin' about colour, the other day when I took the dogs for a walk, I see summut growin' in the hedge as I never noticed affor, well not in this particular part of the country any road. Course I recognized what 'twas, though its years since I saw any.' We were strolling down the lane behind the shepherd's cottage, the dogs running excitedly in front.

'Yer 'tis then,' Mark cried, 'Spindleberry en't it? Now 'thas what I calls a nice bright colour.' The gaudy, pinky yellow berries hung like little lanterns on the almost leaf-bare branches. We picked a few sprays.

'Very hard wood the spindle tree is', Mark went on, ''thas what it was used for years ago, to make spindles, the sort they used for weaving. Mind you, you don't want to encourage it to grow near yer garden; attracts the black fly summut dreadful, that do.

'This is what I bin fillin' me time with fer the past few wiks,' Mark said as he proudly showed me a section of dry stone walling. He had almost rebuilt the entire wall that circled his garden. It looked as good as if it had been done by an experienced tradesman.

'Where did you learn how to do that?' I exclaimed, amazed at the workmanship.

'Ah, I watched the old fellows,' he replied. 'You see, thurs a tidy bit of dry stwon wallin' round these parts, specially on the farm wur I worked. And some mornin's when we got to work arter we'd had a heavy rain overnight, like as not thur'd be a piece of wall fell down. And as soon as our gaffer got to hear about it 'ed shout, "send for Breakspear". He was a retired stone mason what lived over at Delly Green, and he was glad to do a bit of work now and then. Wonderful craftsman he was, 'twas a pleasure to watch him at work; he'd got an eye as keen as an eagle when it come to cuttin' and shapin' stwons.

'You see, you got to get um to fit in right, and he could pick up a stwon from a gret pile and place it just right, sometimes without havin' to chip even an inch awf.

'I often used to watch him at work. We was very good pals too, 'e used to set along wi' I to have his victuals. And sometimes 'ed get on about his younger days. Mind you, 'e bin dead and gone this twenty years—lived till 'e was ninety-odd though. He started work when 'e was twelve year old and fer years 'e walked backurds and forrods from Bladon to Oxford—six days a wik fer 1½d. a day—apprentice 'e was, and ended up as one of the finest stone masons anywur round yer. I expect, in his time, he'd worked on every college in Oxford. I don't mean buildin' 'um, I means repairin' the stwon-work, although now I comes to think of it he did help to build one of they newish uns. And I'll bet thur's many a wall or buildin' whats standin' today as he helped to build, good solid cotswold stwon places, and they'll still be standin' long arter you and I be gone.'

'How do you begin to build a dry stone wall?' I asked.

'First,' he said, 'you must start right at the bottom. Even a wall has to have footin's, not as deep as a house mind you, about three or four inches below ground. Then you lays some good big flat stwons fer the base, like this.' He paused, showing me a piece that he had just started to build.

'You see, when you starts, its like two walls, but as you works up you binds 'um together here and there with a very big stwon, what they calls "threws", and that sort of ties it together. Then you fills the middle up wi' all yer small stwons and rubble. And you'll notice, as the wall gets higher it gets very slightly narrower. Then you gets what we calls an "edger", 'thas a nice shaped un, they be kept for finishin' awf, by a gateway or end of a wall.

'This is what I shapes the stwons with', he said, picking up a rather clumsy looking hammer; the head was sort of boat-shaped. 'Old Jim Breakspear give I that', Mark said, ''twas one 'ed used fer years. Then you tops the wall up with these copin' stwons or double coulters, as we calls 'um. See, you places 'um upright like this,' Mark said, demonstrating how he finished off the wall top.

'Mind you, handlin' stwons all day don't half make yer fingers sore, 'cos you can't wear gloves 'er nothin'. But', Mark went on, 'I think wallin's a very satisfying job, you be sort of creatin' summut; well 'thas how I feels when I be doin' this. When you comes to think of it, my wench, I was all they years shupperin' and I really ent got nothin' to show for it, only me shupherd's crook and a gammy hand. But a man what builds a house or a wall or a church have left his mark, summut as you can remember him by,' he said seriously.

'How do you manage to work with your bad hand?' I enquired.

'Ah, some days it plays I up that much as I can't even hold a pen, leave alone a stwon. Then other days, when 'tis dry-like, I gets on quite well. Mind you I takes me time, thur yent no cause fer I to do it if I don't feel like it,' he told me laughingly.

'I had to smile to meself 'tother mornin'' he went on, changing the subject, 'thurs two old fellows, Ted Oliver and Bert Norridge what lives up the road a bit, and most days one or 'tother comes down yer and watches I, and gives a bit of advice too. Well 'issday they met just about wur we be standin' now, and Ted Oliver ses "Wur be you awf to this mornin' then Bert?" and old Bert said, "I byent goin' nowur I be just come back." I had to chuckle to meself, that did sound so funny to I.'

Mark picked up a piece of fossil-filled stone and turned it over in his great hand. 'I'll bet that stwon's thousands and thousands of years old, look at all they tiny shells fossilled in thur. Ah, stwons a wonderful thing when you come to think of it, and course this county's famous for its quarries, though thur yent so many being worked as thur was. Do you know, my wench, the stwon what they used to build St Paul's mostly come from this area. I suppose any cotswold building fer miles around was built from local quarried stwons. And you must admit they buildings be lastin' memorials to the craftsmen who built 'um—summut that generations of people have looked at. And folks 'ull still be lookin' at 'um fer a good many years to come.'

Before I left Mark was already chipping away at the stones, fitting them into the wall. I watched him, his head slightly on one side as he surveyed his handiwork. Here was a truly contented man. His needs were few, yet he was rich in character and wisdom. And having seen the beautiful dry stone wall that he was re-creating, with all the skill and knowledge that he had gleaned over the years, I felt sure that if people didn't remember him as a shepherd they would remember him for the way he built this wall.

15

Whitey Smith

I FIRST met Whitey Smith in a pub; I was delivering the wartime ration of cigarettes and crisps, from the wholesale grocers where I worked, to the Inn where Whitey could often be found propping up the bar. He was getting on for seventy then, and had worked hard for well over fifty years, so he reckoned that he'd earned his half pint and daily chatter with the other old worthies who made the bar parlour their meeting place.

The Inn Keeper said to me one day, 'That's the fellow to tell a tale, I can never remember 'um, but 'e reels 'um off by the dozen, buy him half a pint and he'll go on fer hours.'

The trouble was, in those wartime days I was usually pushed for time—six long weary years they were, and I was very glad when the time came to hand the lorry back to its former driver, a soldier returning from the wars, and I was able to settle down to being a housewife once more. Then one day I suddenly thought of Whitey and his tales, and hied me off to see if the old fellow was still propping up the bar in 'The Black Boy'.

There he was, still in the same place. His hair was thinner than when I'd last seen him, otherwise he'd changed very little. I was given a great welcome.

'Ju remember 'er,' Whitey said to the other customers, 'used to come round durin' the war, drivin' that gret lorry—I've sin 'er carry a two hundern-weight bag of sugar on 'er back into that old bakehouse next door—she carried it as if 'twas a couple of pounds,' and they oh'd and ah'd and remembered.

I told him that I'd come to hear some of the stories that I'd never had time to listen to before, and Whitey, the great talker

377

that he was, settled for 'something tu wet me whistle' and started—

'I'll tell you 'ow I come by me nickname fust go awf—I was christened Herbert you see, arter me uncle, but I bin called Whitey fer years, on account of the colour of this old thatch of mine. Ah, it bin snow white like this since I was seventeen, went white overnight it did, as true as I set yer that is.

'You see, I was a learnin' to be a carter, and Sid Baker, 'e was over I on this biggish farm wur we was employed. Well, when we come home from the fields at night, old Sid 'ud clear off home and leave I to feed and water the hosses. Well on this particular day, well 'twas night-time really, we comes home from ploughin' and as usual off goes old Sid.

'I goes out to the well to draw up some water for the hosses and before you could say Jack Robinson I'd slipped on the wet ground and went headfust down the well. I hit the bottom then struck out as if I was swimmin' in the river and comes to the surface—course 'twas as black as pitch down thur. I hollered and shouted but nobody heard. I thought I'd had it, for 'twas a deep well and the stone sides was damp and slippery without much of a place to hang on to. I kept tryin' to climb the wall of the well, keepin' me eyes on a little bit of half light at the top. But as fast as I climbed I slipped back into the water again, till I was damn near exhausted. Well, I couldn't tell you what happened arter that, but when I "come to" I was lying on the muck heap in the yard; and thas wur Gaffer found I when 'e and his wife drove in from market.

'They took I home—I had a couple of days in bed—and when I got up me hair was as white as it is now and thas fifty odd years ago.'

Whitey paused for a swig and went on, 'I was a-tellin' this same tale to one a they clever sort of town fellas one day, and 'e ses to I a bit cocky-like, "How long were you down the well young man?" And I answers him pretty smartish and said "I dun't know sir, I never looked at me watch", ha ha, 'e never asked I any more silly questions arter that.'

Somebody called for drinks all round and the 'customers' settled down again as Whitey rambled on. 'And I'll tell 'e another funny thing that happened to I. I was puttin' some barbed wire fencin' round one of Gaffer's fields; you see we'd had a lot of trouble with the cattle gettin' out. I was getting on very well with the fencing when suddenly I drops me hammer and as I bent down to pick it up I caught me trousers on the barbed wire and damn near tore the backside out.

'Well, I couldn't go all the way home like that, 'twasn't decent, so I goes up to the farmhouse and asked Gaffer's wife if 'er could cobble it up, rough like, just to last I till I got home at night.

' "Come on in Whitey" 'er said, "and bend over that chair and I'll see what I can do." Mind you, 'er was a bit heavy handed with that thur needle, two or three times 'er jabbed I in the backside.

'Well, when 'er'd finished I stands up and ses to 'er, "thank you kindly Mam, I be most grateful, and I'll do the same fer you if you be ever likewise fixed."

'Her looks I strait in the eye and said "I sincerely hope that occasion never arises Whitey."

'Mind you, I didn't mean what I said, about doin' the same fer 'er, but I could hardly stop from bustin' out laughin'.

'Then thur was the time when my young nephew come down this way to work, durin' the war it was, when the government used to send the workers wur they was needed most. Well, young George, that was his name, was about eighteen at the time, and his Mother, my missus's sister, thought it 'ud be a good thing if 'e come and lodged with us. 'Twas the lad's first visit to the country—lived in London all his life 'e had. It was one a they real hot days when young George arrived, a Sunday if I remembers rightly. Well 'e goes indoors to say hello to my missus, then comes out into the garden to I and ses "Uncle", 'e ses, "Where's your toilet?" so I ses to 'im "wurs the what?" "Well where's your lavatory then?" he said, a bit urgent like. So I ses to 'im, "ah, that's the place, that little old stwon place thur at the bottom of the gyarden—just behind that thur boxbush."

'So down the gyarden path 'e goes a bit quick like, but 'e comes back again strait away and said "I can't go in there uncle 'tis full of flies", so I looks at me watch and ses to 'im, "Ah-h thee try and hang on fer ten minutes, missus is goin' to dish up the dinner, they'll all come up yer then", and I laughed. Course 'e didn't know how to take what I'd said and I thinks it put 'im off 'is dinner, for 'e never 'et a thing, but 'e soon got used to they flies— you has to when you lives in the country. We used to hang Elderflower branches up in the dyke (lavatory) years ago, they was supposed to keep the flies away. Nowadays my missus takes one a they airysole things down with 'er. Fust time 'er done that, 'er squirted it so much as 'er sat thur, 'er nearly passed out 'erself. Come staggerin' up the path as if 'er was drunk 'er did. Damn that, I'd rather put up wi' the flies meself.

'Well now,' Whitey went on, looking at his pocket watch, 'we ent got a lot more time today, otherwise the landlord will be chucking us out, it looks as if we just got time fer a short 'un.'

'Ah-h and a quick 'un,' one of his mates said, and I nodded to the landlord to fill the glasses again.

'What about the caretaker story?' he said as he brought the drinks to us.

'Oh ah, I'd fergot that 'un,' Whitey said, smacking his lips over the fresh cool beer.

'Now this happened over at Tanfield Bottom a few years back; I knows its gospel 'cos it was my second cousin and his missus as was the caretakers thur at the time, and all they 'ad to do was keep this big country house tidy like and show folks round—they as might want to buy it.

'Mind you, they was new at this caretakin' lark and thur first "customer" was a portly gentleman who seemed quite interested in the property. After he'd had a good look round he turned to

Fred, me second cousin, and said, "How many windows face north and where's the W.C.?"

'Course old Fred didn't know what 'e meant so 'e looks at his wife and 'er whispered to him "Wesleyan chapel you fool." So then Fred turned to the gentleman and said, very important like, "Thur are five windows that face north Sir, and the nearest W.C. is half a mile away. I went thur six months ago, but I had to stand up all night so I ent bothered since." Oh dear,' Whitey went on, 'we've had many a chuckle over that I can tell you. Now I'd best get off home, my missus got a bacon and onion puddin' on fer our dinner, 'er wunt like it if I be late.' He called cheerio to his mates. Then he turned to me.

'Why dun't you come down home along wi' I' he said, 'I expect I could think of a few more stories, arter I've had me dinner like.'

'Tell you what Whitey,' I said to him, 'I'll have a look round the village and find somewhere in the cool to eat my sandwiches, then I'll come along to your house and meet your wife, in about an hour's time.'

'Ah, perhaps thas the best idea,' he replied as he turned for home. 'And don't ferget 'tis the last cottage on the left-hand side down Spittalls Lane.'

The village itself was small and scattered, yet the church was a huge magnificent building, built on the brow of a hill rising up from the river Evenlode. Two elderly men sat on a bench under the giant Elm trees, dark and heavy with summer leaf, and down the lane the blackberry flowers and white convolvulus climbed and looped their way over the hedgerows.

Whitey was on the look out for me. His cottage was very picturesque, built of Cotswold stone and roofed with lichen-covered Stonesfield slates.

'My Grandfather most likely quarried they very slats (slates) his-self, out of one of the local mines,' Whitey told me proudly as we stood and surveyed his little castle. 'You see, he worked in the next village, ah, quite a lot of the men hereabouts was employed in they old slat mines. Course 'twas a hard job and the conditions was a bit grim too. You see the mines, or pits as some folks call 'em, was only about three or four foot high and the men often had to work all day long a-creepin' along on thur hands and knees, peckin' out all the waste soil and small stwons to get to the rocks. Then they loaded these rocks, gret stwons they was, on to a thing called a "jack barrow", they then was hauled to the surface. And then the rocks was laid out all over the ground and the village folk used to pray for good, hard, frosty winters. You see that was what split the rocks into slats, and sometimes the men would pour water over the rocks to make sure the frost got right through and split 'um properly. Mind you,' he went on, 'the slats had to be shaped properly afterwards and that was a very skilled job too. The men what done this often set up a little bit of shelter in the field, like a little workshop it was. Sometimes 'twas just a couple of hurdles covered with straw, anything to keep out the cold wind. Then they'd get a gret big stwon that served as a work bench and the slat was rested on this while the man tapped away turnin' out a slat shaped summut like a luggage label only a lot bigger, then he'd make a small hole in the top, then when the tiler come to fix the slat on a roof he would drive a small wooden peg into that hole so that the slat could be hung on a lath when it was in its right position on the roof.

'Ah,' Whitey went on, 'they slats had names accordin' to thur size, I knowed 'um all at one time, thur was "Cussems" and "Long Becks", "Muffities", and "Long Elevens", but I can't remember no more. I en't quite sure when the last Stwonsfold (Stonesfield) slats was quarried—pity they dun't do it now, but perhaps they run out of the right sort of rock in this district. Course the only way you can get hold of any now is when an old barn or cottage is pulled down. Worth thur weight in gold damn-near they be.

'Course thur must have bin thousands of tons of 'um quarried round yer at one time. Now the only thing left is all they hummocks and mounds in the fields; thur's four or five big 'uns just as you goes out of Stwonsfold. They piles be all the waste stuff what was left behind after the men had dug the rocks out. I went into one a they mines some years ago,' he said, 'just to have a look like. Damp and dark it was, and creepy—I was glad to get out in the fresh air agen I'll tell 'e.

'Well my gel, I thinks I'll go and have forty winks now; I do most afternoons, so do my old lady. You come and see I agen one of these dinnertimes, you knows wur to find I, in "The Black Boy". We never did get round to any more story tellin' this afternoon did us? Still, thur's always another day, ent thur?' he said, as he waved me goodbye.

But it was mid-winter before I saw Whitey again. I'd had a card from his wife to say that he was 'in bed with his leg', but that he wanted to see me.

I found him propped up in a huge brass bed. He looked frail and tired, and his white hair stuck out rough and untidy like an old bird's nest.

'Ah my gel,' he said after I had asked after his health, 'I don't think I shall be able to get down to "The Black Boy" again. You must remember I be goin' on fer ninety five, I be well past me four score years and ten. I've bin lucky really, this is the fust time in me life as I've bin bed-bound'. He went on, his pale eyes watering, 'I wanted to tell you that thur's going to be a village do at Stwonsfold later on this year, and when old Ted Gammage come to see I the other day he said that the farmer who owns the only slat mine what 'ent bin filled in is goin' to let folks go down it, fer a small fee. Not for his-self mind you, but fer church funds. And I thought as you'd like the chance to see down one, bein' as you be interested in that sort of thing. Mind you, the numbers 'ull have to be limited, so you'll have to get yer oar in quick, cos they reckons that this might be the last time that the public 'ull be allowed to go down.' Here Whitey paused for breath. He went on, 'all the other pits have bin filled in and blocked up to make 'um safe-like, but somehow this un was left. Mind you I thinks it was a very wise thing, otherwise the present generation 'ud never knowed what the working conditions was like.'

I thanked Whitey for the news, then turned to his wife to remark on the wonderful patchwork quilt that covered the bed. It was a beautiful thing and an absolute galaxy of colour. She told me proudly that her grandmother had started it, then her own mother had had a go, and she herself had finished it off.

'This here's a bit of my granny's wedding dress,' she said, pointing to a blue-grey patch of shot silk, 'and this was a piece of my mother's wedding dress', she went on, moving her hand across to a bit of sprigged muslin. 'Course that had to have a piece of firmer material on the back of that. And this here's a scrap from my wedding frock and further over here's a bit from our daughter's; lovely brocade it was, looked like a queen in it she did. Ah, there's memories of four generations sewed into this old quilt, though who 'ull want it when we be gone I don't know,' she said sadly.

The Church festival that Whitey had told me about, which was to include the reopening of the old slate mine, was held the following May. By then Whitey had moved to 'pastures new', having died quietly in his sleep about three weeks after I'd visited him.

The trip down the old slate mine was certainly worth while. We descended the thirty foot shaft by means of two long ladders which were roped together, and to me it seemed that we were going to the very bowels of the earth. The bottom of the shaft was damp with spring water, gently oozing from the sides of the shaft, which was skilfully built with local stone; and from where we stood, waiting for our guide, it looked as if we were standing at the bottom of a great well.

We worked our way along the narrow tunnel, which was never more than four feet high and in some places only three feet, and only about five feet wide. Some crawled crabwise while others went along on hands and knees; soon we were covered in thick yellow mud. Most of us carried torches, but the men who once toiled down there must have had to work with the aid of lanterns.

Our guide explained the working conditions, which must have been appalling, to say nothing of the pay which was 8s. 0d. a week at the time when most of the pits closed around 1910. Apparently most of the rock was hewn out of the pits from about October to January, and men used to walk for miles to Stonesfield during that period to try and get a few week's work there. The rocks were laid out on the surface, and if the weather was mild and dry they would be carefully covered with any vegetation that was available, so that the pit moisture wouldn't dry out; if this happened, the slate flaked off in layers and was useless as a roof tile. As soon as the frosty weather came the vegetation was taken off, and if a very severe frost was imminent the men of the village would be called out during the night (by the ringing of the church bells) to pour water over the rocks.

But the men who worked down the pits envied the fellows who cut and shaped the tiles, for their work lasted all the year round. Sitting in their little huts made from hurdles and straw they turned out slates at £2 a 1,000. At the turn of the century there were two such men employed here at this job—both elderly and loth to show anyone else their trade, for a younger man working faster could have put them out of work.

Around 1910 it was decided that it was uneconomical to work the pits and one by one they closed down. But the strong men of Stonesfield (and they must have been strong men to put up with those conditions) left their mark all over the country: on castles, colleges, cottages, and cowsheds, in the form of lovely, grey, lichen-covered Stonesfield slates.

Conclusion

A few weeks after the completion of this book, I was asked to join the cast of the BBC's famous long-running serial 'The Archers'. My part is that of an ordinary cheerful village woman. Such a person can be found in any English village, as indeed can the rest of the Archer cast. And as *Another Kind of Magic* deals with the lives of country folk, I didn't want the book to go to press without paying tribute to the painstaking accuracy and attention to detail that goes into the making of 'The Archers'. In fact, the script writers and producer are so exact in their interpretation of country life today that the whole story could easily be happening in any village in this green and pleasant land of ours.

The farming people and their kin, the village shop with its harmless chatter, the pub—a popular meeting place for the men-folk—the threat of closing the village school 'meals on wheels', the old people's club, good crops, bad crops, the knowledge and experience of the older workers blending with the modern methods of the younger generation, all these help to make the serial a true picture of the present day.

Until I joined this happy group of actors I had no idea of the amount of hard work that goes into making such a programme successful. One thing to which, rightly, great importance is attached is getting the right sound effects. These are taken from a huge library of tape recordings made from actual country sounds—Sunday morning church bells, rooks in the elms, lambs bleating, the cry of a dog fox, the harsh sound of a tractor or a harvester, all combining to make the programme as true to life as possible.

Having always lived in the country, and worked on a farm for several years, I feel quite at home with 'The Archers'. In *Another Kind of Magic* you will have met ordinary, earthy countrymen and women, as I met them on the farms and in the villages of Oxfordshire and Gloucestershire. And in 'The Archers' programme you can meet their like again, very faithfully portrayed.

OXFORD

MORE OXFORD PAPERBACKS

This book is just one of nearly 1000 Oxford Paperbacks currently in print. If you would like details of other Oxford Paperbacks, including titles in the World's Classics, Oxford Reference, Oxford Books, OPUS, Past Masters, Oxford Authors, and Oxford Shakespeare series, please write to:

UK and Europe: Oxford Paperbacks Publicity Manager, Arts and Reference Publicity Department, Oxford University Press, Walton Street, Oxford OX2 6DP.

Customers in UK and Europe will find Oxford Paperbacks available in all good bookshops. But in case of difficulty please send orders to the Cash-with-Order Department, Oxford University Press Distribution Services, Saxon Way West, Corby, Northants NN18 9ES. Tel: 0536 741519; Fax: 0536 746337. Please send a cheque for the total cost of the books, plus £1.75 postage and packing for orders under £20; £2.75 for orders over £20. Customers outside the UK should add 10% of the cost of the books for postage and packing.

USA: Oxford Paperbacks Marketing Manager, Oxford University Press, Inc., 200 Madison Avenue, New York, N.Y. 10016.

Canada: Trade Department, Oxford University Press, 70 Wynford Drive, Don Mills, Ontario M3C 1J9.

Australia: Trade Marketing Manager, Oxford University Press, G.P.O. Box 2784Y, Melbourne 3001, Victoria.

South Africa: Oxford University Press, P.O. Box 1141, Cape Town 8000.

OXFORD REFERENCE

THE CONCISE OXFORD COMPANION TO ENGLISH LITERATURE

Edited by Margaret Drabble and Jenny Stringer

Based on the immensely popular fifth edition of the *Oxford Companion to English Literature* this is an indispensable, compact guide to the central matter of English literature.

There are more than 5,000 entries on the lives and works of authors, poets, playwrights, essayists, philosophers, and historians; plot summaries of novels and plays; literary movements; fictional characters; legends; theatres; periodicals; and much more.

The book's sharpened focus on the English literature of the British Isles makes it especially convenient to use, but there is still generous coverage of the literature of other countries and of other disciplines which have influenced or been influenced by English literature.

From reviews of *The Oxford Companion to English Literature*:

'a book which one turns to with constant pleasure . . . a book with much style and little prejudice' Iain Gilchrist, *TLS*

'it is quite difficult to imagine, in this genre, a more useful publication' Frank Kermode, *London Review of Books*

'incarnates a living sense of tradition . . . sensitive not to fashion merely but to the spirit of the age' Christopher Ricks, *Sunday Times*